WHAT YOUR COLLEAGUES ARE SAYING . . .

Sheninger's Digital Leadership, Second Edition, *is straight from the heart of practice and it shows. Well advanced and consolidated from the first edition, more than anyone else Scheninger has integrated technology, learning, and change leadership. The seven pillars of learning are comprehensive. Leadership for quality implementation is captured beautifully. And the prominent positioning of efficacy and competencies nails impact.* Digital Leadership *is comprehensive for educators who want to advance learning with the latest know-how.*

—Michael Fullan
Author, Professor Emeritus
Ontario Institute for Studies in Education, University of Toronto

I'm glad to see that Sheninger revisits Digital Leadership *for a second time. There is great value in the fact that Eric looked at this topic through a lens of efficacy during this revisit. He focuses on the fact that it's not that educators are resistant to technology, but that they often don't have the confidence to keep up with the changing nature of it all, and Eric presents us all with a way to do that.*

—Peter DeWitt, EdD
Author, Consultant

Digital Leadership *is quite simply a tour de force of a book. It is timely, relevant, and essential reading for those leading educational change within a fast and furious digital world. The book is fundamentally about learning and pedagogy rather than software or hardware. It is a manifesto for change in a digital age and is fundamentally concerned with using technology to enhance the learning outcomes and life chances of all students. It is a must-read!*

—Professor Alma Harris
Head of the School of Education
Swansea University, UK

There can be a perceived hysteria when it comes to integrating technology into education, especially from a leadership perspective. As an administrator, I know how full our plate already is. This book helps simplify what YOU can do as a leader on your campus or in your district. The problem is our students today crave an environment that we struggle to provide. Sheninger provides a calming, thoughtful framework in Digital Leadership. *Educators of all levels will benefit from his unlocking of a "solution" that combines where most districts are and where we should all strive to be. It is full of sound, relevant information that guides strategic thinking, problem solving, collaboration, and decision making—all to the benefit of the ones we serve. There are plenty of people lining up to offer up problems when it comes to how to lead in this digitally focused era; thankfully, we have* Digital Leadership *to help offer solutions.*

—Amber Teamann
Principal, Whitt Elementary, Wylie ISD
Wylie, TX

I'm thrilled that Eric decided to put out a second edition of Digital Leadership. *Since the first edition's release back in 2014, we've seen changes in the digital landscape due to advances in technology. As school leaders, we must continue to adapt to these shifts in order to lead sustainable and meaningful change in our schools. As a highly acclaimed educator, leader, writer and speaker, Eric has dedicated his career to providing pedagogical frameworks, practical ideas, and real-life examples that he has gathered from practitioners in the schools in*

D1088396

which he serves. *Regardless of your role in schools, I am confident you will find this second edition applicable to your work and inspire you to want to shift your practices as you continue to evolve as an educator.*

—Jimmy Casas
Educator, Author, Speaker, Leadership Coach

If you were not an inspired leader and advocate for technology before reading this book, you will be by the end of it. As technology advances and becomes a way of being for students, Eric challenges school leaders not only to keep up but to excel. The book is thought provoking, encouraging, and—most important—practical for today's leaders.

—Dr. Russell J. Quaglia
Author, Executive Director
Quaglia Institute for School Voice & Aspirations

The role of a leader isn't to tell others what to do. It's to show them what they can become. The world of education doesn't change annually, it changes daily. The digital connection to how we lead is an ever-changing landscape and one all leaders need to know how to navigate. Creating leadership capacity in others moves the whole system. Eric Sheninger not only provides a pathway to get there, but he also provides the connections to move forward. The intersection of ISTE standards, Future Ready Frameworks, and organizational change makes this a must-read for leaders in a changing world.

—Dr. Joe Sanfelippo
Author and Superintendent
Fall Creek School District, ICLE Most Innovative District 2016–2017

Five years ago, Eric Sheninger cemented the importance of digital leadership at all levels of a school district. In the time since the first book's release, the 4th industrial revolution has continued to accelerate changes on the outside of the school walls. To remain relevant throughout this evolution, school leaders must work to create the learning experiences today's modern learners need to thrive in their future workforce. In this second edition, Sheninger solidifies his leadership pillars, through a refined underpinning of evidence and research, to ensure efficacy and deeper learning experiences, while avoiding the low-level fluff that has pervaded the education space. If you want to ensure a return on instruction and work to create schools that are future ready, this book will be a foundational support for your journey.

—Thomas C. Murray
Director of Innovation
Future Ready Schools, Alliance for Excellent Education
Washington, D.C.

Eric Sheninger has done it again! As I read through the second edition of Digital Leadership, *it was clear to me that the title of the book alone tells a very "compelling story." Eric is not one who simply studied digital leadership and then started consulting on it—he walked digital leadership for years as a highly successful principal. He literally led his school digitally and resultantly the school experienced tremendous success. Through* Digital Leadership, *he has taken those strategies and infused them into this invaluable second edition. If you are in school leadership and you are looking for proven strategies toward successfully incorporating technology into your academic program, the second edition of* Digital Leadership *is your resource.*

—Principal Baruti Kafele
Education Speaker, Consultant, Author

Digital Leadership

Second Edition

To my amazing wife, Melissa. Your unwavering support, love, and understanding further ignite my passion for the work that I am engaged in.
Thank you for your unwavering support in all that I do.

Digital Leadership

Changing Paradigms
for Changing Times

Second Edition

Eric Sheninger

Foreword by Sugata Mitra

JOINT PUBLICATION

A SAGE Publishing Company

FOR INFORMATION:

Corwin

A SAGE Company

2455 Teller Road

Thousand Oaks, California 91320

(800) 233-9936

www.corwin.com

SAGE Publications Ltd.

1 Oliver's Yard

55 City Road

London EC1Y 1SP

United Kingdom

SAGE Publications India Pvt. Ltd.

B 1/I 1 Mohan Cooperative Industrial Area

Mathura Road, New Delhi 110 044

India

SAGE Publications Asia-Pacific Pte. Ltd.

18 Cross Street #10-10/11/12

China Square Central

Singapore 048423

Publisher: Arnis Burvikovs

Development Editor: Desirée A. Bartlett

Senior Editorial Assistant: Eliza B. Erickson

Project Editor: Amy Schroller

Copy Editor: Cate Huisman

Typesetter: C&M Digitals (P) Ltd.

Proofreader: Sally Jaskold

Indexer: Molly Hall

Cover Designer: Scott Van Atta

Marketing Manager: Sharon Pendergrast

Copyright © 2019 by Corwin

All rights reserved. Except as permitted by U.S. copyright law, no part of this work may be reproduced or distributed in any form or by any means, or stored in a database or retrieval system, without permission in writing from the publisher.

When forms and sample documents appearing in this work are intended for reproduction, they will be marked as such. Reproduction is authorized for educational use by educators, local school sites, and/or noncommercial or nonprofit entities that have purchased the book.

All third-party trademarks referenced or depicted herein are included solely for the purpose of illustration and are the property of their respective owners. Reference to these trademarks in no way indicates any relationship with, or endorsement by, the trademark owner.

Printed in the United States of America

Library of Congress Cataloging-in-Publication Data

Names: Sheninger, Eric C., author.

Title: Digital leadership : changing paradigms for changing times / Eric Sheninger; foreword by Sugata Mitra.

Description: Second Edition, Revised Edition. | Thousand Oaks, California : A joint publication of Corwin ICLE, [2019] | Includes bibliographical references and index.

Identifiers: LCCN 2018059105 | ISBN 9781544350837 (Paperback : acid-free paper)

Subjects: LCSH: Educational technology—Planning. | Educational leadership. | Education—Effect of technological innovations on. | School management and organization. | Education—Aims and objectives.

Classification: LCC LB1028.3 .S4426 2019 | DDC 371.33—dc23

LC record available at https://lccn.loc.gov/2018059105

This book is printed on acid-free paper.

19 20 21 22 23 10 9 8 7 6 5 4 3 2 1

DISCLAIMER: This book may direct you to access third-party content via Web links, QR codes, or other scannable technologies, which are provided for your reference by the author(s). Corwin makes no guarantee that such third-party content will be available for your use and encourages you to review the terms and conditions of such third-party content. Corwin takes no responsibility and assumes no liability for your use of any third-party content, nor does Corwin approve, sponsor, endorse, verify, or certify such third-party content.

Contents

Foreword

Imagine if you wanted to build and manage a school on a piece of land in a prime location in a city or a village somewhere. Or, even more difficult, imagine if you head a school that is old and respected, but you know it needs to be rebuilt to meet the needs of a new world. Where would you start?

Only about 25 years ago, around the 1990s, you would have gotten a lot of help from the past. You would have standard designs, with classrooms and corridors and lots of stairs going up and down. A playground, a library, labs, an art room, a music room, and an "assembly hall." You would attract trained teachers by advertising, have a curriculum from the government, and inherit established ways in which to get your students to do well on standardized tests. Then you are all set—a few newspaper ads, a little word of mouth, and the parents would come flocking.

But things change. Today, close to the 2020s, you would probably pause a bit. You might wonder, "What kind of a building should I have? Should I have classrooms? What will happen in them? Is the playground too close to the main road? What about pollution? What kind of teachers do I need? From where will I get them? Do I need separate 'labs' for the arts and the sciences? What's a maker space? Everything is digital, I can do a math experiment in the music room, can't I? What will I tell the parents, and how will I communicate with them? Why should they send their children to my school? What's my school for, anyway?"

At this point, you might consider reading this book.

"You get what you model," says Eric Sheninger in his new edition of *Digital Leadership: Changing Paradigms for Changing Times*.

That traditional school model was nearly static for over 300 years; in fact, the older a school looked the more respectable and better it seemed.

Now you need to make your new model; the old ones don't work anymore. The strength of this book is that it won't tell you what the new model is—it will tell you what questions to ask to make your own model. This book is for school leaders and, I think, for school makers. After all, you need to have something to lead before you can lead it.

Learners are changing. They have shorter attention spans, they can focus on multiple things at the same time. Some research says this is good, some says it is bad. Eric takes us through it all—not taking sides but pointing at options. Schools should reflect real life, but how much of "real" life is real?

Teaching is changing into learning—at last. Eric treads gingerly into the world of digital learning. Gingerly, because I think he knows we are all out there ready to pounce on every idea with bared fangs. I know, believe me—I go through this every day with my own work on self-organized learning.

When the first electric trams rolled down the streets of London and Calcutta, people asked, "Where have they hidden the horses?"

This book deals with learning environments and spaces—some real, some not. The internet, and the digital tools that utilize it, are diffused through the physical spaces of the school. The internet is real, of course. But where is it? Where have they hidden the horses this time?

Eric Sheninger has an advantage over the classical academic. He himself has done what he is suggesting in this book. In real schools. The book is full of examples from his own work and the work of others around the world. These are words from real teachers talking about themselves and the work they do.

What should teachers do? How should they develop their skills and acquire new ones? To me, the teacher today is an enabler and a communicator. In this book there are guidelines for how to develop these new skills. Like most things in the world today, the key is networking. And remember, networks don't exist in real space, they exist somewhere else.

Beginning with Chapter 8, the book heads into management and marketing. Very strange subjects for the schools of yesterday, but necessary for the schools of today.

Schools need to communicate—with learners, teachers, parents, governments, and the public at large. It is a new challenge in digital leadership. Leaders have the means to communicate with the whole world instantly.

Schools need to have a face, to tell a story, and they need dedicated resources and technology to do so.

And, lastly, schools and their leaders need to keep abreast of our rapidly changing world. To avert new threats to learning. To seize new opportunities as they arise.

Keep this book around!

—Sugata Mitra
Professor and Principal Research Investigator
Newcastle University, England

Preface

Society continues to evolve at an exponential rate thanks to unprecedented advances in technology. This has led to shifts in the way people communicate, collaborate, solve problems, create projects, and consume content. These changes have placed all educators in a position to reflect upon the effectiveness of teaching, learning, and leadership so that the noble goal of ensuring learner success now and well into the future is achieved. Therein lies the key focus of the work of schools. There must be an emphasis on cultivating competent learners who are equipped to thrive and survive in a digital world. A secondary goal is the building of powerful relationships with key stakeholders in education (parents, students, community members) by authentically engaging them where they are at. Are you up to the challenge?

The increasing dominance technology plays in our lives can easily be experienced through behavioral observations of professionals, businesses, parents, children, and even grandparents. As of December 2017, approximately 54% of the world's population was on the internet (Internet World Stats, 2018). New tools are popping up faster than ever. Have school structures and procedures taken these shifts into account? More important, do leaders know how to adapt to these shifts and thus lead meaningful, sustainable change in their schools? The point is that we need to be better, and not only because of the changes we are seeing outside the walls of our schools. Change begins with each and every one of us and spreads from there. The truth is that there is no perfect lesson, project, classroom, school, district, teacher, or administrator. There is, however, the opportunity every day to get better.

AUDIENCE

The primary audience for the book is school leaders (supervisors, assistant principals, principals, directors of curriculum, superintendents, and teacher leaders). Professors of higher education can also integrate this book in their preparation programs, as many people would agree that exposure to this style of leadership is desperately needed. Even though the book is directed at school leaders—because they have the decision-making power to implement schoolwide and districtwide changes—teachers can easily incorporate the principles at the classroom level to improve their pedagogy and communication with students, colleagues, parents, and community members.

THE CALL

Leaders today must establish a vision and implement a strategic process that creates a teaching and learning culture that provides students with critical competencies—creativity, communication, collaboration, critical thinking, problem solving, entrepreneurship, technological proficiency, and global awareness. The twenty-first century skills movement is played out, as we are well into this century. The development of competent learners in the digital age is the key to the future. This focus should be at the heart of every decision a leader makes, and it is key to providing students with the tools to succeed in jobs that have not yet been created. Consistent innovation, purposeful use of technology, meaningful professional learning, connecting beyond the walls of a brick-and- mortar building, and an open mind are all mandatory duties of a leader in the digital age.

The call to prepare students for the unknown jobs of tomorrow is made more difficult as mounting challenges such as budget cuts, new standards, seemingly constant changes to standardized tests, value-added evaluation of staff using test scores,·and what seems like a relentless attack on the profession of education have taken their toll on staff morale. Quality leadership therefore becomes imperative in order to cultivate a school culture whose primary focus is on the learning and achievement of each and every student while anticipating needed changes in a society that is evolving at a dizzying pace.

It can also be argued that these changes have created a new type of learner that schools are entrusted with educating, as well as key stakeholders with shifting needs in terms of how they prefer to engage with schools. In this digital age, we are experiencing amazing advances in educational technology that have the potential to enhance the teaching and learning process, as well as establish powerful connections with our communities and among an array of stakeholders. These advances have also unlocked the creative potential of many students, teachers, and administrators.

The challenge for school leaders is to acknowledge these societal changes and embrace them. If schools continue to follow an outdated educational model focusing on preparation for an industrialized workforce, they run the risk of becoming irrelevant to our students and communities. More often than not there is a fundamental disconnect between learners and the schools they attend. Relevancy is just as important as achievement. It is hard to increase the latter if there is not a consistent focus on the former. Why are schools not meeting the diverse learning needs of students today at scale? Do school leaders leverage available technology and social media to do what they already do better? Are our decisions and behaviors taking into account future shifts and changes, or is the status quo still coddled? Why are so many slow or fearful to change? If these pressing questions are not squarely addressed by leaders, our system of education will continue to devolve into irrelevancy and inadequacy.

Digital leadership consists of a dynamic combination of mindset, behaviors, and skills that are employed to change and enhance school culture through the strategic use of technology. As leaders across virtually every sector began to evolve and take advantage of an interactive web, they began to embrace change, demonstrate transparency, increase engagement, employ collaboration, focus heavily on sharing, initiate global dialogue, and build community. Leaders quickly found the value in a plethora of digital tools to support and enhance traditional aspects of leadership (i.e., management, productivity, collaboration, evaluation, feedback, and communication) while forging new pathways to initiate change leading to transformation. Many would argue that this leadership style is still prevalent today.

Digital leadership considers changes such as ubiquitous connectivity, open-source technology, artificial intelligence, robotics, mobile devices, and personalization. It represents a dramatic shift from how schools have been run and structured for over a century. The shift has already started for many leaders through their use of technology for personal reasons. If there is value here, then surely there must be for professional practice as well. There is no time like the present to ride the digital wave and incorporate it seamlessly into every facet of leadership. You must be the change that you wish to see in education, but more important, you must be the change your learners yearn for.

The evolving web and other technologies provide an opportunity for each and every one of you to work smarter, not harder, with the goal of improving results. A new path can be forged when improved thinking is applied to the way you lead. Digital leadership can thus be defined as establishing direction, influencing others, initiating sustainable change though access to information, and establishing relationships in order to anticipate changes pivotal to school success in the future. Leaders must learn to better anticipate the learning needs of students and staff, the desire for information from stakeholders, and the necessary elements of school culture that address both rigorous standards and needed competencies. They must also be "change savvy" (Herold & Fedor, 2008), which involves

- careful entry into the new setting;
- listening to and learning from those who have been there or been at it longer;
- engaging in fact finding and joint problem solving;
- carefully, rather than rashly, diagnosing the situation;
- forthrightly addressing people's concerns;
- being enthusiastic, genuine, and sincere about the change in circumstances;
- obtaining support for what needs to be fixed or improved; and
- developing a credible plan for making a fix or improvement.

THE NEW DIGITAL LANDSCAPE

A great deal has changed since the initial publication of *Digital Leadership*. New tools have been developed, while old ones that many of us loved have been shut down. The pace of change in the digital age continues to increase at an exponential rate, and as a result, disruptive innovation has taken hold in virtually every sector. We are moving further into the fourth Industrial Revolution and eventually the fifth, and it is incumbent on digital leaders to adapt and embrace needed shifts to practice. In a world with advanced robotics, enhanced automation, and evolving artificial intelligence, the need to teach, learn, and lead not only differently, but better, must be a priority. Whereas the first edition focused a great deal on tools and skills, this new edition provides greater attention to the specific competencies needed to transform teaching, learning, and leadership that are vital no matter how fast technology evolves. This edition moves past trends and fads to focus on the essence of leading innovative change in education now and in the future.

CENTRAL PURPOSE AND FOCUS OF THIS BOOK

Digital Leadership: Changing Paradigms for Changing Times, Second Edition presents a framework for leaders to harness the power of innovative ideas and digital strategies in order to create school cultures that are transparent, relevant, meaningful, engaging, inspiring, and primed for better results. In order to set the stage for increasing achievement and to establish a greater sense of community pride for the work being done in our schools, we must begin to change the way we lead. To do this, leaders must understand the origins of fear and misconceptions that often surround the use of technology and implementation of innovative ideas. Once the fears and misconceptions are placed on the table, leaders can begin to establish a shared vision for the effective use of technology to improve numerous facets of leadership. The challenge for school leaders is why, how, and where to begin. Digital leadership is not about flashy tools; it is a strategic mindset that leverages available resources to improve what we do while anticipating the changes needed to cultivate a school culture focused on efficacy. This book will present an evolved construct of leadership that grows out of the leader's symbiotic relationship with the digital world.

Talk is cheap. Leaders must be able to back up talk with action that leads to improvement at scale. This book provides readers with research-aligned strategies and evidence to transform the teaching and learning culture in any school or district. A good deal of the ideas presented come from my days as a practitioner, as principal of New Milford High School in New Jersey, where digital leadership paved the way for improved outcomes and achievement. *Digital Leadership* tells the story of how I radically changed my beliefs on how a school should be structured and function, with the end result being sustainable change in programs, instruction, behaviors, and leadership involving technology. The book examines how shifting a leadership style from one of mandates, directives, and buy-in to one grounded in empowerment, support, and embracement is the key to sustainable change. My story is only one component. This second edition covers the stories of other bold leaders who are creating schools that work for kids.

Figure 0.1   Pillars of Digital Leadership

Source: Copyright © 2018 by International Center for Leadership in Education, a division of Houghton Mifflin Harcourt. Used with permission.

The Pillars of Digital Leadership

The Pillars of Digital Leadership are the specific areas embedded in the culture of all schools that can be improved or enhanced through the purposeful use of technology.

> **Student engagement, learning, and outcomes:** We cannot expect to see increases in achievement if students are not learning. Students who are not engaged are not likely to be learning. Engagement is not a silver bullet though. Students need to be empowered to think at the higher levels of cognition while applying what has been learned in relevant contexts. Leaders need to understand that schools should reflect real life

and allow learners the opportunity to use real-world tools to do real-world work. As technology changes so must pedagogy, especially assessment and feedback. Pulling from real-world examples, a blueprint is provided for improving instructional design and accountability protocols to ensure efficacy in digital learning.

Innovative learning spaces and environments: Would you want to learn under the same conditions as your students do, or in similar spaces? More often than not, the answer is no. Research has shown the positive impact that innovative spaces can have on learning outcomes. Leaders must begin to establish a vision and strategic plan to create classrooms and buildings that are more reflective of the real world while empowering learners to use technology in powerful ways. In order to do so, leaders must be knowledgeable of the characteristics and dynamics that embody innovative learning spaces and environments that support Bring Your Own Device (BYOD), 1:1, more personalized pathways such as blended and virtual learning, and maker education.

Professional learning: Leaders need and should want access to the latest trends, research, and ideas in the field. With the continual evolution of digital tools and increasing connectivity, schools can no longer be silos of information. As such, leaders do not have to feel like they are on isolated islands, have answers to every question, and feel pressured to always have to come up with the next big idea. This section discusses how leaders can form their own Personal Learning Network (PLN) to meet their diverse learning needs; acquire resources; access knowledge; receive feedback; connect with experts in the field of education as well as practitioners; and discuss proven strategies to improve teaching, learning, and leadership. Readers will learn how to develop their own PLN for free and access this priceless resource anywhere at any time. This section will also discuss the move from professional development to learning. Digital leadership also compels educators to create more personalized learning pathways for adults during the school day and year.

Communication: You will not find an effective leader who is not an effective communicator. Leaders can now provide stakeholders with relevant information in real time through a variety of devices by meeting them where they are at. No longer do static, one-way methods such as newsletters and websites suffice. Discussion will focus on types of information that can be communicated through various tools and simple implementation strategies to create a more transparent culture.

Public relations: If you don't tell your story, someone else will, and more often than not, another's version will not be the one you want told. Leaders need to become the storyteller-in-chief. This section will focus on how leaders can use free social media tools to form a positive public relations platform and become the de facto news source for their school or district. It is time to change the narrative by sharing all of the positives that happen in schools every day to create a much-needed level of transparency in an age of negative rhetoric toward education.

Branding: This is how your school or district is defined. It is not something that you want to leave up to others. Businesses have long understood the value of brand and its impact on current and potential consumers. Leaders can leverage social media to create a positive brand presence that emphasizes the positive aspects of school culture, increases community pride, and helps to attract/retain families looking for a place to send their children to school. Tell your story, build powerful relationships in the process, and empower learning.

Opportunity: It is important for leaders to consistently seek out ways to improve existing programs, resources, and professional learning opportunities. This section highlights how to leverage connections made through technology and increase opportunities to make improvements across multiple areas of school culture. Leaders will see how the other six pillars connect and work together to bring about unprecedented opportunities that would otherwise be impossible, such as securing donations, resources, authentic learning experiences for students, and mutually beneficial partnerships.

Leaders need to be the catalysts for change, and the Pillars of Digital Leadership pave the way. Each is critical in its own right to transforming and sustaining a positive school culture. This book defines each pillar, uses research to emphasize its importance and value, and provides an overview of specific strategies that can be used regardless of budget obstacles. I use not only my experiences and successes in each of these areas, but also those of other innovative leaders, schools, and districts who are not just talking the talk but are actively walking the walk. These practitioner vignettes offer powerful voices that establish a context for each pillar and illustrate the *why* and *how* so that readers will be able to implement the strategies in their own contexts.

By addressing each of these pillars, leaders can begin changing and transforming their respective schools into ones that prepare learners for success in a digital world while building critical relationships with stakeholders through improved engagement strategies. Be sure to share your thoughts, ideas, reflections, and work on social media using #digilead.

After reading this book, you will be able to

- Identify obstacles to change and specific solutions to overcome them in order to transform teaching, learning, and leadership in the digital age.

- Work smarter, not harder, by aligning a digital-leaning mindset to leadership practices to enhance school culture and improve stakeholder relations.

- Leverage digital resources and personalized pathways to grow professionally like never before.

- Readily implement practical digital leadership strategies aligned to research and proven in action, as told through practitioner vignettes.

New features in the second edition include

- Revamped organization throughout to emphasize the interconnectivity of the Pillars of Digital Leadership to drive sustainable change that gets results.

- A reduced focus on tools and a greater emphasis on leadership dispositions to create a more evergreen resource.

- New and updated vignettes from digital leaders who have successfully implemented the strategies presented.

- New insights from my experiences working in schools and organizations all over the world.

- Informative graphics in full color that add more context.

- A new foreword.

- Guiding questions at the end of each chapter to help you reflect on and apply the lessons offered in the book.

- A brand-new Chapter 12 with a focus on efficacy and competencies (as opposed to skills).

- New online resources.

As you read, answer the guiding questions, and be sure to engage and share on social media using #digilead.

Acknowledgments

Like many pieces of writing, *Digital Leadership: Changing Paradigms for Changing Times* has been a labor of love for Eric. For him, digital tools were a catalyst for conversation that not only provided him with ideas and inspiration, but also connected him with some of the most amazing educational leaders in the world: leaders such as David Britten, Dwight Carter, John Carver, Spike Cook, Robert Zywicki, Cheryl Fisher, Robert Dillon, Lyn Hilt, Patrick Larkin, Joe Mazza, and Pam Moran. Each of them has modelled the essence of digital leadership and continuously provides Eric with the support and guidance to lead change and grow professionally. One could not forget business maven Trish Rubin, who taught Eric about the importance of branding in education. Her insight and continuous mentoring have given Eric a fresh look at what education can and should be.

As much as digital influences and influencers played a role in the development of this book, the traditional elements have been just as important. Many of the ideas and strategies laid out in the book originated and/or evolved at New Milford High School (NMHS). Eric will forever be indebted to the NMHS community—students, teachers, administrators, parents, and other stakeholders—for their support, confidence, feedback, and inspiration. His family has also been instrumental in bringing this project to fruition with their patience and advice on how to craft a manuscript that not only makes sense, but also has value to an array of educators.

Finally, Eric would like to thank the staff of Corwin: publisher Arnis Burvikovs, who would not take no for an answer and convinced Eric to write this book focusing on his work as a digital leader; development editor Desiree Bartlett, who provided invaluable feedback and suggestions on how to improve the manuscript; Cate Huisman, whose keen eye and sound suggestions greatly assisted in creating this valuable resource; and senior editorial assistant Eliza Erickson, who kept Eric in the know with due dates, permissions, and other materials needed for the book.

About the Author

Eric Sheninger is a senior fellow and thought leader on digital leadership with the International Center for Leadership in Education (ICLE). Prior to this he was the award-winning principal at New Milford High in New Jersey. Under his leadership his school became a globally recognized model for innovative practices. Eric oversaw the successful implementation of several sustainable change initiatives that radically transformed the learning culture at his school while increasing achievement.

His work focuses on leading and learning in the digital age as a model for moving schools and districts forward. This has led to the formation of the Pillars of Digital Leadership, a framework for all educators to initiate sustainable change to transform school cultures. As a result, Eric has emerged as an innovative leader, best-selling author, and sought-after speaker. His main focus is purposeful integration of technology to facilitate student learning, improve communications with stakeholders, enhance public relations, create a positive brand presence, discover opportunity, transform learning spaces, and help educators grow professionally.

Eric has received numerous awards and acknowledgments for his work. He is a Center for Digital Education Top 30 Award recipient,

Bammy Award winner, National Association for Secondary School Principals Digital Principal Award winner, Phi Delta Kappa Emerging Leader Award recipient, winner of Learning Forward's Excellence in Professional Practice Award, Google Certified Innovator, Adobe Education Leader, and ASCD 2011 Conference Scholar. He has authored or coauthored six books, including best sellers *Uncommon Learning: Creating Schools That Work for Kids* and *Learning Transformed: 8 Keys for Designing Tomorrow's Schools, Today.*

Eric began his career in education as a science teacher at Watchung Hills Regional High School in Warren, New Jersey. He then transitioned into the field of educational administration, first as an athletic director and supervisor of physical education and health and then as vice principal in the New Milford School District. During his administrative career, he has served as district affirmative action officer and is the current president of the New Milford Administrators Association.

Eric earned a bachelor of science degree from Salisbury University, a bachelor of science from the University of Maryland Eastern Shore, and a master of education in educational administration from East Stroudsburg University.

To learn more about Eric's work, visit ericsheninger.com, or follow @E_Sheninger on Twitter. For booking inquiries, you can email him at esheninger@gmail.com.

A Day in the Life of a Digital Leader

Since 2009 I have been a digital leader. Each day as a principal, my day began like any other. I would arrive at school, greet the administrative assistants, and then boot up my computer. For the next couple of minutes, I put the finishing touches on the staff e-mail message of the day. This is the point at which things might be a bit different for me when compared to other administrators.

As I worked on the daily e-mail, my Twitter stream was also visible though an application called TweetDeck. I browsed the many tweets from members of my Personal Learning Network (PLN) to look for resources to include in the e-mail to my staff. Typically, I would find free web-based tools that my staff could integrate into their lessons to review prior learning, check for understanding, or provide digital closure. These tools were also curated in Diigo, a social bookmarking site, and in Pinterest for my staff and me to refer to when needed. I then quickly finished up my e-mail, sent it off, and again browsed my Twitter and Flipboard streams to catch up on the latest developments in education.

My next morning tasks consisted of updating announcements for students on a Google Doc that they could access on the school website. Once these were finished, I posted the link on our school's Twitter and Facebook pages, and a notification was sent out through our official school app the NMHS students helped to develop. Prior to homeroom beginning, I updated all of the school social media accounts to keep stakeholders abreast of the latest developments and news related to the school.

The day finally began around 8:00 AM. Armed with my smartphone and tablet, I would proceed to walk the halls, observing classes and conducting walk-throughs. My admin team and I conducted numerous walks a day, and information was collected using a Google Form and then later reflected upon, so teachers could receive timely, non-evaluative feedback related to improving pedagogy. I also conducted one to two formal observations a day using a digital platform from McREL. After each observation, teachers uploaded artifacts related to pedagogy and school culture for review, feedback, and an eventual discussion on how to grow and improve.

As you can see, the majority of my time during the school day was spent in classrooms. I used this time to not only evaluate instruction, but to also look for opportunities to consistently share student work and accomplishments using social media tools such as Twitter, Instagram, YouTube, and Facebook. I loved to capture innovative lessons and projects that my teachers had implemented, where technology was used in a purposeful way aligned to deeper thinking and relevant application. It was quite common to see teachers using web-based response tools to have students text in their answers to a do-now question. There was nothing more exciting than seeing students using their mobile learning devices to answer questions, engage in vibrant discussion, and collaborate on digital projects. This not only enhanced the learning experience but also prepared my students better for the real world, where digital devices are essential tools in many professions.

I eventually would pop back into my office to attend to the usual management tasks that often consume school leaders. However, time was always allocated to peruse through and comment on articles that my digital journalism students posted regularly on *The Lance,* the school's official newspaper, which was available only in digital format. I usually learned about this as they posted updates on the Twitter page that was created for the class in order to report stories in real time and promote their work.

During lunch, my administrative team and I would take turns supervising in order to free up teachers so that they could use the time to learn and grow professionally. As we were a Bring Your Own Device (BYOD) school, students were seen freely using their devices to socialize, complete assignments, conduct research, or organize their day. I seized the opportunity regularly to get Minecraft tips for my son, but also to catch up on completing observation write-ups using either my laptop or tablet. Thanks to our school's Wi-Fi and mobile charging stations, I could work seamlessly anywhere in the building. Working in the presence of my students was an added bonus.

The afternoon was usually composed of the same tasks and instructional duties as the morning. As I travelled the halls, I peeked into classrooms and would see students using their mobile learning devices to take pictures of notes the teacher had placed on the board, create learning artifacts, and collaborate on assignments. As the student day ended, I worked to make sure every managerial task had been completed. I then used the next couple of hours to blog about the great things I saw during the day and catch up on the chatter in social media spaces to acquire resources for my teachers and improve professional practice.

I was a digital leader, connected not only to my school, but also to a global network of educators that had evolved into my most treasured resource. This network consisted of tens of thousands of educators from six different continents. As a building leader in a small school, I was able to attend to and complete every major job task, such as observations, walk-throughs, new standard alignment, curriculum revisions, preparing for new teacher evaluations, budgeting, master scheduling, meetings, and other managerial issues. What distinguished me from most other school principals, though, was that I had learned to integrate a variety of digital tools and strategies to enhance all the facets of how I led. Digital leadership was not an add-on, but a complement to everything that I did as a principal and what I now do as a thought leader in the education space. It is not a time sap, either; instead, it is a different way of leading that is richer, more effective, more efficient, and better informed.

iStock.com/peshkov

How the Learning Landscape Has Changed

1

Today's kids are born digital—born into a media-rich, networked world of infinite possibilities. But their digital lifestyle is about more than just cool gadgets; it's about engagement, self-directed learning, creativity, and empowerment.

—Edutopia (2012)

THE FOURTH INDUSTRIAL REVOLUTION

Change isn't coming, it's already on our doorstep. Do you like change? If you do, then living in the present is an exhilarating experience. For those who don't, buckle up, as we are only going to see unprecedented innovation at exponential rates involving technology. You can't run or hide from it. The revolution, or evolution depending on your respective lens, of our world will transform everything as we know it. We must adapt, but more important, prepare our learners for a bold new world that is totally unpredictable. Welcome to the fourth Industrial Revolution.

In *Learning Transformed*, Tom Murray and I looked in detail at the disruptive changes we are all seeing currently, and also those that are yet to come. Here is an excerpt:

> Today's pace of technological change is staggering, and the speed of current breakthroughs has no historical precedent. Consumers may seem well-versed with the latest personal gadgets, yet growth in artificial intelligence (AI), robotics, autonomous vehicles, the internet of things (IoT), and nanotechnology remains hardly known except to technology gurus who live and breathe ones and zeros. The coming interplay of such technologies from both physical and virtual worlds will make the once unthinkable, possible.
>
> We believe that we are in the first few days of the next Industrial Revolution and that the coming age will systematically shift the way we live, work, and connect to and with one another. It will affect the very essence of the way humans experience the world. Although the 2000s brought with them significant change in how we utilize technology to interact with the world around us, the coming transformational change will be unlike anything mankind has ever experienced (Schwab, 2016).
>
> The Fourth Industrial Revolution, toward which we are facing as a society, is still in its infancy but growing exponentially. Advances in technology are disrupting almost every industry and in almost every country. No longer do natural or political borders significantly reduce the acceleration of change.

Today, we are taking our first steps into the Fourth Industrial Revolution, created by the fusion of technologies that overlap physical, biological, and digital ecosystems. Known to some as Industry 4.0, these possibilities have been defined as "the next phase in the digitization of the manufacturing sector, driven by four disruptions: the astonishing rise in data volumes, computational power, and connectivity; the emergence of analytics and business-intelligence capabilities; new forms of human-machine interaction such as touch interfaces and augmented-reality systems; and improvements in transferring digital instructions to the physical world, such as advanced robotics and 3-D printing" (Baur & Wee, 2015). Such systems of automation enable intelligence to monitor the physical world, replicate it virtually, and make decisions about the process moving forward. In essence, machines now have the ability to think, problem solve, and make critical decisions. In this era, the notion of big data and data analytics will drive decision-making. (2017, pp. 16–17)

To prepare learners for success during the fourth, or even fifth, Industrial Revolution, the notion of education has to change at scale. If all of the change we are seeing has taught us one major lesson, it is that schools must prepare kids to do anything, not something. Having current and future generations go through the motions and "do" school just won't cut it. Just because it worked for us as adults, does not mean it works—or even serves—well for our learners. The transition to the fourth Industrial Revolution does not spell doom and gloom for society as we know it. The idea here is to be proactive, not reactive, and to understand where opportunities lie for growth and improvement in education systems across the globe.

Figure 1.1 provides insight on what students need to compete in an automated world.

TECHNOLOGY AND SOCIETY

Societal shifts involving technology are beginning to have a profound impact on teaching, infrastructure, resources, stakeholder relations, and our learners. The opportunities include greater access to rich, multimedia content; the increasing use of online courses that offer classes not otherwise available; the widespread availability of

Figure 1.1 Automate This

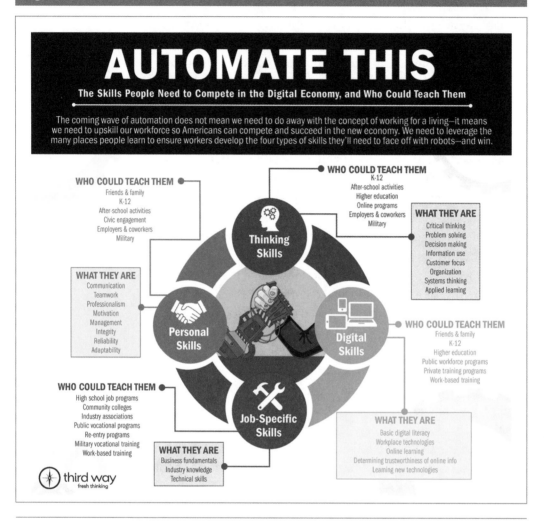

Source: Third Way (2018)

mobile computing devices that can access the internet; the expanding role of social networking tools for learning and professional growth; and the growing interest in the power of digital games for more personalized learning (*Education Week,* 2016). For our learners, a big part of their world is now online in some way. Understanding these shifts is key to developing a culture of learning that best meets the needs of our students while showing value to stakeholders.

There is a growing trend when it comes to people's use of technology, and that is use continues to increase exponentially. All one has to do is take a peek at the data sets, publications, and fact sheets compiled annually by the Pew Research Center (www.pewinter net.org/) to see not only the latest use, but also historical trends. The proliferation of technology and ease of access has resulted in changes to behavior. A study conducted by Andreu Casero-Ripollés (2012) found that young people's news consumption was oriented toward new media, especially social networks, while newspaper readership among young people declined. Wi-Fi is a staple in the industrialized world, and over time will be the new normal for even some of the world's most rural and isolated areas. Kids will enter a workforce that is influenced by new technologies. To be successful in a changing economy, students must learn to think algorithmically and computationally, and to solve problems with varying levels of abstraction (Jacob & Warschauer, 2018).

It is apparent that the majority of our students, stakeholders, teachers, and administrators are engaged in online spaces and have ample means to access the internet. Within this space, they are creating, communicating, collaborating, and discussing. This is occurring on and across a variety of sites and through the use of both mainstream and emerging tools. People from all walks of life find value in the amount of time spent using technology to connect with friends, read digital content, play video games, and create their own unique content. It is hard to deny the high level of engagement and interactivity that is taking place, all of which supports the outcomes that schools claim they want to enhance. This is the world into which our students are born and within which all members of society are immersed. The conversation needs to shift from one that focuses on digital natives and immigrants to one that looks at the fact that technology now permeates virtually every facet of society. As technology and the world continue to evolve, learners will continue to adapt. There is no time like the present for schools to follow suit and embrace change.

The statistics and facts the are continually shared by the Pew Research Center paint a general picture of society's increasing use, reliance, and infatuation with the internet and other technologies. Access to information in real time has become the standard, spearheaded by the continuous rise and evolution of social media sites. With the proliferation of evolved mobile technology, cheaper devices, and advances in wireless connectivity, it can be assumed that the majority of the world will be connected sooner than we think. With this information in hand, it is best to be proactive rather than reactive. Will your learners be adequately prepared for a world that is now almost impossible to predict based on exponential advances in technology? If not, then what are you willing to do to get your classroom, school, district, or organization moving in a better direction?

Society has a craving for accessing the internet for a variety of purposes and now possesses the means to connect in many ways. In response to these shifts, some educational leaders have begun to recognize that the current structure and function of institutions of learning are not in tune with the real world that is continuously advancing beyond the walls of schools. Finally, conversations are taking place on how schools and leaders can take advantage of the phenomena associated with this digital-age renaissance. Once sparsely connected, schools now invest in wireless networks that connect throughout buildings to the internet. Having the infrastructure in place is one thing; using it to advance learning and enhance other facets of leadership is another. Schools can no longer be wary of venturing into the world of social networking during school hours. We now have a generation of learners who are comfortable with and enthusiastic about using digital tools to collaborate and participate as creators rather than consumers. The calling now for all educational systems and leaders is to empower students to learn in powerful and meaningful ways like never before.

Change at scale has progressed at a snail's pace as a result of fear, lack of initiative, unwillingness to change, or not knowing where to begin. This has led to a natural disconnect in many cases between schools and those they serve—our learners. The longer this disconnect continues, the more meaningless and irrelevant our schools become to our students, who yearn for—and quite frankly deserve—more from the education they receive. It is time to transform schools into vibrant learning communities that are connected and allow access to numerous avenues that can unleash the creativity of our learners. This will increase engagement and, ultimately, achievement. By understanding how reliant all stakeholders are on the internet, leaders can develop strategies to better communicate information, enhance public relations, collaborate with other practitioners, discover opportunities to improve school culture, and be open to a nonstop pathway of new, innovative ideas.

The internet is not the only thing that continues to change. The advancement of existing technologies as well as the introduction of new tools has created a rich market for schools to utilize. Schools adopt educational technology to

- increase student engagement.
- improve learning (i.e., achieve higher standardized test scores).
- improve the economic viability of students (i.e., increase students' abilities to succeed in new work environments through teaming, technology fluency, and high productivity).
- close the digital divide (i.e., increase technology literacy in all students).
- increase relevance and real-world application of academics.
- build twenty-first century skills (e.g., critical thinking, sound reasoning, global awareness, communication skills, information and visual literacy, scientific reasoning, productivity, and creativity). (Lemke, Coughlin, & Reifsneider, 2009)

There seems to be no shortage of technology tools that are being used to increase student engagement, access and manage information, foster creativity, assess and curate content, and aid in conceptual mastery. Whether it is the result of societal pressures, marketing techniques, or a shift in vision, educational technology has become more prevalent in schools. Some schools have been adept at keeping up with those changes, while many others are falling far behind, creating a digital divide based largely on the quality of the educational technology they use, rather than just simple access to the internet (Herold, 2016). How this technology is ultimately used and its relative effectiveness in improving teaching, learning, and leadership will be discussed later in this book.

Desktops and laptops have long been considered the standard when it comes to educational technology in schools. As these devices have evolved, their prices have dropped, making them much more attainable within school budgets. Laptops today are 99% cheaper than they were in 1980. No wonder many schools are adopting devices at a feverish pace. Many computer suppliers have instituted lease programs, which make their products even more attractive in difficult economic times. It goes without saying that we will only continue to see price drops in not only computers, but other types of technologies as advances continue.

In addition to computers, there are many common educational technologies that are being utilized in schools today and have begun to reshape pedagogy, conceptual mastery, and professional learning, as well as content consumption and creation. The choices for school leaders can be overwhelming, and with tight budgets, sound decisions need to be made to ensure that any purchase makes the most sense to improve learning. Let's take a look at some common technology investments schools make. It is important to understand though that over time tools will evolve, and some will be phased out. The key here is to focus on why a certain piece of technology is a sound investment and how it will improve student learning.

Interactive Whiteboards (IWBs) and Displays

Some of us remember the days of the overhead projector as the gold standard for presenting information during direct instruction. The invention of the IWB not only replaced this dated piece of technology but provided an interactive experience in the classroom for both teachers and students. The appeal of IWBs lies in the opportunity for use of dynamic, interactive images, animations, video, and text of a size visible to an entire classroom (Lemke, Coughlin, & Reifsneider, 2009). Advances in software packages that come with a typical IWB purchase have made the device even more appealing. Educators can now access interactive lessons from the web or create their own, share content with colleagues near and far, and utilize integrated student response technology to facilitate a more connected learning experience for kids.

Research has found that IWBs and other display technology can have a positive impact on learning. Haystead and Marzano (2009) conducted 85 studies in 50 different schools and found large percentage gains in student achievement under the following conditions: The teacher had 10 or more years of teaching experience, had used the IWB for two years or more, had used the IWB 75%–80% of the time in the classroom, and had possessed high confidence in using the technology. Overall though, when it comes to the real benefit of IWBs in the classroom, it is what the learner, not the teacher, does with the device as a means to better understand concepts. It is important that any piece of display technology does not become a glorified direct instruction or presentation tool.

Tablets

Tablets are an attractive option for schools, as they are more portable and than laptops, which makes them very attractive centerpieces for 1:1 initiatives or station rotation models in blended learning environments. Tablets are a powerful educational tool, because they provide access to informational tools for creative learning and productivity, and they can be used for research. Tay (2016) conducted a three-year study in an all-girls' secondary school where the iPad was piloted by half the school. Empirical data through lesson observation was triangulated with perception surveys and group interviews of both teachers and students. The study found that the use of iPads was associated with more learner engagement and collaboration. It also found that iPad-using students, particularly those in the lowest and highest ability groups, performed better than their non-iPad-using peers in comparable groups on year-end examinations. Other studies have also found that tablets improve learning when utilized as a component of project-based learning and when used to support students in an inclusive setting (Cheu-Jey, 2015; Maich & Hall, 2016).

Recent advances in digital publishing have resulted in many traditional textbooks now being available on tablet devices for a fraction of their paper-published cost. In addition, schools have the ability to replace the overpriced textbook, which is still a crutch in many schools across the world. For example, students and educators can access iTunes U for free and access entire courses of educational content for K–12 schools. Apple has dominated the tablet market with its iPad, which launched in 2010. Even with the iPad's dominance, the tablet market has become saturated with stiff competition from Android tablets such as those manufactured by a variety of companies. As of 2019, the Apple App Store supports over 2 million apps for the iPad, while the Android Marketplace allows users to choose from 3.8 million apps.

Document Cameras

These devices are very similar to their ancestor, the overhead projector. Document cameras are connected to a projector in order to display the image of anything put underneath the camera. What makes these devices more dynamic is their ability to record both video and sound, a useful feature that allows teachers to capture lessons and notes to make available to their students through a website or to create flipped lessons. Students can even use them to display their work or thinking to an entire class. They are cost-effective, small, and portable. Some models even use wireless technology, so they don't have to be hardwired to a projector.

Chromebooks

Google developed this one-of-a-kind device that contains no operating system or hard drive. When the computer boots up, it connects directly to the internet, and the entire process takes around 10 seconds. Chromebooks are cheap and easy to manage, making them popular with budget-constrained schools with limited tech-support staff. With Wi-Fi now common in schools across the globe and in homes, an internet-dependent device has become practical for students (Jesdanun, 2017). Many models cost hundreds of dollars less than typical laptops and popular tablets. Users can create a free Google profile and log on to any Chromebook to access their G Suite, favorite websites, or the web-based applications that they have added to their account. There is even functionality offline through certain apps that don't require an internet connection.

All of the factors above have made the Chromebook a logical choice by schools as the device for 1:1 rollouts. Price and management aside, these programs have been found to lead to academic benefits among learners. Zheng, Warschauer, Lin, & Chang (2016) conducted a meta-analysis of 15 years' worth of research studies on K–12 schools where students were given a computing device. Using statistical techniques to analyze already-completed studies, they found that 1:1 laptop programs on average had a statistically significant positive impact on student test scores in English/language arts, writing, math, and science as well as providing a modest boost to twenty-first century skill attainment.

Mirroring Devices

These devices mirror exactly what is on digital devices such as laptops, smartphones, and tablets without the hassle of wires. Apple TV has the ability to mirror the screen from any Apple device to a projector or television. The Apple TV device is connected directly to either an HDMI projector or HDMI port on a television. Once the mirroring setting is enabled on any Apple device, the image appears on the television or projector screen. Many schools have now begun purchasing and using an Apple TV, HDMI projector, and iPad to create a wireless IWB. Best of all, this setup costs a great deal less than a mounted IWB but maintains all of the benefits of this technology. Apple TV is not your only option. Chromecast from Google allows screen mirroring on Android devices of web pages from any type of computer.

Augmented and Virtual Reality

Both augmented reality (AR) and virtual reality (VR) have the unique ability to alter our perception of the world and in turn provide our learners with enhanced ways to understand concepts. AR is where real life is modified and enhanced by computer-generated sights and sounds. A great example that many of us can relate to is Pokémon Go. A review of existing research by Saidin, Abd Halim, and Yahaya (2015) found that AR has been shown to have good potential in making the learning process more active, effective, and meaningful. This is because its advanced technology enables users to interact with virtual and real-time applications and brings the natural experiences to the user. In the context of education, it allows students to be immersed in realistic experiences, thus increasing relevance and allowing for deeper understanding.

VR on the other hand invites users into an artificial world that consists of images and sounds that are affected by the actions of a student who is experiencing it. The learning environment is provided through the use of a headset viewing device, including high-quality units such as the Oculus Rift for around $500 or the cheap Google Cardboard that runs between $10 and $15. All one has to do with the latter is insert a smartphone that has compatible apps downloaded, most of which are free, such as Google Expeditions. Schools are using VR for virtual field trips, content creation, distance learning, improved collaboration, game-based learning, and investigating certain concepts in more detail.

There has been a consistent rise in the use of VR content to enhance teaching and learning in 3-D environments. From specialized projectors to visual learning solutions, content providers are continuing to build upon their products to immerse students in virtual learning environments where they not only see, but hear and feel as well. These technologies are having a positive impact on learning. JTM Concepts of Rock Island, Illinois, began collecting data on the educational impact of its 3-D content in 2003. The results were impressive. Data showed that students who observed the 3-D simulations made a big jump from their prelesson to postlesson test scores while outperforming control groups who received traditional instruction (Gordon, 2010). A smaller study showed that students who observed the 3-D lesson improved an average of 32% from pretest to posttest, with substantial gains in every subgroup. A meta-analysis conducted by Merchant, Goetz, Cifuentes, Keeney-Kennicutt, and Davis (2014) found that VR-based instruction was effective in improving learning outcome gains.

Cloud Computing

This term refers to any hosted service that can be accessed over the internet. Many schools have invested in virtual servers, which are much more cost-effective than traditional ones. For schools and administrators, using the "cloud" has become a more effective and efficient way of managing documents, projects, and general information, as they can all be stored virtually and accessed anywhere. This has resulted in the adoption of either Google's suite of free tools or of Microsoft's Office 365 by many schools and educators alike. As cost-effective and enticing as cloud computing is, many schools fear losing control of private student information, especially in the United States.

The Family Educational Rights and Privacy Act (FERPA) (20 USC §1232g; 34 CFR Part 99) is a federal law that protects the privacy of student education records. The law applies to all schools that receive funds under an applicable program of the U.S. Department of Education. FERPA does not offer much guidance for schools on the selection and maintenance of cloud providers and the resulting relationships. The good news for school leaders, though, is that nothing in FERPA prevents schools from using cloud-based services, and schools across the country have embraced these solutions. When contracting any cloud-computing solution, it must be clear that the party to whom the information is disclosed will not disclose the information to any other party without the prior consent of the parent or eligible student. If this condition is not met, it is a violation of FERPA.

COPPA, the Children's Online Privacy and Protection Act (15 U.S.C. §§ 6501–6506), deals with how websites, apps, and other online operators collect data and personal information from kids under the age of 13. Schools can grant COPPA consent in cases where a tool is used solely for an educational purpose. When consent on behalf of parents can be determined, schools should also ensure they are in compliance with COPPA by thoroughly vetting products and providing appropriate information to parents. Information should include the names of sites or services the school has consented to on behalf of parents as well as information about those sites and services' information-sharing and security practices.

If you are based in a country other than the United States, be sure to reference your country's specific privacy laws as they relate to protecting the identity of students when using digital tools in schools.

Web-Based Tools

Within the cloud are many applications commonly referred to as web tools. Many of these tools are free and work to promote essential competencies such as collaboration, communication, creativity, entrepreneurship, and global awareness. Tools are always coming, going, or evolving. Thus, it is pointless to list specific favorites. The trick to finding the best tools to support your needs and those of your students is to learn about them in digital spaces. Social media tools such as Twitter, blogs, and digital discussion forums have become widely accepted as means to grow professionally. The only downside of web applications is that they are generally grouped together with mainstream social media sites such as Facebook and YouTube. As a result, many schools in the United States block them and prohibit access, feeling that their use is a violation of the Child Internet Protection Act (CIPA) (20 U.S.C. §§ 6801, 6777, 9134 [2003]; 47 U.S.C. § 254 [2003]). Congress enacted CIPA in 2000 to address concerns over children accessing inappropriate content over the internet. The Federal Communications Commission (FCC, 2011) provides details that schools need to know about CIPA:

> Schools must certify that they have an Internet safety policy that includes technology protection measures. The protection measures must block or filter Internet access to pictures that are: (a) obscene; (b) child pornography; or (c) harmful to minors (for computers that are accessed by minors). Before adopting this Internet safety policy, schools and libraries must provide reasonable notice and hold at least one public hearing or meeting to address the proposal.

So why are the majority of schools blocking these amazing tools? School leaders are well aware of CIPA but are misinformed when it comes to access to web-based digital applications. All that CIPA requires in order for schools to be eligible to receive e-Rate funding is that inappropriate websites are blocked. In a 2011 interview, the Department of Education's director of education technology, Karen Cator, explained that accessing YouTube and similar social media sites is not a violation of CIPA, and web-based tools do not have to be blocked for teachers (Barseghian, 2011). The takeaway here is that leaders must become advocates for the use of web applications in schools, working with all stakeholders to create an environment focusing on responsible use. They need to be active in creating and sustaining a safe online environment for students and acceptable use policies (AUPs) that address misuse, and also ensuring that adequate supervision is provided at all times.

As in the case with student identity, if you are based in a country other than the United States, be sure to reference your country's specific laws as they relate to keeping students safe when using digital tools in schools.

Mobile Technology

As mentioned earlier in this chapter, mobile technology (i.e., mobile phones, tablets, e-readers) continues to explode into the marketplace and into homes. This trend has not gone unnoticed in the education world. Schools and leaders in many areas have seen the value in purchasing mobile technology for 1:1 initiatives, while others are opting for more cost- effective programs that utilize the technology that students already own. These latter initiatives are commonly referred to as either Bring Your Own Device (BYOD) or Bring Your Own Technology (BYOT) programs. Regardless of the acronym, digital-rich environments are created as leaders begin to rethink existing policies that prohibited access to sites that have educational value and prevented use of student-owned devices that can be leveraged for learning. Mobile learning devices hold great potential, since they can be used by a variety of stakeholder groups for assessment, content curation, research, organization, collaboration on projects, classroom walk-throughs, and observations. As discussed previously in this chapter, research by Zheng et al. (2016) found that mobile learning has led to improved student learning outcomes.

Video Conferencing

As the internet has evolved, so has video-conferencing technology. Long past are the days when this tool was only available to schools in affluent areas or through sparse grants. All one now needs is a webcam-enabled device (i.e., desktop, laptop, tablet, or smartphone), an internet connection, and either a program or an app (e.g., Skype, FaceTime, Adobe Connect, Google Hangouts, Zoom) to create a video feed. Schools now have the means to conduct virtual field trips, connect with authors, and collaborate with colleagues from across the globe. Using tools like Facebook and YouTube Live, schools can not only broadcast live events, but can even archive the footage for viewing at a later time.

Open Education Resources (OER)

These resources, commonly referred to as OER, are accessible for free on the internet. They consist of openly licensed text, media, and other digital resources that can be used to support and enhance teaching, learning, and assessment. Some OER assets can even be used for research purposes. OER Commons (www.oercommons.org) is a great place to start. It is a public digital library of open educational resources where you can explore, create, and collaborate with educators around the world to improve curriculum. Here you can access lesson plans and projects aligned to specific content areas, standards, and education levels.

One of the major recent advancements in educational technology has been the availability of OER content and entire courses from some of the nation's most prestigious universities and professors free of charge. The movement began with the Massachusetts Institute of Technology (MIT), which believed that making OpenCourseWare (OCW) available would enhance human learning worldwide by providing a web of knowledge (Vest, 2004). Harvard, Yale, Stanford, and the University of Michigan are just a sample of some of the universities offering access to their courses online through massive open online courses (MOOCs).

OCW is composed of content in the form of university lectures, notes, and assignments, with little emphasis on cohesiveness. MOOCs, on the other hand, are structured around lengthy courses aligned to online learning. In this setting, lectures are scheduled by professors or facilitators with associated deadlines, assignments, assessments, and community engagement. The accessibility and quality of OCW hold the promise of providing students and educators with more personalized learning options that can cater to diverse needs. If you or your students ever want to access some amazing, free learning opportunities, then check out either Coursera (www.coursera.org) or edX (www.edx.org), where OCW courses are curated.

Virtual Schooling

Also known as cyberschooling or distance learning, this is a service that schools can invest in, available to students anywhere at any time. Traditional schools can increase their current course catalogues by hundreds of new courses that cater to student interest. Key characteristics of virtual schools include credit attainment to complement studies at a local campus, and ability of students to work at their own pace; instruction is available year-round, courses are taught by highly qualified teachers, and there is a wide range of courses available that are updated frequently (Kelly, McCain, & Jukes, 2009).

Electronic delivery provided by a virtual school can occur using synchronous communication, in which class members all participate at the same time, or asynchronous communication, where participants are separated by time (Mielke, 1999). In a synchronous course, students meet with a live instructor at set times. The content is delivered using videoconference technology, and students submit their assignments to the instructor when due. In an asynchronous course, students can access the learning materials at times convenient for them, but all work and assignments are due within a specified period of time. As in a synchronous course, assignments are sent to a certified teacher. Virtual schooling offers students considerable benefits, including convenience of time and place (LeLoup & Ponterio, 2000). Popular providers include the Virtual High School (vhslearning.org/) and the Florida Virtual School (www.flvs.net/Pages/default.aspx), which are accessible all over the world.

Gaming

Long thought only to be a distraction, research has a different story about gaming in education. James Gee (2007) derived a set of 36 learning principles from his study of the complex, self-directed learning each player undertakes as he or she encounters and masters a new game. He suggests that adherence to these principles could transform learning in schools both for teachers and faculty and, most important, for students. Steve Johnson (2006) found that video games, from *Tetris* to *The Sims* to *Grand Theft Auto,* raised IQ scores and developed cognitive abilities, skills that even books can't foster. In a study of more than 500 second graders, Wexler et al. (2016) found that math and reading scores on school-administered tests increased significantly more in children who used a brain-training game during the school year than in children in control classes. The effect on math achievement scores was greater than what has been reported for 1:1 tutoring, and the effect on reading scores was greater than what has been reported for summer reading programs.

Some innovative schools have begun to seize the opportunity with educational gaming by investing in popular game consoles such as Nintendo Wii and Microsoft's Xbox. Both of these systems can be used to support tactile and kinesthetic learning styles. This is significant, as research shows that students learn more quickly and easily with instruction across multiple modalities or through a variety of media (Lemke, 2008). Many researchers continue to build upon these studies and continue to find positive impacts of gaming on learning (IGI Global & Information Resources Management Association, 2018). One of the hottest games has been *Minecraft* (minecraft.net), a world-building game that some educators have embraced to teach physics, geography, and the English language. Another exciting tool is VR Quest, where students can design 3-D virtual reality games aligned to standards. To learn more, visit www.vrquest.net.

A NEW LEARNER

> Our students have changed radically. Today's students are no longer the people our educational system was designed to teach.
>
> —Mark Prensky (2001, p. 1)

The world has changed, as have the learners that schools are responsible for educating. They may be referred to as the iGeneration, Millennials, or Generation Y. Whether we like it or not, students today are immersed in an environment rich in digital media and tools. These tools have become status symbols, means of communication, and digital-age organizers. Many people would agree they have also become a student's nerve center, because so much of a student's life is now influenced by the tools of the age. The attraction ultimately begins at a young and innocent age. All one has to do is observe a toddler with an iPad or a slightly older child building a virtual world in *Minecraft* or immersed in *Fortnite*. Observe enough, and it is tough to deny how technology sparks curiosity, ignites ingenuity, and fosters collaboration.

Students are engaged in their digital worlds, and they are learning without us. It has become a much more active process due to that ease of accessing information on the internet and a wide range of tools that support constructivist learning. Students are constructing meaning through the use of technology in ways that are relevant, meaningful, and fun.

Leaders of schools need to acknowledge that learners today are "wired" differently as a result of the experiential learning that is taking place outside of school. The learning styles of the active, digital learner conflict with traditional teaching styles and preferences. How can we possibly meet the needs of these unique learners if our practices are suited for a time that has long since passed? Ian Jukes, Ted McCain, and Lee Crockett (2010) provide the following characteristics of learners today and the resulting disconnects that they are experiencing in schools:

- Digital learners prefer to access information quickly from multiple media sources, but many educators prefer slow and controlled release of information from limited sources.

- Digital learners prefer parallel processing and multitasking, but many educators prefer linear processing and single tasks or limited multitasking.

- Digital learners prefer random access to hyperlinked multimedia information, but many educators prefer to provide information linearly, logically, and sequentially.

- Digital learners prefer to learn "just in time," but many educators prefer to teach "just in case."

- Digital learners prefer instant gratification and immediate rewards, but many educators prefer deferred gratification and delayed rewards.

- Digital learners prefer to network simultaneously with others, but many educators prefer students to work independently before they network and interact.

- Digital learners prefer processing pictures, sounds, color, and video before text, but many educators prefer to provide text before picture, sound, and video.

- Digital learners prefer learning that is relevant, active, instantly useful, and fun, but many educators feel compelled to teach memorization of the content in the curriculum guide.

The learners that we now embrace in our schools grew up with laptops instead of books. They use keyboards more than they do pens.

Students today want to know things all of the time. In their world, they can use numerous digital tools to learn whatever they want, any time and from anywhere. These students have been raised in a technology-rich environment, they accept that this environment is the norm, and they have grown up surrounded by digital devices that they regularly use to interact with other people and the outside world (Prensky, 2001). They are what many refer to as Millennials or active learners.

As a result of the growing disconnect between their world and the world where they are supposed to receive a formal education, many students are bored with the classroom. The environment outside of school is more engaging, relevant, and meaningful. They routinely communicate with friends, see faces, hear voices, create works of art, and engage in conversations with other learners on the other side of the school world. *Their* world is drastically different from that of the schools they attend and the educators tasked with teaching them. The active learner often seeks knowledge online rather than using a textbook and has little tolerance for delays. This makes it important for educators to provide feedback to their queries. For many active learners, the idea of constructing knowledge within a social community has a great deal of appeal (Skiba & Baron, 2006).

Society has created these active learners that schools need to keep up with, not the other way around. They crave choices and want to be connected. Their connections mean everything. When they discover something they like, they are excited to share it with their friends using digital devices and social media tools. This is how they want their educational experience to be. Active learners want to learn collaboratively and to apply what they have learned through creative pathways. They prefer learning on their own time and on their own terms and want to be involved in real-life issues that matter to them. They want to use their personal devices to take notes or, better yet, take pictures of teacher notes using a cell phone. At New Milford High School in New Jersey, this became widely accepted by both students and teachers. The traditional way of doing things does not have the same impact it once did. We as educators need to think about our own behaviors in the digital age and work to apply them for the betterment of learners of all ages.

It is important to understand that, even though today's active learners have grown up with technology, it does not always follow that they know how to use it effectively for learning. This is the responsibility of schools. We are tasked with preparing students for success in a world that is becoming more dependent on technology, a world that is also in need of a workforce that can think critically, solve real-world problems, and function entrepreneurially.

SUMMARY

Leaders need to be aware of the changing educational landscape inherent in the fourth Industrial Revolution (and eventually in the fifth one), which includes societal shifts in technology use, advances in educational technology, and a new type of learner. Acknowledging and beginning to understand these changes are the first steps to developing a vision and strategic plan for creating a learning culture that provides access to tools that support the development of critical competencies, celebrates success, supports innovation, and inspires students to learn and ultimately achieve. Digital leadership can and should begin here. If we discount the shifts occurring outside our walls and fail to embrace what learners today need and expect, we will never develop the capacity to anticipate needed changes that will transform school culture for the better.

GUIDING QUESTIONS

1. How has your district, school, or classroom changed to align with societal shifts? Where is improvement warranted? If change has been slow, where will you begin?

2. In what ways are you preparing your learners for the fourth Industrial Revolution (and eventually the fifth one)? Where are the opportunities for growth?

3. What types of technology have been adopted in your school or district? Has it been successful in improving learning outcomes? Why or why not?

4. How have you been responsive to the needs of learners today?

iStock.com/courtneyk

A Compelling Case for Change

2

Those who work in a school system are the victims of TTWWADI—That's the Way We've Always Done It. Schools have operated this way for such a long time that most people who work there don't really know the reasons why they do the things they do.

—Kelly, McCain, and Jukes (2009)

During the nineteenth century, there was a dire need to prepare students for assimilation into a workforce in response to the rapid increase in manufacturing. As our nation and the world became industrialized, school became the central institution to provide students with the skills to succeed in this new work environment, which aligned itself to the pressing needs of manufacturing. As these organizations evolved and competition increased, the need for workers who were more efficient and possessed specialized skill sets also increased. As the twentieth century approached, innovation continued to have a profound impact on formal schooling. The increased efficiency and productivity of Henry Ford's assembly line trickled down and eventually impacted school structure and function. For all intents and purposes, schools modelled themselves after these assembly lines, and teachers became specialized to teach only one general subject throughout the school day. A school's raison d'être became that of organizing students into distinct roles in order to prepare them for the various industry-specific jobs that awaited them. America's system of education changed forever, and schools across the globe mirrored the assembly lines where many of their graduates would end up. Curricula leaned heavily on the memorization of facts, and the skills taught were those that were pivotal to success in the industrial age.

Obviously, many things began to change as technology became more advanced, requiring a different type of workforce with skills that exceeded those needed in manufacturing. The transition from agriculture to manufacturing eventually gave way to a variety of new occupations in service, professional, and technical areas; thus, more and more students began to seek additional education upon graduating from high school. A bachelor's degree became a prerequisite for a job. This soon changed to the requirement of a master's degree in many professions, as society moved from an industrialized to a globalized economy. Despite these major changes over the years, one thing remained unchanged: the structure of schools. To this day we need to ask ourselves this question: Are schools preparing learners for their future or for a world that no longer exists?

If you walk into any secondary school building, chances are it will eerily resemble any other one you've seen. The day will be structured into periods, and bells will signify movement from one class to the next. Students will have a different teacher for each subject as well as a textbook or workbook. Each room will have desks aligned in rows where students will obediently take notes, answer questions, and complete either group or individual work. Lectures or other direct forms of content delivery will dominate class time. The day will typically end with the assignment of homework in some or all of the classes. After everything is said and done, all of the students will be assessed using either standardized methods or internally generated tools chock-full of fill-in-the-blank and multiple-choice questions. Sure, technology might be used in some way, but the chances are it is in a way that acts as a direct substitute for the ineffective practices just described. In this way, public education has become nothing more than a cog factory, churning out workers who can be successful in a factory or consumers who will purchase what is being produced (Godin, 2010). Is this what your school looks like? More important, is this what the real world looks like?

Standardization and efforts to reform education that have always been heavily dependent on high-stakes testing are further reducing the education system to a model that does not work for our learners. Many kids are not motivated by standardized tests, as they find no true meaning and value in them. Educators can become motivated for all the wrong reasons, including job security or financial incentives. A focus on standardization narrows the curriculum and creates a learning culture where creativity, exploration, and critical thinking are scarce or nonexistent. It creates a culture that learners dislike, one that can only be sustained with the use of "if-then" rewards or "carrots and sticks." There has to be a better direction. If schools continue down the same course, they risk inhibiting creativity, stifling passion, and reinforcing an outdated model that will not prepare our students for their future.

Standardization continues to follow in the footsteps of the century-old model of education that is focused on industrialization. Such a model stifles the growth of teachers, students, and administrators. This entrenched system produces learners who lack creativity, are fearful of failure, comply (do homework, study for tests, do not question authority), and eventually leave schools with skills that are obsolete in a postindustrial society. Schools, for the most part, focus more on filling the minds of students with useless facts and knowledge, rather than giving them essential competencies that they can't demonstrate with a #2 pencil. The measure of a school is not just how well students do on standardized tests, but on whether or not kids love and appreciate learning. The latter is a better indicator of future success.

Learners are not fond of what is described above. Both of my kids have been a part of what was just described at some point during their K–12 education and can attest to this fact. I want both of my kids to love learning and know that they are so much more than a score. The job of schools is to help all learners believe that. Kids today expect and deserve different and better, which is why a course reset is needed at scale. The world, as described in Chapter 1, continues to change at an exponential pace. Learners have embraced the Information Age, while many schools continue to function as they have for well over a century. The conundrum is that we want our learners to be prepared for whatever the future holds for them. Life will be dramatically different for our kids in the near and far future, given the pace of change in a technologically driven world, but our current education system does not adequately prepare them for the kinds of jobs and challenges they are likely to encounter in their lifetimes (Schrum & Levin, 2015). Kelly et al. (2009, p. 9) note the fundamental disconnect between students and the schools they attend:

- The industrial efficiency model envisioned for teaching in the early twentieth century is not reflected in learning efficiency for students in the twenty-first century.

- The learning styles of today's digital learners are significantly different from those for whom our schools were originally designed, especially high schools. They work, think, and learn differently—and our schools are not designed for them.

- Instruction is primarily based on teachers talking in classrooms, textbooks, memorization, and content-based tests; as such, schools are out of sync with the world around them.

- Schools focus on linear, sequential, left-brain thinking in a world that requires both left- and right-brain capabilities.

- The segregation of skills and tasks that typified the industrial approach is reflected today in our approach to creating schools for the future—and it does not serve us well.

Everything is changing—society, the educational landscape, and learners—and it is time for educational leaders to embody a modern, progressive form of leadership. More often than not, the individuals trusted with leading change in the present are the least knowledgeable about the present and future needs of learners. Education is at a crossroads, and it needs innovative leaders who possess the competencies and fortitude to move schools forward. We can no longer sit back and watch our schools become less and less relevant while failing to meet the needs of our learners and other stakeholders. The actions of school leaders will ultimately determine the fate of schools as we continue to advance further into the fourth Industrial Revolution, and eventually the fifth. Digital leadership is about establishing a vision and implementing a strategic process that creates a teaching and learning culture that provides students with essential competencies: creativity, communication, collaboration, critical thinking, problem solving, entrepreneurship, technological proficiency, and global awareness. It is also about how each of us approaches our work through the lens of these skill sets; this will redefine not only the structure of schools, but also our capacity to lead and initiate sustainable change. Digital leadership focuses on a consistent pursuit of innovation, purposeful use of technology, quality professional learning, transparency, celebration of successes from which others may learn, establishment of relationships with stakeholders, an open mind, and anticipation of continued change. It flies in the face of TTWWADI and allows us to reinvent education.

This imperative has become more difficult because of budget cuts and what seems like a relentless attack on the profession of education, which have taken their toll on staff morale. Digital leadership thus becomes even more essential for cultivating a school culture whose primary focus is on the learning and achievement of each and every student.

A SCHOOL LEADER'S NEW PATH FORWARD

Architect Louis Sullivan once said, "Form ever follows function." In no place has that precept ever been truer than in our schools, from cafeterias to classrooms. Yesterday's students, often destined for the factory floor or service work, attended schools functionally designed to teach institutional compliance. In the 1990s, America outsourced its factories; yet today's factory schools continue to warehouse young people, despite the fact that America no longer needs a workforce trained for the last century. This is why Dr. Pam Moran's district began to usher in significant changes in their work beginning in 2006 to optimize learning among young people for this century. Pam worked in the Albemarle School District adjacent to Charlottesville, Virginia, from 1986 to 2018, and was its superintendent for 12 of those years. She was the first female superintendent in the district (P. Moran, personal communication, 2018). In 2016 she was named Virginia Superintendent of the Year. In that same year she was one of four finalists for National Superintendent of the Year.

It seems like Pam was on to something. Schools in her county were preparing students for a world that no longer existed. The National Academies Press emphasized the way in which schools should be structured in its publication *Education for Life and Work: Developing Transferable Knowledge and Skills in the 21st Century,* which aligned with Pam's push for change:

> When the goal is to prepare students to be successful in solving new problems and adapting to new situations, then deeper learning is called for. Calls for such 21st century skills as innovation, creativity, and creative problem-solving can also be seen as calls for deeper learning—helping students develop transferable knowledge that can be applied to solve new problems or respond effectively to new situations. (National Research Council, 2012, p. 70)

As noted in Chapter 1, current learners inhabit a world in which multimodal communication, face-to-face and virtual teamwork, self-initiated problem solving, and creative solution finding have become the normative expectation, not the exception, at work, in homes, and across communities. Young people don't depend on home editions of encyclopedias, the library, or their teachers for basic information or "do-it-yourself" solutions (Riedel, 2012). They go straight to Wikipedia, YouTube, Twitter, Facebook, Siri, or Alexa—or they text a friend. With the rapid acceleration of new technologies, the world has changed for these neomillennials, and for their grandparents and their parents. But the schools that they, themselves, attend haven't evolved much at all.

Young people still often languish in mass-standardized schools where desks in rows, the dominant teaching wall, print on paper, one-size-fits-all testing, bell schedules, and an outright focus on compliance are key to controlling and limiting learners' work. Frederick Taylor's "cult of efficiency"—essential to assembly lines, piecework, and the repetitive processes of the factory floor—remains well established inside schools, regardless of the build date. This is not true of other professions.

Over time, the practices, tools, and work spaces of physicians have changed to reflect contemporary research and new technologies to better serve patients. Lawyers use online research resources to prepare briefs and contractual agreements on behalf of clients.

Automotive technicians download data from vehicles to determine what repairs and maintenance are needed. Amazon shipping facilities have become more and more automated, so that many boxes that arrive on your doorstep have received less than a minute of human contact. Even trash trucks and taxis have quick response (QR) codes affixed to them to lead potential customers to their websites. Every sector, every job, every employee today has had to respond to exponential change, often because of new technologies. All one has to do is look at how Netflix, Uber, and Airbnb have flourished at the expense of their rivals who either did not change or failed to change fast enough.

Educators Pam worked with in her district sought to understand the dynamic of global changes that young people would face in their future. They asked,

> Isn't it past time for education and educators to respond to twenty-first century changes as well? Isn't it time to move from teaching places limited by the walls of classrooms and schools to learning spaces, limitless in possibilities, that extend educational opportunities beyond school walls and district boundaries? Isn't it time to stop paying attention to political and private sector agendas that promote twentieth century standardization methodologies and, instead, attend to the need to "destandardize" curricula, assessment, and pedagogy so we can get to unlimited, deep learning?

Pam routinely walked through schools inside or outside her own district. She looked at how staff reconfigured their use of space so that learners could work privately or together in larger or smaller groups and teams, and with a choice of tools, both virtually through the internet and face to face. The concept of space, both physical and virtual, provided a critical entry point for instructional change to occur, so that educators could personalize, individualize, and differentiate learning through the use of new technologies. Creative flexibility and the adaptability of space in schools served as starting points for students to produce artifacts showing what they had learned, not just consume what an adult taught. Space matters. Tech matters. According to Pam, though, it is our teachers who remain the determining factors in whether learning will be transformed to represent what young people need for today and tomorrow, not for yesterday's world.

At one point she visited a new school outside of her district that was built as a series of interactive learning spaces—a school for the present and future, not the past. Its design served any level of school, elementary to high. She was part of a small group inspecting this "best-in-class" school, which was constructed to reflect advances in neuroscience and educational design research that teach us that learners benefit from fresh air, movement, and natural light in a learning environment. It was a school built for project-based learning. Pam wanted to experience a school designed from the ground up with progressive learning at its core, because her district was similarly committed to transforming pedagogy, resources, and learning spaces.

Created with experiential learning in mind, the airy spaces in this school were designed so that active learners could collaborate, create, and share. Faceted light tubes brightened hallways and the gym with natural light on days when winter clouds darkened the morning sky. Window seating, wide enough for two or more children to curl up with a good paper or e-book, punctuated swaths of glass that stretched across outer classroom walls. The art room and library opened onto spacious decks designed to entice learners into open air. In addition to integration of a food lab, a learning lounge, state-of-the-art composting facilities, a "teaching kitchen," and a performance area that opened into the dining space, cafeteria doors led to large raised-bed vegetable gardens irrigated from a rainwater harvesting and collection system.

A combination of open and closed flexible learning spaces linked nooks and open areas—labelled "nest," "canopy," "cave," and "woodlands"—to natural environments outside the school. Furniture and technology tools afforded a continuum of choices and zones of comfort for learners and educators alike. It was what many educators would characterize as a dream of a school.

Despite these innovations, Pam found that teachers and children were not doing the work she had anticipated. A teacher commented to her openly, "I'd prefer desks with built-in storage areas for textbooks. When the kids need to go get their social studies texts, it takes 10 minutes out of the block." Pam watched learners complete worksheet after worksheet, read in round-robin style, and listen to teacher-directed instruction. The message—whether posted as reading rules, library rules, or class rules—was, in essence, "Be compliant. Sit down. Be silent." Whiteboard and other technologies lay mostly unused, expensive devices lost to learning.

In a school filled with state-of-the-art learning spaces, tools, and resources, students' work mirrored the traditions of a twentieth-century education. Despite the innovative space design and tools present in this school for the future, it was still a teaching place of the past. On the surface everything had changed, yet in the reality of learners, nothing had really evolved. The district had invested significant resources in advanced technologies and learning spaces. Some would say there should be no barriers to contemporary learning in this new school. There was a glaring issue though. Pedagogy and mindset had not changed at all.

Why do some educators resist change, particularly in the face of the significant shifts occurring around us in the world? Is it that we do not notice the shifts or that we see them as irrelevant to our own work? Perhaps we do not know what we need to do differently or why we need to change anyway. Could it be that we simply resist change because of our own fears of failure? Is it because of the standardization movement that's embedded in schools everywhere? Or, in the best tradition of the iconic multiple-choice test, is it all of the above?

Pam discussed with her school board and staff how traditional trends of education represented the same multiple governmental failures identified by the 911 Commission: failure of policy, management, organizational capacity, and imagination. In the education sector in general, we build policy based on old paradigms, still work mostly in silos, lack strategies to build consistent capacity to use new pedagogies and tools, and fail to imagine a future that will be substantively different from yesterday or even today. Pam believes that as leaders, we must question at every opportunity our commitment to sustaining practices that need to be abandoned for the sake of contemporary learners.

Moore's Law represents a norm in our world—that is, there will continue to be rapid shifts in the evolution and extinction of technologies in the workforce, our personal lives, and our social communities. People go to work today not in cubicles or on assembly lines but in their own homes and highly active spaces in which technologies seamlessly blend into jobs—whether at McDonald's, Google, or an automotive repair shop. A visit to an advanced manufacturing "collaboratory" at the University of Virginia provided Pam with a glimpse of contemporary engineering work areas: a multipurpose space that combined lounge seating with programming and design space, partitioned only by a glass wall from a construction laboratory filled with 3-D printers and test spaces. The chair of the department explained that classical engineering curricula, like current medical school curricula, is evolving from disciplines taught in isolation to transdisciplinary learning, and that the field of engineering no longer operates singularly, but as one in which engineers must draw from multiple fields to design, engineer, test, and manufacture.

This kind of change is everywhere in the workforce. However, change being advanced in schools isn't *just* about the workforce. It's also about how humans search, connect, communicate, and create as members of a global community, and within our own families. It's about citizenship, including digital responsibility. If we expect learners to continue to evolve in their experiences with us and throughout their lives, why would we not expect them to power up their learning in our schools with contemporary tools to connect with peers and experts across our schools, districts, the nation, and the globe?

People live today, as Google's Pascal Finette (2012) explained, in "a culture of participation plus technologies plus networks" that will, in his opinion, change the course of human history. One spring, high school seniors in Pam's district conversed via Skype with an Egyptologist who was boots-on-the-ground in the revolutionary streets of Cairo. Their connection? A student teacher with family in Egypt. Kindergarten children in two different schools explored *J* words in a lesson cotaught by their teachers and an educator from Michigan—via their class Twitter account. Pam was regularly invited to comment on first- and third-graders' blogs. She watched from her couch the live broadcast of three schools' winter orchestra concerts via Ustream and observed sixth graders characterizing contemporary lyrics as poetry in their own virtual, multimedia "op-ed" posts. She visited multiage coder dojos where students, age 6 to 18, informally learned from and with one another and teachers to use multiple programming tools.

Pam believes that students in our schools are winners or losers depending on whether they are the recipients of annual random acts of excellence or not. A learner can end up in a state-of-the-art-school facility where pedagogy still remains in command-and-control mode, driven by a "one-to-some" teaching model through curricula, assessment, and instructional standardization that minimize opportunities for young people to pursue interests, passions, and possibilities. Or a child can enter a school district or class where he or she is afforded opportunities that evoke passion, capability, resiliency, and self-direction. In such learning spaces where questions, curiosity, and risk taking are nurtured, young people don't power down their tools or their minds when they cross the threshold of school. Instead, they learn today what they need for today—and tomorrow. That's what she believes every young person deserves in school.

The Albemarle County Schools recognize that deep, necessary change does not come from changing spaces, tools, or other resources alone. It comes from supporting professionals to invest in studying, connecting, communicating, and learning together, beginning with their own questions, curiosity, and interests as learners. We expect young people, regardless of whether they attend a school built in the 1930s or one built today, to acquire lifelong learning competencies that transcend the knowledge they need in the present, knowing it will be different tomorrow.

The deep changes Pam observed have come from years and years of ongoing professional work by teachers, principals, and central staff—educators working together in vertical and horizontal learning communities and leadership teams. Each summer they came together to study, plan, and develop curricula that were concept centered and standards aligned. They took the time to identify, use, and evolve instructional practices that were personalized, differentiated, and individualized to how young people learn. Teachers created open and interdisciplinary performance tasks designed to inform assessments in an effort to move beyond standardized testing as the measure of success.

Was everyone on board in Pam's district with the changes being made? Absolutely not. However, the ethos and culture of learning communities in her previous district, and everywhere for that matter, continue to shift among its educators, who are more tuned in than ever to considering and answering the question, "Why change?"

EXCUSES HOLD US BACK

We can no longer afford to sustain a school structure built for a time long past. What will it take for the lightbulb to finally go on and the long, difficult process of change to begin? Success in this endeavor relies on us to take a no-excuse attitude. Ask yourself this: What am I prepared to do to improve all facets of my classroom, school, or district? How will I accomplish more with less? Leaders must think and reflect upon the ways to accomplish established goals as opposed to worrying about the challenges, roadblocks, and pushback that they will surely experience. These are all common complications that arise during the change process and should not be excuses not to push forward. If it is important to you, you will find a way. If not, you'll make an excuse.

Leaders must be the pillars of their respective institutions and focus on solutions rather than problems. The role of a leader isn't to tell others what to do. It's to show them what they can become. Succumbing to the negative rhetoric, abiding by the status quo, and having a bunker mentality will do nothing to initiate needed changes in buildings to improve teaching and learning. Each day leaders are afforded an opportunity to make a positive difference in the lives of students. One's passion for helping all students learn and desire to assist staff in their growth should be the driving motivational forces to make schools the best they can be, regardless of the obstacles. Keep in mind this important point. The most impactful change doesn't come from people with a title, power, or position in education. It happens at the ground level with our teachers, as it is they who have to implement ideas for the direct betterment of students. Let your actions, not role, define you.

As noted in Chapter 1, everything is changing—the world, learners, the job market, technology, access to information—yet the sad reality in many (not all) cases is that schools are not. Digital leadership emphasizes the need for current leaders to be catalysts to drive sustainable change that will transform school culture. Only then will schools produce learners ready to take on the world and able to succeed in a demanding society ever more reliant on digital fluency and an entrepreneurial thought process. Leaders must begin to map out collective responses that focus on positive solutions to the problems inherent in school culture.

YOU GET WHAT YOU MODEL

Jobs have changed radically due to the rise of globalization, the continuous surge of outsourcing by many businesses and industries, increasing immigration, and a flattened world (Friedman, 2005). Think about the fact that this was written in 2005. Now just imagine not only what we are seeing now, but what might be on the horizon. Schools need to change in the face of this challenge if they are to create the next generation of entrepreneurs, scientists, politicians, and engineers who work in a technology-rich and technology-driven world. With this modern workforce as the goal, what do we want our schools to look like? Why do we need to change? Are we doing what's best to meet the needs of our learners who have grown up in the digital age with ubiquitous access to information?

Leaders must articulate a clear vision that, if we are to change, we must be willing to shed some strongly embedded ideals, opinions, and behaviors that have shaped schools for over a century. The consensus has to be that every student can and should learn, and that educators must learn how to push each other to become ever better. Getting everyone to embrace these concepts is at the heart of digital leadership. I prefer to use the word *embracement* rather than *buy-in,* a more commonly used word synonymous with change efforts. We should not be trying to "sell" others on pedagogical techniques and other initiatives that will better prepare our learners for success in today's constantly evolving society once they graduate. The envisioning and resulting strategic planning process need to address the interconnected questions of *why, how, where,* and *what* in this order (Jones, 2008):

- *Why* involves convincing all stakeholders why a school needs to change.

- *How* is the process of change and involves determining how to change the school once people understand and embrace the *why, what,* and *where.*

- *Where* defines the location and direction, which involves assessing the present status, agreeing on a common direction, and defining ways to measure improvement in student achievement. In the case of digital leadership, it also must define ways to measure improvement in professional learning, communications, and public relations.

- *What* is the content of the change, built through a common focus. It involves using good data, research, and best practices to determine what needs to change once people understand why.

An honest dialogue centering on these questions will provide a rationale and direction for why the school or leader must change.

In order to promote the embracement of new ideas, strategies, and techniques, we need to collaboratively work with staff to transform traditional classroom environments into vibrant learning communities where all students are authentically engaged. Consistently engaging staff in brainstorming sessions in order to develop a collective vision on how to transform the school for the betterment of all students should be a routine practice. Leadership isn't about making yourself happy. It is about helping others find purpose and joy in the pursuit of goals.

EMBRACE INNOVATION

A vision begins with talk, but it will only become reality with action. As society evolves due to advances in technology, we as digital leaders must ensure that instruction, learning, and other leadership functions follow suit, or we run the risk of our schools becoming irrelevant. By irrelevant I am referring to our ability to prepare students with the competencies to think critically, solve problems, demonstrate learning through creation, and compete in a global society. How well we model these essential competencies goes a long way in changing attitudes, beliefs, and behaviors.

As instructional leaders, it is your primary responsibility to observe, evaluate, and provide meaningful feedback to improve instruction. With this comes the responsibility to ensure that teachers are provided the freedom to take risks, knowledge of effective practices, resources to make change happen, and flexibility to incorporate innovative teaching strategies. With these parameters in place, leaders must then be able to consistently identify, foster, support, and promote digital pedagogy. An easy way to ensure this is to incorporate the four Cs—*creativity, communication, critical thinking,* and *collaboration*—into curriculum and lesson design.

Inherent within this shift is the need to reevaluate the curriculum and pedagogy, as the digital age presents new challenges to instruction and student learning. The time is now for us to lay the foundation to ensure that our students evolve into critical consumers and producers of content; understand the importance of digital citizenship; and possess the ability to create, analyze, and interpret an array of media messages. Leaders have to make concerted efforts to see where educational technology aligns well to the curriculum and pedagogy. Figure 2.1 provides some key elements associated with twenty-first century pedagogy. Chapter 1 presented a snapshot of the many tools and resources available to schools today that can assist with the transformation in this area. With all of the choices available today, as well as the relentless marketing campaigns by educational technology companies, it is easy to succumb to making rash decisions. Our focus shouldn't be on what the adult does with tech in schools. It is about how we empower our learners to use tech to learn in ways that they couldn't without it.

Leaders must be cognizant of this and ask themselves what they want students and teachers to do with these tools to enhance learning instead of what they want to buy. Enhancements to pedagogy, curriculum, and instruction rely on leaders taking the time to evaluate technology to justify its expense while ensuring that it will have a positive impact on learning. As you progress through this book, you will be taken on a deep dive into the Pillars of Digital Leadership. Gather key stakeholders to review each pillar and collaboratively revise your instructional, curriculum, professional learning, and leadership practices to incorporate the right technology and innovative ideas to emphasize what today's learners need to excel beyond the building walls.

BOLD IDEAS FOR A BOLD NEW WORLD

All around the world, there are ideas that are put into action. These ideas, for the most part, put student learning front and center and

Figure 2.1   Pedagogical Framework for the Twenty-First Century

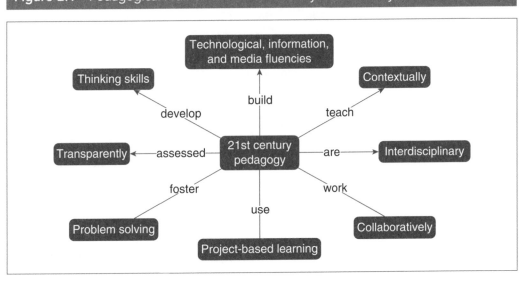

Source: Churches (2008). Used with permission.

consist of experiences that enhance their ability to think and apply what has been learned. As I have alluded to up to this point, we don't need skilled learners, but instead competent learners. The twenty-first century skills discussion and debate has waged since before the onset of this century and continues to wage on. The ensuing conversations have provided an opportunity for schools, districts, and organizations to critically evaluate what students need to know and be able to do in order to succeed in the new world of work. As we have moved further into this century, the number 21 has less meaning.

One day I was speaking with Rose Else-Mitchell, a wickedly smart educational leader, who pushed my thinking on the whole skills conversation. As I was reviewing a talking point for a webinar that I was to facilitate, I brought up an image and discussed the skills that students needed to be critical thinkers in the twenty-first century and beyond. After looking at what I had on the slide and listening to my analysis, she commented that I was (or should be) referencing and explaining competencies, not just skills, that students will need. This really got me thinking.

As I reflected on her feedback, I began to dive deeper into what the difference is between competencies and skills as well as their implications for learning. I am now more focused on how we can begin to address competencies to really prepare students for success in a disruptive world. While skills are an important part of learning and career paths, they're not rich or nuanced enough to guide students toward true mastery and success. Skills focus on the "what" in terms of the abilities a student needs to perform a specific task or activity. They don't provide enough connection to the "how." Competencies take this to the next level by translating skills into behaviors that demonstrate what has been learned and mastered in a competent fashion.

In short, skills identify what the goal is to accomplish. Competencies outline "how" the goals and objectives will be accomplished. They are more detailed and define the requirements for success in broader, more inclusive terms than skills do. There is also an increased level of depth that takes into account skills, knowledge, and abilities. To succeed in the new world of work, students will need to demonstrate the right mix of skills, knowledge, and on-the-job ability. A skill is a practical or cognitive demonstration of what a student can do. Competency is the proven use of skills, knowledge, and abilities to illustrate mastery of learning by solving problems.

In order to really see the difference between a skill and competency I came across this great communication example provided by the human resources management company HRTMS (2016).

> A person can become a good presenter through practice, learning from others, and education but in order to be a strong communicator one must rely on a combination of skills *PLU*S behavior and knowledge. A person can learn how to be a good presenter but only a strong communicator has advanced language skills, the knowledge of diverse cultures, and behaves patiently when communicating. In short, skills are specific learned activities like mopping the floor, using a computer, and stocking merchandise, while competencies are skills + knowledge + behavior like problem solving, communication, or professionalism.

Competencies, therefore, may incorporate a skill, but are much more than the skill. They include a dynamic combination of abilities, attitudes, and behaviors, as well as knowledge that is fundamental to the use of a skill aligned to a learning outcome. Success in a digital world will rely on much more than skills. It's time to shift our focus and energy to developing and assessing core and innovative competencies (Figure 2.2) that will serve all students now and in the future.

Figure 2.2 Developing Twenty-First Century Critical Thinkers

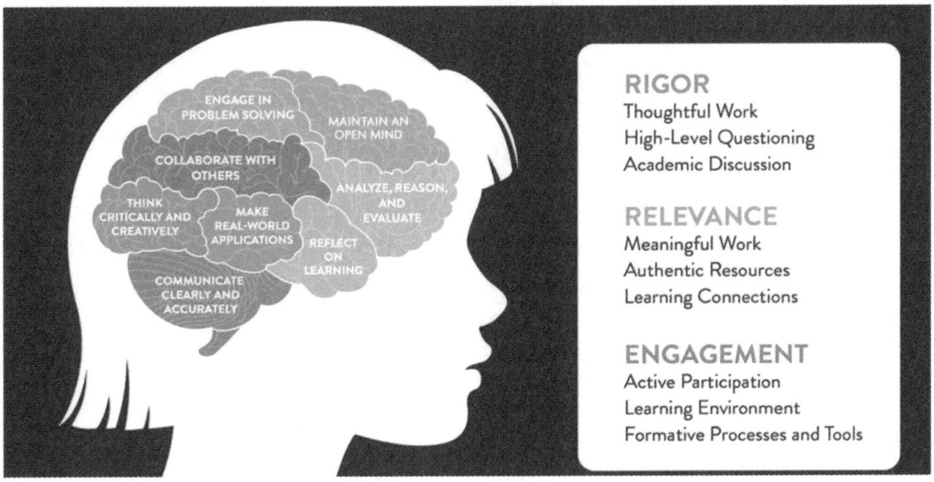

Source: ICLE (2018)

As leaders, it is our duty to be agents of change. We must collaboratively develop and implement our own bold ideas to improve the learning process in a way that emphasizes our students' cognitive growth, passions, and strengths, while challenging them to push their own boundaries. It is difficult work to transform a culture of learning that has been embedded for nearly a century, but every problem in education has been solved sometime or somewhere before. Now is the time for all of us to critically analyze our respective schools and take a stand against the status quo in order to do what is best for our students. Bold ideas revolve around respecting the learner, authentic problems, real tools and materials, expanded learning opportunities, collegiality, and lessons from outside of education.

Respect for Each Learner

All kids have greatness hidden inside them. It is the job of an educator to help them find and unleash it. Respect for each learner is pivotal if leaders want to create schools where digital tools are used responsibly and routinely. We need to have actual conversations with our students. Respecting students means regarding them with special attention, honoring them, showing consideration toward them, being concerned about them, appreciating them, relating to them, admiring their strengths, and caring for them (Tomlinson, 2011). They must be part of the transformation efforts, and their voices can provide invaluable feedback in efforts to reshape everything from curriculum to pedagogy, to technology purchases, to how time for learning is allocated. Respect also entails consistently seeking paths to grow professionally in order to discover and implement new ideas on their behalf. All children in our schools deserve adults who believe in them.

Authentic Problems

Authentic problems provide a meaningful and relevant context for learning. This is as "real world" as it gets. Through problem-based learning, students learn how to use an iterative process of assessing what they know, identifying what they need to know, gathering information, and collaborating on the evaluation of hypotheses in light of the data they have collected (Stepien & Gallagher, 1993). In addition to a focus on a real-world problem that mimics the work of professionals, authentic learning involves a presentation of findings to audiences beyond the classroom; engages students in discourse and social learning in a community of learners; has students direct their own learning in project work; and actively uses open-ended inquiry, thinking skills, and metacognition (Rule, 2006). This type of learning can be messy and unstructured at times, which is why solid leadership is needed to embed it as an embraced pedagogical technique that is employed regularly, not sparingly. In my opinion, there is no more powerful learning strategy than to have students exposed to and tackle problems that have meaning and relevancy.

Students are using technology and innovative strategies to solve problems outside of school. They are also creating their own technology in some cases. Learners are capable of incredible things if they are placed in the right environment and afforded the opportunity to use real-world tools to engage in real-world work. It is our responsibility to create these environments. To do so, we must relinquish control, provide support (i.e., purchase the right tools, provide and engage in quality, job-embedded professional learning), encourage calculated risk taking, exhibit flexibility, and model expectations. The last point is the most important. Don't expect others to do what you are not doing (or have not done) yourself.

Expanded Opportunities

The adoption of more challenging standards has placed pressure on schools to ensure that students are college and career ready upon graduation. A curriculum, instructional strategies, and assessments aligned to standards can only go so far in preparing students for the challenges they will experience in either college or careers. Expanded opportunities that serve as an extension to the curriculum have the potential to greatly increase students' readiness for whatever the future holds. We made great strides in this area in my former district through the development of the Academies at New Milford High School. Through this initiative, all students had the opportunity to be exposed to authentic learning experiences, online courses, specialized field trips, independent study, credit for learning experiences outside of school, internships, and capstone projects. More detail on this will be presented in Chapter 11.

Collegiality and Collaboration

Let's face it, as educators, we need to work together in order to successfully implement the best ideas to improve teaching and learning. We must overcome personal agendas, bring the naysayers on board, implement a system focused on shared decision making, and move to initiate a change process that is sustainable. The best ideas will become realities only through collegiality and collaboration. Divided we fall, but together we can achieve greatness.

Lessons From Outside Education

Some of the best ideas for why schools need to change and how to go about it come from outside the field of education. In *Linchpin*, Seth Godin (2010) writes,

> Every day I meet people who have so much to give but have been bullied enough or frightened enough to hold it back. It's time to stop complying with the system and draw your own map. You have brilliance in you, your contribution is essential, and the art you create is precious. Only you can do it, and you must. (p. 8)

Godin's work focuses on the concept of a linchpin, the essential building block of great organizations. To Godin, linchpins are indispensable, love their work, understand that there is no playbook, and challenge the status quo. Every day, linchpins set out to turn each day into a work of art. Creating a school and culture that parallel the real world is, in itself, a work of art. Linchpin leaders, although not entirely indispensable, are creative, see or are able to discover solutions to issues, develop strong connections with a variety of stakeholder groups, and help others solve problems. Digital leadership is about inspiring students and educators to think rather than follow rulebooks and ace tests. It is about making a profound difference, and it begins with acknowledging the shortcomings of the system, building a plan to lead schools differently in the digital age, and then doing something about it.

In *Drive*, Daniel Pink (2011) takes a look at what truly motivates us based on scientific research. Drawing on four decades of research, he reveals society's need to use a carrot-and-stick approach or an if-then rewards system as the means to extrinsically reward people for the work they do. Our educational system is brimming with extrinsic rewards that we need to move away from if transformative change is the goal. As Pink discovered, a carrot-and-stick approach worked well in the twentieth century, just like the industrialized education model worked well for creating the workforce needed, but it does not work well for the creative work that is now in demand in schools or the real world.

It definitely does not work well for leaders interested in change. Extrinsic motivational forces crowd out good behavior, diminish performance, crush creativity, encourage shortcuts or unethical behavior, foster short-term thinking, and essentially eliminate intrinsic motivation. "Carrots and sticks are so last century. For current work in this century, we need to upgrade to autonomy, mastery and purpose" (Pink, 2011, p. 203). For schools to change, leaders must work on creating cultures that focus on intrinsic means of motivation driven by autonomy, mastery, and purpose. Autonomy is the desire to direct our own lives. Mastery is the urge to get better and better at something that matters. Purpose is the yearning to do what we do in the service of something larger than ourselves.

Google understood the importance of fostering a climate fueled by intrinsic motivation. As a result, the company developed an 80/20 innovation time-off model (ITO), where 80% of employee time was spent on core projects, and about 20% was spent on activities of personal interest that ultimately impacted Google's bottom line. During the time that this program was in existence, Google recognized that relinquishing control and unleashing creativity were the keys to innovation and change. This model fit nicely with the elements of intrinsic motivation identified by Pink. Imagine a school where students and teachers could spend time working on projects that they own, that could make them think differently and passionately about their work during the other 80% of their time?

Digital leadership focuses on fostering intrinsic motivation as the primary catalyst for change. It is about developing our own innovation ideas and strategies using inspiration from outside education to initiate meaningful change. As leaders, this is the type of teaching and learning culture that we should want to foster and cultivate, one where creativity flourishes, students find relevancy and meaning in their learning, and teachers are given the support and autonomy to be innovative. Think about how you can apply the concepts of autonomy, mastery, and purpose to your work and that of your students and staff. Chapter 7 will highlight how schools have incorporated the 80/20 model as an intrinsic innovative force to change instruction and improve learning based on both student and teacher interests, not those dictated from the top down.

Every child can learn, regardless of his or her innate level of intelligence, and gaps in achievement can be mitigated through research and understanding of differences in individual background and opportunity (Glazer, 2009). This holds true for leaders as well. In *Outliers,* Malcolm Gladwell (2008) takes a detailed look at the characteristics and secrets of successful people. He defines outliers as people who, for one reason or another, are so accomplished and so extraordinary and so outside of ordinary experience that they are puzzling to the rest of us.

A great deal can be learned from Gladwell and applied to educational leadership. Successful leaders are not necessarily those with the highest IQs. Instead, they are those who are "smart enough" to recognize and take advantage of the unique opportunities that present themselves. Digital leadership is about discovering, recognizing, and taking advantage of the many opportunities that the digital age presents. This represents an entirely different construct, as it breaks away from the mold associated with traditional leadership. It is about seizing the opportunity to pursue any possible learning path or area of interest to improve the schools we work in and ourselves.

If we think about outliers not as leaders who fall beyond the normal boundaries of the education system, but rather as individuals whose leadership makes them fall beyond society's expectations of what an educational leader looks like, everything falls into place. Leaders who position themselves to be outliers are, in a natural way, facilitating the type of innovative and creative thinking that is necessary to thrive in an information-based economy. Isn't this what our schools need? In a world where the creation and dissemination of new information is the key to economic viability, leaders today actually have to be outliers to some extent in order to initiate and sustain the type of change needed in our schools—especially those schools still functioning to prepare learners for an industrialized workforce—and as a result have become unaligned with society. The very nature of the internet and the vast and constantly changing educational opportunities available on it need to be harnessed by leaders for their own development and that of their schools. Those who recognize and act on this will ultimately become outliers as the resulting changes create a paradigm shift in leadership style as well as school structure and function.

GROW INTO A DIGITAL LEADER

Have you ever been complacent when it comes to undertaking or performing a task? Of course, you have, as this is just a part of human nature. In our personal lives, complacency can result if we are happy or content with where we are. Maybe we don't change our workout routine because we have gotten used to doing the same thing day in and day out. I know I love using the elliptical for cardio, but rarely use any setting other than manual. Or perhaps our diet doesn't change, as we have an affinity for the same types of foods, which might or might not be that good for us. So, what's my point with all of this? It is hard to grow and improve if one is complacent. This is why we must always be open to finding comfort in growth. If we don't, then things might very well never change.

The issue described above is prevalent in not just our personal lives. Complacency plagues many organizations as well. When we are in a state of relative comfort with our professional practice, it is often difficult to move beyond that zone of stability and, dare I say, "easy" sailing. If it isn't broke, then why fix it, right? Maybe we aren't pushed to take on new projects or embrace innovative ideas. Or perhaps there is no external accountability to improve, really. Herein lies the inherent challenge of taking on the status quo in districts, schools, and organizations. Celebrate where you are and what you have accomplished, but never become complacent. The pursuit of being where you ultimately need and want to be is a never-ending journey.

There are many lenses through which we can take a more in-depth look to gain more context on the impact complacency has on growth and improvement. Take test scores for example. If a district or school traditionally has high achievement and continues to have it, the rule of thumb is that no significant change is needed. The fact that a school or educator might be "good" at something doesn't equate to the fact that change isn't required in other areas. It is also important to realize that someone else can view one's perception of something being good in an entirely different light. Growth in all aspects of school culture is something that has to be the standard. It begins with getting out of actual and perceived comfort zones to truly start the process of improving school culture.

Joani Junkala (2018) shares some great thoughts on the importance of stepping outside our comfort zones:

> Stepping out of our comfort zone requires us to step outside of ourselves. If we are going to strive for progress, whether professionally or personally, we have to get comfortable with the idea of being uncomfortable. This isn't easy for

everyone. For someone like me, who is a self-prescribed introvert, this can be difficult. Stepping out of our comfort zone requires extra effort, energy, and sometimes forced experiences. It requires us to set aside our fear and be vulnerable. We have to be willing to try something new, different, difficult, or even something that's never been done before. We have to put ourselves out there—trusting in ourselves and trusting others with our most vulnerable self. It's a frightening thought. What if we get it wrong? What if we look silly? Will it be worth it in the end? Will I stand alone? What if I fail? Oh but, what if I succeed and evolve?

Change begins with each and every one of us and spreads from there. Finding comfort in growth and ultimately improvement begins with being honest with ourselves. Let me be blunt for a minute. The truth is that there is no perfect lesson, project, classroom, school, district, teacher, or administrator. There is, however, the opportunity every day to get better. This is not to say that great things are not happening in education. They most definitely are. My point is that we can never let complacency distract us from continually pursuing a path to where our learners need us to be.

Are you comfortable where you are at professionally? What about your school, district, or organization? Where are opportunities for growth? By consistently reflecting on these questions, we can pave a continual path to improvement. Questions lay the path forward. Actions are what get you to where you want to be.

It is time to grow into being a digital leader if you haven't already. You don't have to like technology, but at this point in time you need to accept that it is not going away. All leaders, regardless of their experience, need to understand this in order to prepare learners for success now and well beyond in the future. For schools to truly be relevant, meaningful centers for learning in today's digital age, it will take leaders who are not afraid to go beyond their comfort zones to lead. Many of the changes schools need are dependent on the ability and desire of leaders to hone specific skills, behaviors, and characteristics associated with technology. The National Association of Secondary School Principals (NASSP) identified the following ten guidelines to assist school leaders in integrating technology in their schools and leadership practices (Demski, 2012):

- Effectively and consistently model the use of the same technology tools they expect teachers to use in their classrooms with the students.

- Be consistent in their decisions and expectations about integrating learning technology in the school.

- Communication about the pace and process of integrating learning technology needs to be clear and reasonable.

- Provide appropriate professional development time and resources to support effective classroom implementation of technology.

- Support early adopters and risk takers.

- Do whatever it takes to ensure that all staff has early access to the very same digital tools that students will be using in their classrooms.

- Educational leaders (teachers, principals, central office) must make it clear to IT that all decisions relating to learning technology will be made by the educational leaders with input from IT, not the other way around.

- Set and support the expectation that student work will be done and stored using technology.

- Ensure that families and the public are kept informed about the school's goals and progress relating to its use of technology as a learning resource.

- Be an active and public champion for all students, staff members, and the school of implementing a vision of fully integrating learning technology for the second decade of the twenty-first century.

Technology has the potential to reshape school cultures and how we learn. Technology is not just a shiny tool that can increase engagement, but a conduit to endless possibilities that can enhance every facet of what we do in education. It is not a frivolous expense that is not worth the investment that many make it out to be. I see technology, along with innovative ideas, as a needed resource in education that can break down the walls of traditional school structures while creating new opportunities to learn.

Technology can engage, connect, empower, and enhance teaching. It can also impact, how educators learn, the work done by schools, and stakeholder relations. The question of why has been definitively answered. Instead, the driving question we should be asking *now* is how all stakeholders, including students, should use the technology that is available to us to improve what we do instead of *why* we should use it to improve what we do. Even in schools that might not have many technology resources, time and energy should be spent figuring out how to maximize what is available instead of making endless excuses for not moving forward.

Technology is here to stay, although there is never a shortage of naysayers who question its value. Its value rests in whether leaders decide to use it effectively to positively impact the lives of our students, achieve learning goals, communicate with stakeholders, share best practices, and connect like never before. The results and impact will speak for themselves in ways that standardized tests never could. Is it a silver bullet or a cure for what ails education? Will it eventually replace teachers? Of course not, but one should think twice before claiming that it is not worth the investment. The results of purposeful use, as you will see throughout this book, speak for themselves. Just ask the students, teachers, administrators, parents, and other stakeholders who witness this on a regular basis. Digital leadership relies heavily on technology combined with innovative thinking as a conduit for change.

SUMMARY

Everything in society is changing at an exponential rate, which compels us to make sure that education prepares learners for a world that is difficult, if not impossible, to predict. It is the duty of everyone who has a stake in education to understand that preparation for an industrialized workforce no longer fits the needs of society or, more important, those of our learners. Digital leadership is about championing change that will transform schools into vibrant epicenters of learning, like the renaissance led by Dr. Pam Moran in Albemarle County, Virginia. Leaders must critically reflect upon all aspects of school culture to determine whether schools are truly best serving the needs of kids today. Once they do, they can begin to create a vision for change that incorporates the bold ideas needed to take schools from ambiguity to relevancy. These are the types of schools that will resonate with all stakeholders, set the stage for increases in achievement, and establish a greater sense of pride for the educational work being done.

GUIDING QUESTIONS

1. Are there still examples of TTWWADI (That's the Way We've Always Done It) in your current situation? If so, what are they, and how will you begin to move in a new and better direction?

2. How do you model a vision for excellence, innovation, and creativity?

3. Changing behavior begins with changing our own mindset first. Identify an aspect of your professional practice that might be held back by a fixed mindset approach. What steps do you need to take to move your thinking in a different direction?

4. Are you comfortable where you are professionally? What about your school, district, or organization? Where are opportunities for growth?

iStock.com/triloks

Leading Sustainable Change

3

> We must move beyond the implementation phase of change when new ideas and practices are tried for the first time, to the institutionalization phase when new practices are integrated effortlessly into teachers' repertoires. This holds true for leaders as well and might ultimately be more important for sustainable change.
>
> —Anderson and Stiegelbauer (1994)

THE JOURNEY OF A PRACTITIONER

Dr. Spike Cook is the principal of Lakeside Middle School in Millville, New Jersey. His story exemplifies how shifting to a new leadership paradigm can initiate change within a school, and eventually a school district, in embracing innovative strategies. In a relatively short time, Spike became a model for digital leadership by setting the example he wanted to see for his teachers, students, parents, and administrative colleagues as principal of his previous school in the district, R. M. Bacon Elementary School. He realized early on in his journey that for change to occur and become sustainable, he needed to establish a vision for both his school and himself as an effective digital leader. This required him to take a reflective look at his school's culture in relation to society and anticipate the types of changes that were needed for improvement. He wanted to become a more relevant leader in order to inspire his staff and learners to reach their potential.

As part of his New Year's resolution years ago, Spike began his journey of becoming a connected leader committed to digital leadership principles. He began by signing up for various social media applications. Following the lead of other like-minded educators, he launched a blog for himself and his school. In the infancy of his leadership transformation, he followed as many connected principals on Twitter as he could find. He studied the articles they tweeted and how they were representing their schools and themselves. Many of the examples Spike followed had blazed a trail for administrators who wanted to become more connected.

Blogging became a reflective tool for Spike. After establishing his blog, *Insights Into Learning* (drspikecook.com), he quickly began to realize the benefits of sharing his professional and personal insights as a principal, husband, father, and teacher. This platform also facilitated the development and communication of his shared vision through conveying the image of an educational setting that would better prepare his learners for success in their future. While using the tool to impart his vision and enhance communication practices with his teachers, he found they began to follow his lead. Before he knew it, he was beginning to see the changes he had set in motion.

Spike realized that to be a digital leader, he would need to commit to reading information on leadership daily and blog at least weekly to set the example for his peers and his teachers. He felt that the consistency of his commitment would not only lead to increased personal knowledge, but also build capacity among his staff. He developed a plan to have his teachers become the most connected in the district. His thought process was simple and direct. He felt that by arming the teachers with the necessary tools to integrate technology aligned to a solid pedagogical foundation, they would eventually become more effective teachers—and the students would benefit. A few had already begun to take steps to embrace the early stages of transformation.

Spike knew that in order to have sustainable change in his organization, he needed to empower a few risk takers. He did this by meeting both formally and informally with these key stakeholders. His main objective was to build resonance and to begin a two-way information-sharing protocol for improving their school. Fortunately for Spike, he had several teachers who were pursuing their master's degrees in educational technology. These teachers joined him and felt reinvigorated by their new principal's excitement with educational technology, seeing this as a way to purposefully integrate technology in more classrooms.

In order to expose the entire faculty to the changes in Spike's leadership, he scheduled meetings to discuss his forays into social media spaces. He felt compelled to share the news with the teachers because he believed wholeheartedly that they would benefit just like he had. After this first meeting, the literacy coach and seven of his teachers signed up for Twitter or updated their existing accounts. Suddenly, numerous educators in his school were talking about social media and discussing whether or not they would take the plunge. Spike knew that in order to get beyond the staff's initial interest in social media, he needed a mechanism to build momentum.

Soon afterward, he began to slowly change his communication style with his teachers. Prior to his transformation, he would send out a weekly e-mail similar to a Monday Memo or Friday Focus (Whitaker, 2003). He wanted to get beyond e-mail and create a place where teachers, students, and parents could meet in an interactive form of the Monday Memo. He created the R. M. Bacon Weekly School Blog as a weekly update of all the activities that were going on and a reflection on the accomplishments that the school made the week past. In this blog, there were videos, pictures, links to supporting artifacts, and relevant information carefully designed to articulate how the school was effectively using technology to support rigorous and relevant learning as part of the school's innovative journey.

It was during this time that he was approached by his literacy coach and another teacher who wanted to build a professional learning program that would allow the staff to experience educational technology in terms of how it could better benefit even more learners. They created "Tech Fridays," designing them in the image of the "unconference" models of professional learning they had seen popping up around the country. For the most part, these Tech Fridays sustained the change needed to provide teachers with hands-on resources to better integrate technology into the classroom to improve learner outcomes.

Spike began to see the impact of the transformation when the district held its annual Technology Showcase. His school had the most participation of the eleven schools in the district. Suddenly, there were community members who were asking about his school and suggesting that all schools embark on a similar digital revolution to that happening at Spike's school.

In addition to the Tech Fridays and the informal networking, Spike began to utilize his faculty meetings as opportunities to expose his teachers to technological tools that could assist them in the classroom. He encouraged teachers to bring their devices to the meetings in order to engage them in hands-on activities. Moving away from a traditional faculty meeting structure, Spike turned this time into an active learning opportunity. He presented the latest tools and modeled how the staff could easily use them to improve learning in the classroom or better engage stakeholders.

Armed with his district-provided iPad, Spike saw the importance of using the iMovie application as a way for the school to create quick, professional-looking videos. At a staff meeting, after showing a video he had made, Spike offered the faculty the use of his iPad. A group of fifth-grade teachers took him up on the offer and created a video for the fifth-grade students. Soon afterward, teachers who taught other grade levels began to use the iPad or their own devices to create videos with their students. These videos showcased not only the effective use of technology, but also other programs and initiatives that increased pride in their school while illustrating beyond the walls of the school the innovative practices that had become the norm, not the exception.

To Spike, summer is not a time to just take it easy and throttle down, but rather an opportunity to continue improving in the areas of digital leadership. He maintained his social media and blogging schedule throughout the summer and realized that his teachers did as well. They were connecting with one another about their plans for the upcoming school year through a variety of tools. Ideas were shared to improve not only how they used technology, but also pedagogy, student agency, curriculum alignment, and time management. Upon their return from the summer break a few years back, there was an increase in activity among the staff in terms of implementing digital strategies to enhance learning (S. Cook, personal communication, 2018).

Spike has never mandated technology integration. Mandates often lead to resistance and animosity, which will often derail change efforts. He has not once asked a teacher to do something with which he or she was uncomfortable. Instead, he feels that modeling (Kouzes & Posner, 2007) is the effective leadership route to help his and all teachers grow. He rewards teachers who take risks and supports them all in an equitable manner in what they need to be successful. He understands that each teacher develops connections in his or her own way and exhibits patience with those who may struggle moving beyond the use of tools that either drive instruction or support superficial learning.

His school benefited from the sustained, focused change in digital learning and innovation, regularly making connections with other schools and educators through Skype, Twitter, Pinterest, Facebook, and blogging. He had a group of fourth-grade students one year connect with other fourth graders in Wisconsin, hosted several Mystery Skype calls, and has had groups visit other schools to learn and collaborate. As a digital leader Spike was motivated like never before to keep providing opportunities to help his teachers and learners grow. To this end he began to bring in outside presenters to assist teachers with more advanced technology integration and support to ensure efficacy in digital learning.

Since the Millville Public School District uses a digital administrative walk-through program, Spike implemented one of the features to track the data on his staff's use of technology. Teachers at his school were observed using technology 29% of the observed time. Spike shared this information with the faculty at the conclusion of the year and vowed to help them raise the use of technology focused on learning goals for the upcoming school year. In the subsequent four months of observations, the staff increased their usage to 42% of the observed time. Student use of technology was observed 45%

of the observed time, up from 32% the school year before. Utilizing the administrative software allowed Spike to chart the data on the school and provide observable reports that show how technology integration had increased under his leadership.

Spike credits Facebook with learning more about his teachers' personal lives. Since becoming friends on Facebook with his teachers, he was in a better position to understand his teachers' life changes, interests, and family. He feels that Facebook networking also increased his staff's knowledge of one another, thereby aiding the collaborative culture of the school. Teachers were able to readily communicate with one another beyond the constraints of the traditional school day and year. Connectivity led to better professional relationships, which in turn helped to sustain innovative change.

As for Twitter, his teachers used the tool to find articles or information to help their classes. In many cases they ended up sharing this information with Spike. With more than 60% of his teachers on Twitter, he saw ideas become reality. For instance, over the summer, teachers were searching for ways to improve their classroom management plans. Through Twitter, an article on ClassDojo was circulated among the staff. ClassDojo, an interactive classroom management application, provides teachers and students with opportunities to reward positive behaviors and track negative behaviors. Spike utilized the data from the teachers to communicate with students and their parents. About 50% of the staff used ClassDojo through their interactive whiteboard, smartphone, or iPad.

Some of his teachers started their own blogs in order to better reflect on their teaching and gain increased parental engagement. They took the practices that Spike modeled for the school and applied them at the classroom level. The teachers who had their own blogs were getting more parents involved and began to "flip" their classrooms in order to enhance the learning process.

Spike has become a more effective principal and leader through his commitment to digital leadership. He has gained a global perspective on the successes and problems in education. This has allowed him to better correlate his effectiveness with the systemic processes that he initiated to support his teachers. He feels that he has created an atmosphere that encourages teachers and students to take risks with new technology. Since his school embraced the transformation process, his vision is no longer singular in thinking but plural in practice.

UNEARTHING THE SECRETS OF CHANGE

The greatest leader is not necessarily the one who does the greatest things. He is the one that gets the people to do the greatest things.

—Ronald Reagan

Spike's journey provides a powerful lesson for all leaders: We must be the change that we wish to see in our schools (or in education, in general, for that matter). Leaders today typically choose one of two paths to follow: telling people what they want to hear or taking them where they need to be. Telling them what they want to hear will only help to strengthen the status quo and continue down a path of doing things the way they have been done forever. This path is also guided by that little voice in all of our heads that continually whispers, "If it isn't broke, why fix it?" The bottom line is that there is an opportunity for growth in all systems, as perfection is a figment of our imagination. Effective leaders are always taking a critical lens to practice, determining when and if change is needed.

Any change process needs a starting point. The keys to sustainable change rely on identifying the problem(s), developing implementation plans to improve school culture, and anticipating future changes. Before moving ahead with change process leaders should possess the appropriate knowledge to guide them during the process. Leading change expert Michael Fullan (2011), through his extensive work in this area, identified six secrets of change (Figure 3.1).

When reflecting on Spike Cook's journey, one can see how Fullan's change secrets were put into practice, with the result being

Figure 3.1   The Six Secrets of Change

1. Love Your Employees
2. Connect Peers With Purpose
3. Capacity Building Prevails
4. Learning Is the Work
5. Transparency Rules
6. Systems Learn

sustainable changes in school culture. The end result was the creation of a learning environment at R. M. Bacon Elementary School that was more attuned with the active learners they were educating and a staff eager to embrace innovative practices. Putting the wheels of digital leadership in motion hinges on mastering the following six change secrets identified by Fullan (2011).

Fullan Change Secret 1: Love Your Employees

Explore the importance of building the school learning culture by focusing on the teachers and staff, students, and the community. The key is enabling everyone to learn continuously while giving them a certain amount of autonomy to take risks and be innovative. Loving your employees is about helping them all find meaning, increased competency development, and personal satisfaction by making contributions that simultaneously fulfill their own goals and the goals of the organization (Fullan, 2011). The best way to love your employees in order to initiate sustainable change is to trust and support them unconditionally. If you are a teacher, consider applying this practice to your learners.

Fullan Change Secret 2: Connect Peers With Purpose

Purposeful peer interaction within and beyond the school is crucial. Student learning and achievement increase substantially when teachers work in learning communities supported by school leaders who focus on improvement. It is also essential to develop relatable goals and associated outcomes with every change initiative. The *why* and the *how* need to be clearly articulated to the staff, and staff members need to be active participants in the change process. Purposeful peer interaction allows teachers to have a voice in the decision-making process and to craft how policies and mandates will be implemented (DuFour, DuFour, & Eaker, 2008).

Fullan Change Secret 3: Capacity Building Prevails

The most effective strategies involve helping teachers and principals develop the instruction and management of change skills necessary for school improvement. Capacity building concerns competencies, resources, and motivation. Individuals and groups are high in capacity if they possess and continue to develop these three components in concert (Fullan, 2011). At the core of the capacity-building model is distributed leadership along with social cohesion and trust (Hopkins & Jackson, 2003). The effectiveness of distributed leadership resides in the human potential available to be released within an organization, an emergent property of a group or network of individuals in which group members pool their expertise (Gronn, 2000). Leaders must continue to develop capacity in all stakeholders while always anticipating the next course of action. Studies on educational change indicate that schools successful in sustaining school improvement build capacity for leadership within the organization (Harris & Lambert, 2003).

Fullan Change Secret 4: Learning Is the Work

Professional learning in workshops, courses, and online environments is only one input to continuous growth and precision in teaching, learning, and leadership. Successful growth itself is accomplished when the culture of the school supports the day-to-day learning of teachers engaged in improving what they do in the classroom and school. Leaders must not only be creative in finding time for teachers to engage in professional learning during the day, but they also must consistently model lifelong learning themselves. Digital leadership dictates that learning is first and foremost. Learning is the fuel of leadership. The best leaders are the best learners.

Fullan Change Secret 5: Transparency Rules

Ongoing use of data for formative feedback, opportunities to see effective practices in use, sharing innovation for others to learn from, and embracing digital tools are necessary for success. It becomes normal and desirable for teachers to observe and be observed in teaching facilitated by coaches and mentors. This is equally important when it comes to leaders sharing and seeing the work of their peers. Leaders, proud of the work being done in their schools, now have the means to continuously tell their story to key stakeholders. Sharing more information will increase engagement in the change process.

Fullan Change Secret 6: Systems Learn

Continuous learning depends on developing many leaders in the school in order to enhance continuity. It also depends on schools being confident in the face of complexity and open to new ideas.

This holds true in a digital world. With access to knowledge and tools like never before, leaders are no longer confined by space and time in their efforts to build capacity in and learn with others to improve professional practice. New ideas are being shared at a furious pace in online spaces, but change does not have to be a reinventing of the wheel. Instead, it can be that an idea that has been tested successfully elsewhere is adapted to meet the unique characteristics of one's own school or district.

THE PROCESS OF CHANGE

There is always a great deal of discussion about change in education in order to better prepare students for success. The stakes have become higher as changes in a globally connected world are far outpacing those in our schools. The proliferation of technology in the world is making it much more difficult to engage our students. This is not to say that meaningful, impactful changes are not evident in schools across the globe. Through my work, I have seen in person, and through social media, some amazing examples of what education can and should be. However, these cases tend to be isolated pockets of excellence as opposed to systemic transformation evident across an entire system, district, or school. It's not just advancements in technology that have to be addressed in our schools. Other elements embedded in school culture cloud our vision as to what is both needed and possible. Issues such as the status quo, traditions, mindset, fear, apathy, funding, infrastructure, and time seem to consistently rear their ugly heads. These real challenges morph into excuses that ultimately inhibit the change process. Every single school on this planet deals with these challenges and many others on a daily basis. The good news in all of this is that they are not insurmountable. If you feel it is important, you will find a way. If not, then human nature will take over and you will make an excuse. The process of change (Figure 3.2) is driven by a desire to focus on solutions rather than excuses.

Now here's the thing with change. It is not easy. Nor will it happen quickly. Sometimes the best examples of sustainable change have resulted from a more organic approach. The ability to initiate, manage, and sustain change relies on a leader's ability to think of it as a process as opposed to an event. This takes vision, planning, patience, and perseverance. If sustainable change is the goal, it is important to clarify the *what, why,* and *how* and to follow with a determination of success.

Figure 3.2 The Change Process

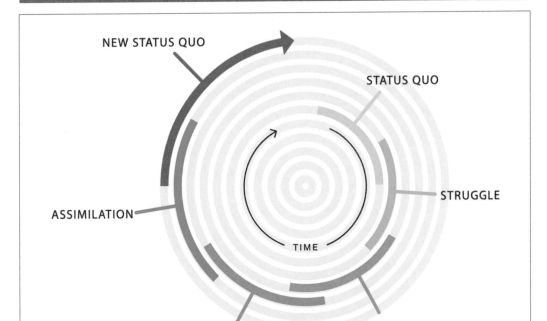

Why

Once you have some data to identify what needs to change, the next step is to build broad support. Aligning supporting research is a sound approach to build a compelling reason as to why the change is needed. This, combined with what the data is telling you, will build a foundation to move the process in a positive direction. To streamline the process, consider using Google Scholar to quickly and easily find research that supports the need for change. When we tackled our grading culture at my school, I first looked at the data (we were failing way too many kids) and then used Google Scholar to find research to guide the direction for a better way. When tackling the why, it is also important to consider the following questions to mitigate potential issues while providing a greater focus:

- Why does change not work?

- Why has it failed in your school?

- What are surrounding schools doing?
- Are we meeting the needs of our students and preparing them for their future?

How

This is where you need to roll up your sleeves and be prepared to get dirty. Change rarely succeeds through mandates, directives, buy-ins, or unilateral decisions. Creating a process that involves honest feedback and consensus is imperative. The best way to approach this is to form a comprehensive committee that includes key naysayers, antagonists, and resisters. You cannot allow them to continue to be a part of the problem. They must be active contributors to a solution. Present the data and supporting research, and together build a shared vision and strategic plan for the identified change. Be prepared though to make some tough decisions. Going back to the grading example, we openly discussed and agreed on a failure floor, no zeros, and a process of retakes/redos. However, I then established seven criteria that had to be supported with evidence before any student could receive a failing quarter grade. You can see the resulting document in Online Resource 3.1 (A More Equitable Grading Philosophy). Accountability was ensured, as I reviewed all failures each quarter and asked for the evidence that everything was done to help students succeed.

What

This seems like a simple step, but more often than not change never materializes or is sustained if we don't identify criteria to determine if change was or is successful. To simplify the process, take a look at data, which can come in many forms. A data review will give you a clear focus that can be used to articulate the why and guide the how. Below are some forms of data:

- Achievement (standardized scores, local measures)
- Attendance rates
- Graduation/promotion rates
- Discipline referrals
- Facilities inventory
- Tech audit
- Perception (find out what kids think needs to change)

Ask better questions to determine what needs to change. Don't ask educators in your school or community how well you are meeting the needs of today's learner. Instead, ask your learners how well your school is meeting their needs.

Success

In the end, a strategic plan for change should bear positive results. If the results are not what you expect, then re-evaluate to improve as opposed to scrapping the idea and giving up. Referring to the grading example one last time, over the course of three years we reduced our student failures by 75% while also increasing graduation and attendance rates as well as standardized test scores. Figure 3.3 emphasizes the critical elements of a strategic plan to help you achieve the results that you are looking for with any change effort.

This change process recipe can be applied to virtually any initiative from homework to mobile learning (BYOD, 1:1), to changes to the school schedule, and anything else. It all comes down to leadership and the will to improve in order to create a better learning culture for all students.

Figure 3.3 Strategic Planning Cycle

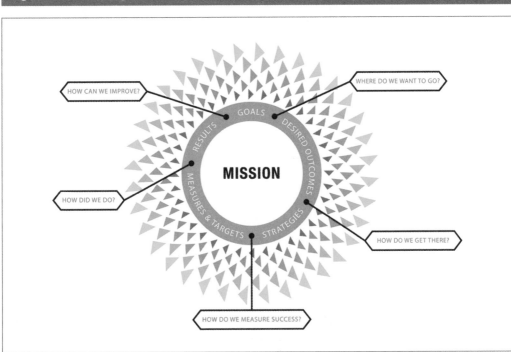

OVERCOMING POTENTIAL ROADBLOCKS TO CHANGE

Fullan's Six Secrets of Change provide a great framework with which to begin the change process, but change can only be sustained if potential roadblocks are acknowledged throughout the process. Putting them on the table at the outset will help to create a vision and plan for implementation. If identified and addressed appropriately, roadblocks like those outlined below can be overcome.

1. **This is too hard.** News flash: CHANGE IS NOT EASY! Please keep this in mind as I continue. Change in the field of education is as elusive as the Loch Ness Monster. If it were easy, we would see countless examples of innovative programs, authentic learning experiences, successful integration of technology, and students yearning to arrive at school each day. The fact of the matter is that nothing in life comes easily, let alone transformational change in education. Educators must be willing to take risks, learn from mistakes, and put in the time.

2. **I don't have the time for this.** Ah, the old "time" excuse. This is probably the most common excuse given when educators and the thought or sight of change come together. We are in a profession with the opportunity to make a difference in the lives of children, leave a lasting impact, motivate them to achieve, instill a sense of lifelong learning, and prepare them for success once they leave our schools. If someone says they don't have time to work toward change that helps to achieve these goals, then they should question why they are in the field of education. Dedicated educators make the time because it is their job! You ask any child who had a teacher that turned his or her life around, and he or she will tell you that the time spent was priceless!

3. **Lack of collaboration.** The field of education has been moving from a profession that hoarded ideas, lessons, and successful strategies to one that is openly willing to share this bounty with as many passionate educators as possible. Innovation and change are a collective process, and schools that understand this concept have personnel who routinely collaborate among one another and with those outside of their schools. "Together we are better" is the motto by which change agents abide.

4. **Directive approach.** Okay, I have been guilty of this when trying to get my staff to utilize technology. Thankfully, I learned

from this mistake and have found that change occurs through shared decision making, consensus, collaboration (see #3), and modeling. As a leader, I had better be able to effectively model what I want my teachers to implement if I have any hopes of seeing the idea succeed and be sustainable. In education, you can't just tell someone to do something because you were mesmerized by a piece of technology, read the latest book on innovative practices, or heard a great speaker discuss professional learning communities. You need to get each and every stakeholder involved in the process (see #3), properly model the strategy, and put the time forth to ensure successful implementation (see #1 and #2).

5. **Hierarchy in schools.** The hierarchical structure in many schools is most often a deterrent to innovation and change. This results in a directive approach (see #4) being prevalent and no chance of collaboration being possible (see #3), because ideas have to go through many layers and red tape even to be considered. Schools that have moved away from a hierarchical structure to support learning cultures are typically more innovative. Educators need to be placed in environments where flexibility and freedom to take risks and try out new ideas and initiatives without fear of repercussion are actively fostered.

6. **No support.** As leaders, how can we expect teachers to be innovative and move toward change if we don't support them 100% of the time?

7. **Fear of change.** This is a given, so it had better be expected. If #1 to #5 above are addressed, this will help to alleviate fear. Passion for helping kids succeed will always work to one's advantage when trying to subdue the fear a group might experience in trying to initiate new ideas. Passion is what drives us! Use it to your advantage.

8. **The naysayers and antagonists.** Well, you should have known this was coming. Some people will never get on board with the change process for a variety of reasons, none of them good ones. Those who embrace change and experience success should be celebrated, honored, and commended. This is the best way to motivate others and inspire them to willingly become part of the process.

9. **Poor professional learning.** How many times have we sat through training sessions that were boring and meaningless, and that didn't provide any practical implementation ideas? Professional learning has to be relevant to teachers, contain numerous choices, and be hands-on. More often than not, this can be done with teacher

leaders present in all buildings. If money is going to be spent, make sure it is on vetted, well-respected presenters, where you will get your money's worth.

10. **Frivolous purchases.** Money does not equate to innovation and change. Just because you purchase the latest technology doesn't mean everyone will use it correctly or productively. Professional learning (see #9) is key.

MOVING LARGE CHANGE EFFORTS FORWARD

Change is a process, not an event. Saying this and fully understanding the intricacies involved with the process of change are two totally different things. Change isn't something that can just be willed on a person, people, or organization. Mandates and top-down directives rarely become embedded and sustained components of school culture, because once the focus changes (and it always does), then all the time, energy, and frustration transfers to the new initiative. These flavor-of-the-month rituals driven by a need to embrace the next big thing drives everyone crazy and only exasperates the whispers of this too shall pass, which eventually morph into a chorus of resistance. Let me be blunt. Change for the sake of change is a ridiculous waste of time and resources. Improvements are needed in every school and district. Some changes will be mandated from your state. In some cases, these will be hard to swallow, but from an accountability perspective you will need to dig deep and display what constitutes real leadership, even if this is not modeled by the people in power above you. Not everyone likes to change, and this includes many of you! Our brains are wired to keep us safe and be risk-averse. This is not to say that many people are not willing to try to implement new ideas and strategies, but when we do there is often a sense of fear and concern as to what happens if we are not successful. Rest assured it is a natural part of the change process.

Large change efforts can stymy even the most ardent leaders who pursue different and better. There are so many moving parts, people to please, and hurdles to overcome that getting derailed is a reality that must be put front and center from the beginning. Below I am going to offer some tips on how to not only move large change efforts forward, but also to ensure sustainability and efficacy. The tips and strategies below are framed around one large change initiative that I helped facilitate as a high school principal—a new teacher evaluation system in our district. New Jersey mandated every district to adopt an evaluation tool that was more detailed and moved away from the traditional narrative report. Here is what we learned:

- **Be a part of the solution.** Large-scale change typically happens at the district level. When I found out that the district was going to be selecting a new evaluation tool, I immediately volunteered to be a part of the process. Regardless of your position, don't sit by idly on the sidelines. Get involved!

- **Do your research.** In this case, we had to adopt a new evaluation tool, and there were many choices available. My team and I did an exhaustive study to narrow down the choices to what we felt were the best four options. We also looked at the research that supported each tool.

- **Embrace the 4 C's.** In this case the 4 C's are communication, committee, collaboration, and consensus. Success of any change, minor or major, begins with effective communication. Your entire staff and community need to know the *what, why, where,* and *when* associated with the change. Communication never ceases to be a prevalent component of this process. Next, form a committee and make sure diverse voices and personalities are represented. For the change to really take hold, supporters and critics alike must come together. Establish committee norms to facilitate an environment where the goal is to collaborate to come to a consensus as to what is the best way to move the change forward. In our case, we reviewed the research on each of the four evaluation tools being considered, allowed each company to pitch their product to the committee, and then openly debated which tool we felt would work best for our school district.

- **Implement with intent and integrity.** Once consensus is reached, it is time yet again to communicate clearly why the decision was made and how implementation will proceed. The focus should be on how this change will improve teaching, learning, and/or leadership. Provide as much information as possible that validates why the change is being implemented, and be honest if any questions or critical feedback arise.

- **Provide adequate and appropriate support.** Needless to say professional learning (not the drive-by variety) is critical for large-scale change to succeed. After deciding on an evaluation tool, we provided in-house trainings on not only the tool itself, but also how the process of conducting observations and evaluations would change. The support continued on an ongoing, as-needed basis until the feeling was that the process was well on its way to sustainability.

- **Evaluate, reflect, act.** Nothing is perfect in the field of education. As such we must always look to improve, not just sustain, a change initiative. The process of reflection and evaluation on a consistent basis helps to create a culture committed to growth and improvement. Leaders who consistently act to make things better lead to a culture of excellence. Actions change things.

There is no recipe for change, but experience informs us on how we can make the process a bit smoother, eventually leading to success.

SUMMARY

Initiating and sustaining change does not have to be a cumbersome process fraught with insurmountable challenges. Fullan's (2011) six secrets of change and the outlined process of change provide guidance from which leaders can work to initiate change. Sustaining change is accomplished by following a process that leads to better results for kids. It's not only about dealing with apparent roadblocks as they appear, but also recognizing potential new ones before they materialize. Digital leadership is not only a change in mindset, but also a change in professional behavior that will pave the way to create a more relevant school through the seamless integration of transformative ideas and technology. It is not changing who we are as leaders but changing the way we do things that will transform school culture to better meet the needs of all stakeholders in the digital age.

GUIDING QUESTIONS

1. Why is change needed?

2. How do Fullan's six secrets of change currently influence your work? Take a critical lens to these elements, and develop specific action steps for improvement.

3. What roadblocks to change most hold you back? How will you work to overcome these? What other roadblocks have you encountered not mentioned in this chapter?

4. Using the Change Process and Strategic Planning Cycle images (Figures 3.2 and 3.3), begin to plan out how a new status quo will be created to improve school culture for your learners.

iStock.com/wildpixel

Leading Through a Digital Lens

4

Leading in a culture of change means creating a culture (not just a structure) of change. It does not mean adopting innovations, one after another; it does mean producing the capacity to seek, critically assess, and selectively incorporate new ideas and practices—all the time, inside the organization as well as outside it.

—Fullan (2001, p. 44)

A SUPERINTENDENT'S JOURNEY

Lieutenant Colonel David Britten, retired following 22 years of military service, brought the importance of teamwork in planning and executing any mission with him to his second career as a public school administrator. He knows that effective teamwork requires that each member fully understand the vision, mission, and plan of execution from the standpoint of the role each member of the team plays in achieving success. There is no room for isolation. Failure to comprehend the role and expectations of each team member, from the leader down to the lowest-ranking soldier, increases the risk of failure.

Those lessons informed his leadership style as an educational administrator for over 20 years, and technology expanded his ability to "lead out loud," with a level of transparency that ensured all members of his team—administrators, teachers, students, parents, and the community—had the real-time information they needed to contribute effectively to success. Social networking and blogging gave Britten the interactive tools that not only informed his decision making, but also built a level of trust the Godfrey-Lee Public School District (Grand Rapids, Michigan) had never before experienced.

Growing evidence as detailed in Chapter 1 has linked real-time, interactive technology tools directly to improved student learning outcomes. Britten knew beyond a doubt that they led to a change in climate and culture throughout his former district that raised the level of student learning significantly. In the nearly nine years he had served as superintendent, bringing with him a broad vision of using digital tools in teaching, learning, and leadership, the community witnessed its high school advance from one of the lowest achieving in the state to ranking in the top third of all public schools in Michigan. This had been brought about by a culture that no longer accepted the idea of low expectations for students in a poor, limited-English-speaking district, and its hybrid 1:1 and Bring Your Own Device (BYOD) technology vision had been at the core of this transformation.

Britten's motto as a superintendent was "leading out loud," and he used social networking and blogging to model both professional learning and transparent leadership for his administrative team. During his time as a school leader, public education was constantly under attack by state leaders and legislators. He led the local effort to advocate for equity in school funding and a broader concept of college and career readiness, unabashedly using Twitter, Facebook, and his personal Rebel 6 Ramblings blog site to point out the shortcomings in state and federal policies. Britten believed that not only did these tools become effective methods for communicating the concerns of the district regarding legislation and funding priorities, but also ensured that everyone throughout the district had real-time updates of information needed to join the effort. Using these tools appropriately and effectively modeled the important skills students could use as they developed their own advocacy roles.

Beyond the Godfrey-Lee District, Britten used technology tools for his own professional learning and developing connections with educational leaders around the world. The use of Twitter in particular led to several valuable partnerships—friendships that provided him with a convenient, real-time mechanism for bouncing off ideas and learning from others. To be the best you need to learn from the best, and for educators in the trenches the best are those people who are currently doing or have successfully done the work. "The professional life of an educational leader is often isolated and lonely, but technology has opened up a whole new avenue for developing learning and social relationships that can support a more successful career" (D. Britten, personal communication, 2013).

The future of educational leadership promises to become even more exciting as real-time communications through evolving technologies combine with the expanding realm of analytics to provide leaders with more powerful, mission-focused tools. The right information focused on the needs of the moment and communicated in real time can only ensure that every member of the team contributes to student learning and organizational success.

BE IN THE DRIVER'S SEAT

I remember one year when my school was recognized as the School of the Month for November/December by *eSchool News*. The resulting article described New Milford High School's many accomplishments pertaining to the use of educational technology and implementation of innovative practices to enhance the teaching and learning process. We were extremely proud of the culture that was created, where technology and innovation converged to improve student achievement and overall success. As technology's role in society continues to become more prevalent, it makes sense to integrate it effectively and in a purposeful fashion so that our learners are not shortchanged in their future. This is an important point. It's not our future we are preparing students for, but theirs. We can ill afford to prepare them for a world that won't exist.

New Milford High became a far cry from its former self. The many shifts, changes, and resulting transformation did not occur overnight, impulsively, or without calculated risks. As I look back on our journey and the path that was taken, I have been able to identify some key elements that drove change. It was these changes that took an average, comprehensive high school and transformed it into a cutting-edge institution that many came to know through social media and traveled from all over the country and world to see in action.

For years technology was viewed as an expensive frill that we would love to have but that was not worth the money when push came to shove. To me, being a digital leader meant making sure our computer labs were up to date and available for staff to use when needed. The notion of using social media was never a thought, since the perception was that it lacked any potential value for learning or education in general. As for mobile phones, the only role they served was as a communication tool for students as they journeyed to and from school. Never under any circumstances would they have been used for learning during my early tenure as principal.

The above paragraph provides a brief, honest synopsis of where we were and the role I played in creating the exact opposite school culture described in the *eSchool News* piece. So what changed? How did New Milford become a digital-rich and innovative school where potential and promise were emphasized rather than problems, challenges, and excuses? How were we able to get everyone on board to initiate and sustain change? Here are some answers to these questions.

Connectedness Matters

It wasn't until I became a digitally connected leader that I truly understood the error of my ways and views. My social media journey has been well documented, but it was this journey that provided me with the knowledge, tools, and ideas needed to initiate change. Knowledge is everything, and it influences our decisions and opinions. For me, I lacked the fundamental knowledge of how technology could truly be integrated effectively and used to either support or enhance teaching, learning, and leadership. Once connected through social media, I was given the knowledge and the kick in the butt I desperately needed. For my school, connected-ness was the original catalyst for change. It also enabled us to form numerous collaborative partnerships with an array of stakeholders who assisted us along the way.

Vision to Action

The seeds for change will only germinate if a coherent vision is established. It is important that all stakeholder groups contribute to a concrete, collective vision and work to create a plan for integra-tion that clearly articulates why and how technology will be used to support education. Without the crucial *why* and *how,* any resulting plan will fail.

Great leaders understand the importance of a shared vision and the need to articulate lofty goals and resulting outcomes. They are for-ward thinking, which turns out to be a highly admirable trait right up there with honesty. To effectively lead change, a shared vison needs to be established. In the words of James M. Kouzes and Barry Posner (2009),

> The only visions that take hold are shared visions—and you will create them only when you listen very, very closely to others, appreciate their hopes, and attend to their needs. The best leaders are able to bring their people into the future because they engage in the oldest form of research: They observe the human condition.

Compelling visions can truly change the world. But staying invested in them can be extremely difficult when hard times arrive. The real work and testament to great leadership is moving past the visioning process by developing a strategic plan to turn vision into reality. I have been a part of, or witnessed, one too many visioning exer-cises that focused on the formation of a mission statement. What resulted for the most part was a hollow vision that was not sup-ported by action. Many, including myself, would consider this a waste of time. I would even go as far to say that getting people in a room for countless hours to develop a paragraph of jargon-filled sentences is more indicative of a boss than a leader. The combi-nation of a mission statement with just a vision does not lead to sustainable change. Forward-thinking visionaries who persistently strive to implement a vision through actions do.

Whereas developing a shared vision is an attribute linked to all great leaders, the best leaders ensure that a strategic plan is developed and then meticulously implemented. A vision has to result in a plan, which provides a focus for the change initiative. The plan then has to be monitored and evaluated if the desired outcome is sustainable change that leads to transformation. The real work comes after a vision has been established. Here are ten crucial elements to successfully move from vision to actionable change:

1. Prioritize it—make digital learning, leadership, and innovation a priority for your district, school, or classroom.

2. Connect strategies to indicators of success—understand how the vision aligns with the strategic goals of the district or school.

3. Communicate a new normal—communicate what achieving the vision will mean for you and your learners.

4. Inspire the masses—leaders must inspire others to move from where they are to where they need to be.

5. Insist on embracement, not just buy-in—the vision should be discussed and supported by all for the inherent value it provides.

6. Promote every chance you get—speak about the new changes whenever possible.

7. Spread the word—communicate the vision at every opportunity.

8. Live it, own it, believe in it—leaders must model the vision and not just pay lip service to or pin it up throughout a building.

9. Drive the bus, don't be a passenger—don't ask others to do what you won't.

10. Delegate certain aspects, but not all.

Great leaders are never satisfied by just developing a shared vision. They work tirelessly to model expectations during the planning and implementation phases of the change process while empowering others to embrace change. It is easy to talk the talk. Great leaders walk the walk while helping others experience greatness and success along the way. Don't settle for anyone else's vision or even your own if it is not persistently put into action. Great visions can, and will, lead to the development of a legacy. Your legacy and that of your school or district will be defined by how well you positively impact the lives of others.

Value

One of the drawbacks to innovation and technology is the perceived lack of value it has in terms of student learning and achievement. As education systems across the globe for the most part place a greater emphasis on standardized test scores, the value of technology in the eyes of many diminishes or is nonexistent. The true value of technology rests on how it is used to support learning and create experiences that students find meaningful and relevant. This, in my opinion, is the key and should be included when establishing a vision. Technology has the power to engage students, unleash their creativity, and allow them to apply what they have learned to demonstrate conceptual mastery. If stakeholders understand and experience technology's value firsthand, change quickly follows. Connecting its use to evidence that clearly shows improvement will also do the trick.

Support

Support comes in many forms. Teachers need to have a certain amount of access to technology in order to experience the types of changes that occurred at New Milford High. We made a commitment at the district level to install a wireless network early on during our transformation efforts and consistently upgraded it over the years. This allowed for the seamless and uninterrupted use of mobile devices by both teachers and students. We also made a commitment to transform a very old building (circa 1928) by outfitting rooms with the latest technology. This was a slow process that occurred over three and a half years. In addition to providing access to technology, another essential support structure is removing the fear of failure and encouraging a risk-taking environment that fuels innovation. Change does not happen without this element. As a leader, it wasn't until I addressed my technology fears head-on and then began to model technology's effective use that many of our initiatives began to flourish.

Professional Learning

Without this element in place, change surely will not occur. Transforming a school culture based on significant shifts in pedagogy requires opportunities to learn how to effectively integrate technology. As there were not many quality professional learning options in place when we started our journey, we made our own.

This was accomplished by leveraging our teacher leaders and available resources. The majority of the knowledge, ideas, and strategies came from the formation of a Personal Learning Network (PLN). By harnessing the power of a PLN, I was able to impart what I learned to my staff. Trainings on various digital tools were held after school. After our first year of holding these trainings, we began hosting our own conference to provide more relevant and meaningful growth opportunities. I even created a Professional Growth Period (PGP), a job-embedded growth model. This resulted in giving my staff the time and flexibility to learn how to integrate the tools that they were interested in, as well as to form their own PLNs, during the school day in lieu of contractual noninstructional duties.

With advances in affordable technology, such as the ultracheap Chromebook, it has been tough for schools to resist spending these funds on devices. Now don't get me wrong, I am all for schools increasing student and staff access to quality technology. However, the cart before the horse scenario has played out in so many schools across the globe. The end result has been a massive influx in tools, but no sound professional learning prior for teachers or administrators to ensure how these powerful tools can, and will, actually impact learning. In the words of William Horton, "Unless you get instructional design right, technology can only increase the speed and certainty of failure." If successful change is the goal, then investments have to be made into job-embedded, ongoing professional learning before, during, and consistently after any technology rollout or implementation of large-scale initiatives.

Embracement

The final element that I found to be critical in driving change was empowering my staff to embrace technology and innovation as opposed to securing buy-in. To me there is a huge difference. Embracement is attained through empowerment and autonomy. Buy-in requires a salesman-like approach that might contain if-then rewards. We had no mandates to use technology at New Milford High School. Empowering teachers to shift their instructional practices and giving them the needed autonomy to take risks and work on effective pedagogical alignment worked to intrinsically motivate them to change. This approach was found to be instrumental in our renaissance, minimizing resistance and resentment. Here are some guiding questions to use to begin thinking about the change process in one's digital leadership journey:

- How can digital leaders create policies and environments that allow educators to harness digital tools to engage learners, unleash their creativity, and enhance learning?

- How can educators and schools effectively use social media to communicate important information (e.g., student honors, staff accomplishments, meetings, emergency information) to stakeholders in real time?

- How can leaders take control of their public relations and produce a constant stream of positive news? If we don't share our story, someone else will, and we then run the risk that it will not be positive.

- How do busy leaders go about establishing a brand presence once restricted to the business world when schools and districts now have the tools at their fingertips to do this in a cost-effective manner?

- How can leaders connect with experts and peers across the globe to grow professionally through knowledge acquisition, resource sharing, and engaged discussion, and to receive feedback?

- Is enough being done to teach students about their digital identity?

- How are leaders tapping into countless opportunities that arise through conversations and transparency in online spaces? Or are they doing this at all?

During my early years as New Milford High School principal, my perspective and philosophy as to what constituted an innovative learning culture was vastly different from what it is now. Back then, I felt that being a digital leader just consisted of purchasing the tools for my staff and letting them use them as they saw fit. I was also adamant that social media had no place in an educational setting. To put it bluntly, no educational organizations in the country would have even thought of approaching me to talk about the innovative use of technology at my school.

We saw many shifts in terms of instruction, communication, and learning at New Milford High, resulting in a transformative culture that was more able to meet the needs of our students while improving achievement in the process. So what changed?

I was just like every other principal on the planet prior to my epiphany. My narrow focus was on sustaining a school culture focused on rules, compliance, conformity, and preserving the status quo. The end goal was to make sure standardized test scores increased (or at least didn't go down) and traditions were preserved. On the inside everything was great. Students and staff seemed happy, while the community was supportive of our efforts. Each monotonous day began with students arriving at school and then going directly to their first-period class, where they sat in desks arranged in orderly rows. After everyone listened to the daily announcements, the delivery of instruction began. My compliant students then went through their rigid eight-period schedule, with each class lasting 48 minutes. At the end of each class, an annoying bell would notify everyone in the school that it was time to continue through the repetitive process. Throw in a few specialized programs, assemblies, and pep rallies, and this was basically the schedule we all followed each and every day.

Then it happened. In 2009 a student had his phone out in the hallway. I got on my walkie-talkie to get some support from my assistant principal, and we proceeded to literally chase the student through the halls. Eventually we cornered him and asked for his device, as it was a violation of school policy to have it out during the day. As he handed me the device, a statement was made that rocked my world: "Thank you Mr. Sheninger for creating a jail out of a school." I was shocked and embarrassed at the same time. Here I was trying to create an "optimal" learning environment, but instead my decisions and actions were making many of my students miserable.

That weekend I happened to read an article about Twitter in the newspaper. Now, I had sworn that I never would get on social media, as I did not see the value it had to support or improve teaching, learning, and leadership. Then the light bulb went on as I saw a connection to professional practice. I then begrudgingly decided to give Twitter a try to improve communications with my stakeholders. Little did I know that this moment in time would totally redefine my purpose in education. As my behavior shifted from communicator to learner, I immediately discovered how blinded I was by a system so entrenched in methodologies and practices designed for a period in time that had long passed. I learned how to unlearn and then relearn through conversations I began having with passionate educators across the globe. These conversations empowered me to begin the process of taking my school in a better direction for the sake of my students.

Now you know how my "Aha!" moment, consisting of a student and Twitter, pushed me to make some small changes on the surface that resulted in some significant improvements to practice. The first small change was my philosophical enlightenment as to the educational value of digital tools, including social media. It was at this time that I saw the error of my ways. I began to leverage the power of new knowledge that social media now provided me to effectively integrate an array of strategies that I had never considered and tools and that were foreign to me. This small change evolved into a philosophy on how schools can and should embrace digital technologies to improve leadership. The short list of elements of my philosophy includes

- Empowering students to own their learning through rigorous and relevant application aligned to standards through improved pedagogical practices.
- Redesigning learning spaces to improve intended outcomes.
- Providing and seeking out research and evidence-based professional learning that is meaningful.
- Effectively communicating with stakeholders.
- Establishing a consistent public relations strategy.
- Developing a brand presence that promises value.
- Discovering opportunity for learners, educators, and schools.

The second small change was educating my staff on the value of innovation in the classroom and beyond. Instead of mandating that every teacher integrate technology, I chose to empower my staff to create to improve the learning environment. Little things such as support, encouragement, flexibility, and modeling went a long way to provide my staff with the confidence to take risks and create meaningful learning activities that fostered creativity, problem solving, critical thinking, and active involvement by all students. This became a collaborative effort, and more and more teachers began to embrace a vision that paired sound pedagogical techniques with technology and innovative ideas.

The third small change was realizing that students had to be instrumental in any effort to transform the culture of our school. We had to give up a certain amount of control in order to successfully implement a BYOD program, where students were granted access to the school's wireless network during the day using their computing devices. We also had to trust that they would use their mobile learning devices responsibly as a tool for learning.

The fourth and final small change was becoming a more transparent administrator and sharing the innovative practices taking place within the walls of my school. With Twitter, I was able to give my stakeholders a glimpse into my role as an educational leader. Facebook had been an incredible tool to share real-time information, student achievements, and staff innovations. Instagram provided me with the ability to share daily how teaching and learning were changing. All of these tools combined gave my stakeholders and the greater educational community a bird's-eye view into my school and the great things happening there.

These small changes, combined with many others, had a huge impact on the teaching, learning, and leadership culture of my school. They also served as the basis for the Pillars of Digital Leadership. Even though I have highlighted changes specific to technology, there were those focused on curriculum, assessment, and programming. Politicians and self-proclaimed reformers routinely throw around the word *change* and think that a one-size-fits-all approach is what's needed to increase student achievement and spur innovation. But each school is an autonomous body with distinct dynamics that make it unique. It's the small changes over time that will eventually leave a lasting impact. Schools and educators need to be empowered to make these changes as they see fit. These are the keys to creating an innovative learning culture in a digital world.

THE PILLARS OF DIGITAL LEADERSHIP

It is incumbent upon leaders to address the above questions, because they hold the key to introducing practical change to leadership and school culture. The Pillars of Digital Leadership represent a basis from which new ideas and practices evolve in order to improve schools and professional practices. Embedded within each pillar are new skills and behaviors that develop either to complement traditional models and methods of effective leadership or create entirely new pathways of doing things. Each provides a context for leaders to lead in different ways that are aligned with societal shifts that place an increased demand on technological fluency and integration. They also connect to or fit in with existing technology standards and frameworks for school improvement in the twenty-first century. The effective integration of readily available technology—especially social media—serves as the main foundation of each pillar. This dynamic resource, available for free to leaders, can be leveraged as a multidimensional leadership tool to spark involvement, creativity, and discussions that truly matter. Once the conversations begin, the seeds of change will quickly be planted. The Seven Pillars of Digital Leadership include

1. student engagement, learning, and outcomes;

2. learning environment and spaces;

3. professional growth and learning;

4. communications;

5. public relations;

6. branding; and

7. opportunity.

ISTE STANDARDS FOR EDUCATIONAL LEADERS

The Pillars of Digital Leadership are aligned to the International Society for Technology in Education's (ISTE) Standards for Educational Leaders (ISTE, 2018). These represent the standards for evaluating the skills and knowledge school leaders need to support digital-age learning, implement technology, and transform the educational landscape. Transforming schools into digital-age places of learning requires leadership from people who can accept new challenges and embrace opportunities, which is at the heart of digital leadership. Now more than ever, the success of technology integration depends on leaders who can implement systemic reform in schools. Online Resource 4.1 (ISTE Standards for Education Leaders) provides a list and description of these standards. Leaders can utilize these as guidelines as they work to implement change through the Pillars of Digital Leadership. Together, these will help pave the way for transformational change. All of ISTE's standards can be found in Online Resource 4.2 (ISTE Standards).

FUTURE READY SCHOOLS

Future Ready Schools helps K–12 public, private, and charter school leaders plan and implement personalized, research-based digital learning strategies so all students can achieve their full potential. Detailed information can be accessed at futureready.org. Central to achieving this lofty goal is the Future Ready Framework (Figure 4.1), a robust structure for digital learning visioning, planning, and implementation focused on personalized student learning. The research-based framework emphasizes collaborative leadership and creating an innovative school culture. The guiding principles focus on seven key areas, called *gears,* with leadership influencing each. The gears are as follows:

1. Curriculum, Instruction, and Assessment
2. Personalized Professional Learning
3. Robust Infrastructure
4. Budget and Resources
5. Community Partnerships
6. Data and Privacy
7. Use of Space and Time

Collaborative Leadership is the outside ring that encompasses the whole cycle of transformation. For the purposes of this book, we'll consider Collaborative Leadership to be the eighth gear:

8. Collaborative Leadership

This framework keeps student learning at the heart of all decision making. The easy-to-use infographic in Figure 4.1 presents a visual that aligns the Future Ready gears and the role of leaders. Online Resource 4.3 (Future Ready Framework) provides more detailed information on the framework.

At the International Center for Leadership in Education (ICLE), we have created a crosswalk that illustrates how the Pillars of Digital Leadership seamlessly align with the Future Ready Schools (FRS) Framework. You can learn more about this alignment as well as evidence-based professional learning solutions that can assist districts and schools in transforming teaching, learning, and leadership in Online Resource 4.4 (Alignment With the Future Ready Framework).

Figure 4.1 Future Ready Framework

SUMMARY

As we move further into the digital age, it is imperative that school leaders develop a vision for the role that technology and innovation will play and establish a strategic plan for implementation across a broad spectrum. Moving from vision to action in this area can be accomplished by emulating the behaviors, techniques, and strategies utilized by highly effective digital leaders. Change in this regard requires establishing a clear vision, an inherent sense of value, embracement as opposed to buy-in, relevant professional learning, and support. The Pillars of Digital Leadership provide the foundational elements to begin the process of transformational change using technological resources that perfectly align with standards for technology leadership and frameworks for school improvement (Figure 4.2).

Figure 4.2   Standards and Framework Alignment for Digital Leadership

Digital Leadership Pillar	ISTE	Future Ready (Gears)
Student Engagement and Learning	1, 2, 3, 4, and 5	1, 2, 3, 4, 7, and 8
Learning Spaces and Environment	1, 2, and 4	1, 2, 3, 4, 5, 6, 7, and 8
Professional Growth and Learning	3 and 5	2, 7, and 8
Communication	2, 3, and 5	5 and 8
Public Relations	2 and 5	5 and 8
Branding	2 and 5	5 and 8
Opportunity	4 and 5	All

GUIDING QUESTIONS

1. How have you helped others see the value in change? Can you be more success-ful, and if so, what steps will you take?

2. How has your school or district put vision into action? Explain the steps taken and the evidence of how these actions have improved school culture.

3. When reviewing the ten crucial elements to successfully move from vision to actionable change presented in this chapter, where do you see opportunities for growth?

4. How does the culture of your school or district align with elements identified in the ISTE standards and Future Ready Framework? Where is improvement needed?

iStock.com/Poike

Improving Student Engagement, Learning, and Outcomes 5

A simple question to ask is, "How has the world of a child changed in the last 150 years?" And the answer is, "It's hard to imagine any way in which it hasn't changed! But if you look at school today versus 100 years ago, it is more similar than dissimilar."

—Peter Senge, senior lecturer, Massachusetts Institute of Technology

SCHOOL SHOULD REFLECT REAL LIFE

Many of us firmly believe in technology's potential to help transform the teaching and learning cultures of schools. Whether it is used to enhance lessons, assess learning, engage students, or unleash creativity, technology has a defined role in a variety of school functions. Even though I am preaching to the choir, many schools still treat education as an effort to prepare students for a world that no longer exists, one in which technology is viewed as either a frill, a distraction, or a nonfactor in improving student achievement.

For many students, school does not reflect real life (Figure 5.1). This results in various levels of disengagement during the teaching and learning process. The question then becomes, How do we move those schools that teeter toward irrelevancy in terms of meeting the diverse learning needs of their students to begin the transformation process? This is pivotal if we are truly to begin to reform education in a way that is meaningful to our students. Our students want to be creative, collaborate, utilize technology for learning, connect with their peers near and far, understand the messages that media convey, and solve real-world problems. Schools and systems of education that do not embrace digital learning and place a high emphasis on standardization will always fail to resonate with our students. It only makes sense to harness the power of technology as a catalyst for authentic engagement and application of concepts among our learners. If schools allow students to use the digital-age tools that they are using on a routine basis outside their walls, chances are they will find more relevancy and meaning in what they are learning.

Digital leadership is a mindset and a call to transform a school's culture into one that unleashes the creativity of students, so they can create artifacts of learning that demonstrate conceptual mastery. It is about providing learners with the knowledge, skills, and confidence to succeed in college, careers, and jobs that have not even been created yet. Most important, it embraces an evolved concept of education, a constructivist, heutagogical approach to teaching and learning. The teachers, learners, networks, connections, media, resources, and tools create a unique entity that has the potential to meet individual learners', educators', and even societal needs (Gerstein, 2013). Digital tools allow for coconstructing knowledge, sharing experiences, reflecting on practice, seeking feedback, and contributing to the learning of others (Killion, 2013). Research has also found that digital learning leads to positive effects on

Figure 5.1 School does not reflect real life.

motivation and learning outcomes when compared to traditional teaching (Lin, Chen, & Liu, 2017).

This is accomplished by allowing students to use real-world tools to apply what they have learned and construct new knowledge. By focusing on how specific technologies can be used to engage students, digital leaders are establishing a foundation for learning that will lead to eventual increases in student achievement. This becomes a reality when school cultures are transformed to meet and anticipate the needs of learners in the digital age.

HOW RESEARCH SHOULD GUIDE THE WORK

Research provides not only some validation of the above points but also some cautious advice. After analyzing numerous studies,

Darling-Hammond, Zielezinski, and Goldman (2014) concluded that technology has a significant impact on students that need it the most—our at-risk leaners. Success relies on technology being used to support interactive learning, to create and explore rather than drill and kill, and the right blend of teachers and technology. The last point is critical. Research has consistently indicated that the number one factor that impacts student learning is the quality of the teacher. Thus, success in improving outcomes through the use of technology means better support for current teachers or finding ways to add more positions.

In *Learning Transformed* (2017), Thomas Murray and I looked at over one hundred studies to glean insight into how technology has been found to positively impact learning. One study by Zheng, Warschauer, Lin, and Chang (2016) really stood out. They conducted a synthesis of results from 96 published studies on K–12 schools that were 1:1 from 2001 through 2015. Of these studies, they critically analyzed 10 that were rigorously designed and examined the intricate relationships between these programs and academic achievement. Not only did they find that test scores increased in science, reading, math, writing, and English, the study also discovered other learner benefits. These included receiving more feedback on writing, routinely publishing more work, increased writing across a wider variety of genres, and more editing and revising of completed work.

Escueta, Quan, Nickow, and Oreopoulos (2017) released a review of more than one hundred experimental studies in education technology. The resulting review paper examined evidence across several areas of education technology: access to technology, computer-assisted learning, technology-based behavioral interventions in education, and online learning. Below are some of the main summaries:

- Computer-assisted learning, in which educational software helps students develop particular skills, is promising, especially in math. This is likely because of the software's ability to personalize learning by adapting to a student's specific level and letting the student learn at the right pace for him or her, as well as the ability to provide teachers immediate feedback on student performance that is actionable. The results here speak to the potential of personalized and blended models of learning.

- Digital behavioral interventions produced consistently improved learning outcomes.

- Initiatives that provide computers to every student in a classroom do not improve learning outcomes. Putting the cart before the horse does not and will not lead to better learning. You can't just put a device in the hands of kids and hope that learning miracles will automatically materialize.

IMPROVING PEDAGOGY WITH A LEANER-FOCUSED MINDSET AND FRAMEWORK

This book might be titled *Digital Leadership*, but don't let that fool you. *Digital* just represents a means to improve teaching and learning in a way that results in better outcomes for our learners. The fact of the matter is if we don't get instructional design right first, then all technology will do is speed up the rate of failure. "Pedagogy first, technology second if appropriate" is the mantra that digital leaders subscribe to. It is important to understand that technology will not improve every lesson, assessment, or learning outcome. For this reason alone, it is crucial that there is always a focus on what we know actually works when it comes to pedagogy. You don't build schools, classrooms, lessons, curriculum, and assessments around technology. The key to success and improving outcomes is grounded in a solid pedagogical foundation . . . period.

> Technology integration has to be strategic to work. Strategic technology use is use that is purposefully chosen for its ability to move you towards defined student learning goals. When technology isn't rooted in pedagogy and hasn't been vetted and tested for its ability to help your students reach learning objectives, then its use is haphazard—this is the opposite of strategic. It's like putting up the sail without pointing [the boat] in the direction you want . . . to go. Or worse, without even knowing where you want to go and why. (Kieschnick, 2017)

There are many technology-specific frameworks out there that are embraced by educators across the globe. Therein lies the issue. Now I am not saying there isn't any value in these, but a tech-centric framework should raise an eyebrow or two. It's not curriculum, instruction, and assessment on one side and technology on the other. The digital aspect should never drive or overshadow what the main emphasis should always be on, and that is learning.

Digital tools are transforming essential elements of the education space. Understanding how they are impacting teaching and learning will help guide your consideration of which tools are useful and how to best implement them.

It is crucial that sound pedagogical techniques and best practices are emphasized in order to effectively integrate technology with purpose to enhance teaching and learning. Students must always be at the center of this process. All too often, technology is infused into the learning environment where the teacher is still employing a direct approach to instruction. It's not what the adult does with technology that ultimately matters, but instead what the learners are doing with it. One of the most important questions a leader needs to answer is, How are students using technology to learn in ways that they couldn't without it? Here is how digital tools can improve learning.

1. **Increase collaboration:** Just as social media has given rise to new definitions of community, digital tools are transforming community and the give-and-take between students and teachers. Platforms for web-based discussion threads and course or class Google Docs alter the types of student involvement in project-based and writing-specific assignments. A piece of student writing can become a diverse and substantive document when it is the basis for a step-by-step exchange of ideas and questions between teacher, peers, authors, and mentors. When digital tools are integrated in a pedagogically sound fashion, they also promote and enhance other essential competencies such as communication, creativity, critical thinking, problem solving, digital literacy, entrepreneurship, global awareness, and digital responsibility/citizenship.

2. **Innovate assessment:** As formats and contexts for assignments evolve, the methods of assessment need to keep pace. The openness of the online environment, and the integration of such things as game attributes, shape all kinds of assessment, especially formative assessment, which measures learning progress (not only endpoints in learning).

3. **Enable learning about information and research:** Research projects will always require substantive research, accurate and relevant synthesis, and defined audience-oriented approaches. However, in an

information-saturated world, students are drawing on tools that help them analyze and understand multiple representations from a range of disciplines and subjects, such as texts, data, and photographs.

4. **Transform time frames around learning:** In many instances, digital tools offer an asynchronous (not simultaneous) environment for response and inquiry not present in brick-and-mortar environments. Written and video discussions online can enable expression of diverse views, opportunities for collaboration, and time to think and plan before responding in ways that in-class discussions do not provide. This is true for both online classrooms and blended classrooms—those integrating online and digital tools into a traditional learning setting.

5. **Ownership of learning:** According to John Dewey, the type of activities that stimulate real involvement "give pupils something to do, not something to learn; and the doing is of such a nature as to demand thinking, or the intentional noting of connections; learning naturally results." There are thousands of free digital tools available that promote the art of doing. Students can now pick the best ones in order to create an artifact that demonstrates conceptual mastery through the construction of new knowledge as well as the acquisition and application of essential competencies. The process of choice increases engagement and authenticity, and ultimately provides more value in the learning process. Unleash the power of digital tools, and empower students to take ownership of their learning.

MOVING FROM TEACHING TO EMPOWERED LEARNING

The Rigor/Relevance Framework is a tool developed by the International Center for Leadership in Education to examine curriculum, instruction, and assessment (Daggett, 2016). The Rigor/Relevance Framework is based on two dimensions of higher standards and student achievement (Figure 5.5). First, a continuum of knowledge describes the increasingly complex ways in which we think.

This knowledge taxonomy is based on the six levels of the revised Bloom's taxonomy as depicted on the vertical axis:

6. Creating

5. Evaluating

4. Analyzing

A PEDAGOGICAL FOUNDATION FOR DIGITAL TOOLS

To ensure that students acquire the necessary digital literacies and competences, it is important that they are presented with a range of digital tools and gain an understanding of those tools' capabilities. The pedagogical framework of eDidaktik (see www.edidaktik.dk) can be the basis for an initial assessment of whether a digital tool is suitable for use in different forms of teaching. The framework is based on distinctions among *monological, dialogical,* and a *polyphonic* forms of teaching. The three forms of teaching can be distinguished by their different theories of how learning takes place, and by their different takes on the relations among subject matter, teacher, and student.

Monological Teaching

Monological teaching is based on Ludwig Wittgenstein's idea that the teacher is the expert within a language game and that teaching is to be seen as the teacher's communication of expert knowledge to the student. Learning is the student's acquisition of this knowledge (see Figure 5.2).

Digital Tool Options: Distributing and integrating tools that facilitate the transfer of information to the student. Additionally, use of tools that aid in the evaluation of student learning outcomes, such as closed tasks and tests.

Figure 5.2 Monological Teaching

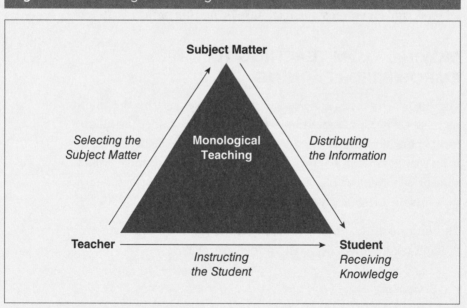

Source: Niels (2012). Used with permission.

Dialogical Teaching

Dialogical teaching is based on John Dewey's (1910) idea that the student has an inherent basis of knowledge that can be developed through interaction with the outside world and by solving problems. The teacher chooses a subject matter; the student chooses to work with the parts of the subject matter that he or she finds relevant and then uses this part of the subject matter to solve authentic problems. If necessary, the student makes contact with the teacher for additional help (see Figure 5.3).

Digital Tool Options: Tools that can facilitate evaluating students' learning outcomes, for example, testing through case assignments and simulations, where students can show that they can use gained experience within different contexts. Tools that support students' problem-oriented work and advanced learning games are especially relevant here.

Figure 5.3 Dialogical Teaching

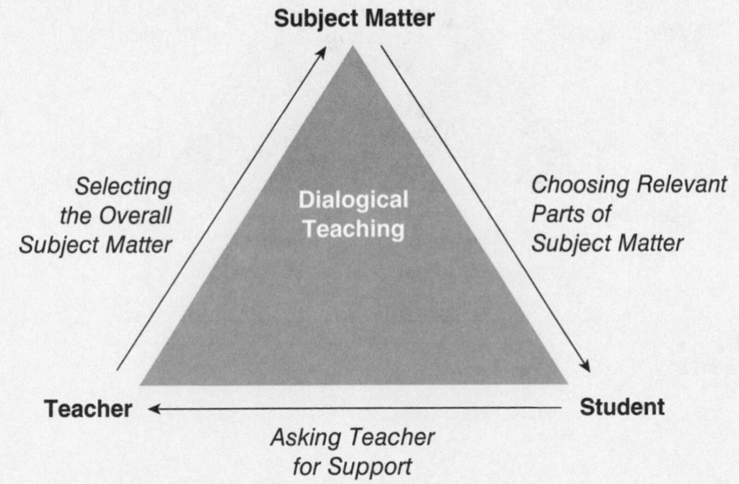

Source: Niels (2012). Used with permission.

Polyphonic Teaching

Polyphonic teaching is based on Knud Ejler Løgstrup's idea that knowledge is created through an equal exchange of many different individuals' perceptions of the world. Learning is the student's participation in this exchange.

(Continued)

(Continued)

The teacher and student jointly select the subject matter to be studied. They are equals in this process, just as they are in their subsequent efforts to process the subject matter and produce common knowledge within the field (see Figure 5.4).

Digital Tool Options: While learning outcomes cannot be easily measured in this collaborative type of learning, digital and online tools that support equal collaboration and the production of common knowledge are especially relevant (Edudemic, 2012).

Figure 5.4   Polyphonic Teaching

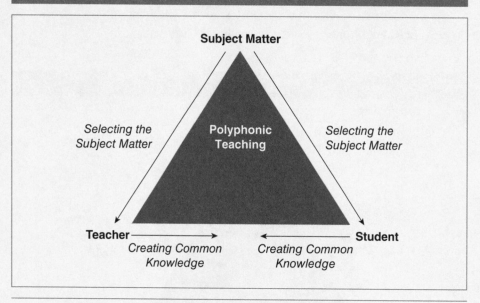

Source: Niels (2012). Used with permission.

3. Applying

2. Understanding

1. Remembering

The low end of this continuum involves acquiring knowledge and being able to recall or locate that knowledge in a simple manner. Just as a computer completes a word search in a word-processing program, a competent person at this level can scan thousands of bits of information in the brain to locate that desired knowledge. The

Figure 5.5   The Rigor/Relevance Framework

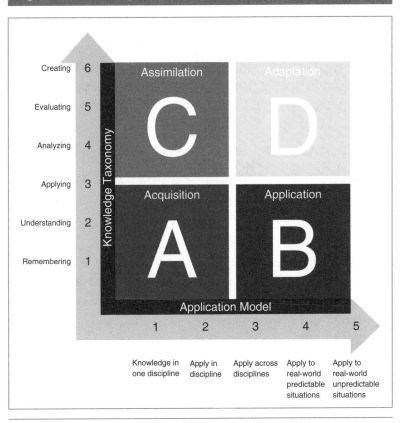

Source: Copyright © 2018 by International Center for Leadership in Education, a division of Houghton Mifflin Harcourt. Used with permission.

high end of the knowledge taxonomy labels more complex ways in which individuals use knowledge. At this level, knowledge is fully integrated into one's mind, and individuals can do much more than locate information—they can take several pieces of knowledge and combine them in both logical and creative ways. Assimilation of knowledge is an accurate way to describe this high level of the thinking continuum. Assimilation is often a higher-order thinking skill; at this level, the student can solve multistep problems, create unique work, and devise solutions.

The second continuum, created by Dr. Bill Daggett (2016), is known as the Application Model. The five levels of this action continuum are as follows:

1. Knowledge in one discipline

2. Apply in discipline

3. Apply across disciplines

4. Apply to real-world predictable situations

5. Apply to real-world unpredictable situations

The Application Model describes putting knowledge to use. While the low end is knowledge acquired for its own sake, the high end signifies action—use of that knowledge to solve complex real-world problems and create projects, designs, and other works for use in real-world situations.

The Rigor/Relevance Framework has four quadrants.

> **Quadrant A** represents simple recall and basic understanding of knowledge for its own sake. Examples of Quadrant A knowledge are knowing that the world is round and that Shakespeare wrote Hamlet.

> **Quadrant C** embraces higher levels of knowledge, such as knowing how the U.S. political system works and analyzing the benefits and challenges of the cultural diversity of this nation versus those of other nations.

> **Quadrants B and D** represent action or high degrees of application. Quadrant B includes knowing how to use math skills to make purchases and count change. The ability to access information in wide-area network systems and the ability to gather knowledge from a variety of sources to solve a complex problem in the workplace are types of Quadrant D knowledge.

Each of these four quadrants can also be labeled with a term that characterizes the learning or student performance.

> **Quadrant A**—Acquisition students gather and store bits of knowledge and information. Students are primarily expected to remember or understand this acquired knowledge.

> **Quadrant B**—Application students use acquired knowledge to solve problems, design solutions, and complete work. The highest level of application is to apply appropriate knowledge to new and unpredictable situations.

> **Quadrant C**—Assimilation students extend and refine their acquired knowledge to automatically and routinely analyze and solve problems as well as create unique solutions.

> **Quadrant D** (Figure 5.6)—Adaptation students have the competence to think in complex ways and apply knowledge and skills they have acquired. Even when confronted with perplexing unknowns, students are able to use extensive

knowledge and skill to create solutions and take action that further develops their skills and knowledge.

The Rigor/Relevance Framework is a fresh approach, future-proofing education by empowering students to think and apply learning in a meaningful way. It is based on traditional elements of education, yet encourages movement from acquisition of knowledge to application of knowledge. The framework is easy to understand. With its simple, straightforward structure, it can serve as a bridge between the school and the community. It offers a common language with which to express the notion of a more rigorous and relevant curriculum and encompasses much of what parents, business leaders, and community members want students to learn. The framework is versatile; it can be used in the development of instruction and assessment. Likewise, teachers can measure their progress in adding rigor and relevance to instruction and select appropriate instructional strategies to meet learner needs and higher achievement goals. A move to Quad D learning is all about future-proofing education by empowering kids to think regardless of changes in society. Don't prepare learners for something. Prepare them for anything!

Figure 5.6 Quadrant D of the Rigor/Relevance Framework

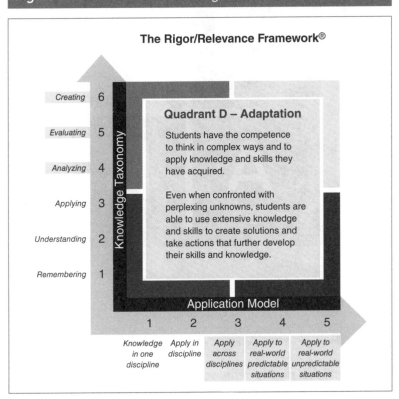

Source: Copyright © 2018 by International Center for Leadership in Education, a division of Houghton Mifflin Harcourt. Used with permission.

RIGOROUS AND RELEVANT LEARNING AS THE STANDARD

When it comes to technology, framing lessons and learning outcomes at the high end of knowledge taxonomy should be the expectation, not the exception. This is not to say that content knowledge is not important. All learners need a foundation to construct essential understandings and new knowledge. The Rigor/Relevance Framework as described earlier in this chapter places an emphasis on higher-order thinking that sets the stage for rigorous learning. It provides a solid lens through which to look at the learning tasks that students are engaged in and redesign them in ways that move away from telling us what they know and instead showing whether or not they actually understand (Figure 5.7).

Figure 5.7   From A to D

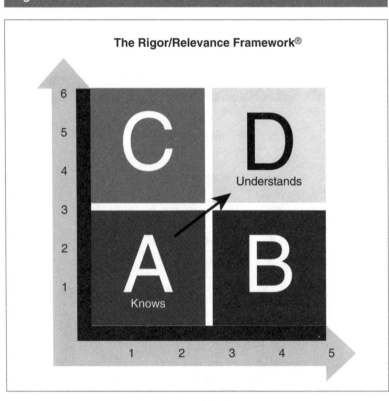

Source: Copyright © 2018 by International Center for Leadership in Education, a division of Houghton Mifflin Harcourt. Used with permission.

The other aspect of this framework is the most important. Are students working, thinking, or both? (See Figure 5.8.) Successful technology integration is totally dependent on the level of questioning that we use with our students (Sheninger & Murray, 2017). This is why I always say that pedagogy trumps technology. Think about the formative and summative assessments you either use or see in your role as an educator. Are students demonstrating high levels of cognitive thought? How do you know whether students have learned or not when integrating technology? What does the feedback loop look like? These are extremely important questions to ask as a teacher or administrator to determine the level of effectiveness.

Figure 5.8 Assess Your Level of Questioning

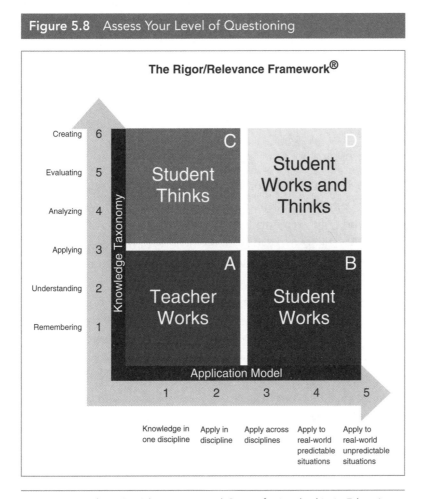

Source: Copyright © 2018 by International Center for Leadership in Education, a division of Houghton Mifflin Harcourt. Used with permission.

Rigor is a concept that describes either an assignment that challenges students to use critical thinking skills or a learning environment that is challenging but supportive and engaging. Rigorous lessons and learning activities ask students to compose, create, design, invent, predict, research, summarize, defend, compare, and justify to demonstrate conceptual mastery and standards attainment.

Rigor is quite simply levels of thinking, including

- Scaffolding for thinking
- Planning for thinking
- Assessing thinking
- Recognizing the level of thinking students demonstrate
- Managing the teaching/learning level for the desired thinking level

Now that a baseline has been established, let's clarify what rigor is not, since there are many misconceptions based on how people interpret various definitions for the word. Rigor is not:

- More or harder worksheets
- AP, IB, gifted, honors courses
- The higher-level book in reading
- More work
- More homework

Whether you call this rigorous or deeper learning is not the point. When it comes to students using digital tools, are they being challenged and empowered to think at the highest levels of knowledge taxonomy? The best way to evaluate the level of thinking learners are engaged in is to look at the level of questioning. Even if a lesson or task begins with low-level questions, digital leaders employ scaffolding techniques to bump them up as a way to develop cognitive flexibility amongst learners. Learners who have developed a competency in cognitive flexibility have the ability to spontaneously restructure their knowledge, in many ways, in adaptive response to radically changing situational demands (Spiro & Jehng, 1990). Engaging their students in addressing increasingly complex questions that have more than one possible answer is something that all educators should try to do, both when they are using technology and when they aren't. Erik Francis created the image in Figure 5.9, which can be used to assess your level of questioning and improve where necessary.

Another main guiding principle of the Rigor/Relevance Framework is relevance. The *why* matters more than ever in the context of schools and education. What one must do is step into the shoes of a student. If students do not truly understand why they are learning what is being taught, the chances of improving outcomes and success diminish significantly. Each lesson should squarely address the *why*. What and how we assess carries little to no weight in the eyes of our students if they don't understand and appreciate the value of the learning experience. In a nutshell, relevance is the purpose of learning. If it is absent from any activity or lesson, many, if

Figure 5.9 Level of Questioning

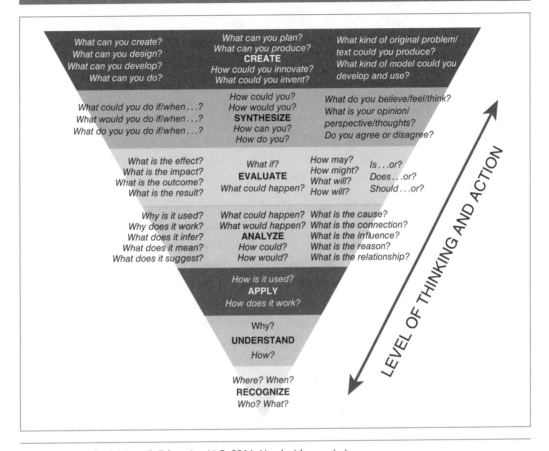

Source: Copyright © Maverik Education LLC, 2016. Used with permission.

not all, students are less motivated to learn and ultimately achieve. Research on the underlying elements that drive student motivation validates how essential it is to establish relevant contexts. Kember, Ho, and Hong (2008) conducted a study where 36 students were interviewed about aspects of the teaching and learning environment that motivated or demotivated their learning.

They found the following:

> One of the most important means of motivating student learning was to establish relevance. It was a critical factor in providing a learning context in which students construct their understanding of the course material. The interviewees found that teaching abstract theory alone was demotivating. Relevance could be established through showing how theory can be applied in practice, creating relevance to local cases, relating the material to everyday applications, or finding applications in current newsworthy issues. (p. 261)

Getting kids to think is excellent, but if they don't truly understand how this thinking will help them, do they value learning? The obvious answer is no. However, not much legwork is needed to add meaning to any lesson, project, or assignment. Relevance begins with students acquiring knowledge and applying it to multiple disciplines to see how it connects to the bigger picture. It becomes even more embedded in the learning process when students apply what has been learned to real-world predictable and ultimately unpredictable situations, resulting in the construction of new knowledge. Thus, a relevant lesson or task empowers learners to use their knowledge to tackle real-world problems that have more than one solution.

Diverse learners respond well to relevant and contextual learning. This improves memory, both short term, and long term, which is all backed by science (Imordino-Yang & Faeth, 2010; Willis, 2010). The research has shown that relevant learning is an effective means for our learners to begin to better demonstrate conceptual mastery. Knowing this should compel all educators to take a critical lens to lesson plans, projects, assessments, and school culture. The dated drill-and-kill model is basically useless from a neurological standpoint. Relevant, meaningful activities that connect with what learners already know and that engage them emotionally help to build neural connections and long-term memory storage (Kember et al., 2008; Imordino-Yang & Faeth, 2010; Willis, 2010).

When it is all said and done, if a lesson or project is relevant, students will be able to tell you

1. What they learned.
2. Why they learned it.
3. How they will use it outside of school in the real world.

Without relevance, many concepts don't make sense to students. The many benefits speak for themselves, which compels all of us to ensure that this becomes a mainstay in daily pedagogy. Figure 5.10 illustrates how rigorous and relevant learning moves learners from just wanting to know the right answer to asking their own questions.

Grounded in rigor and relevance, instruction and learning with digital tools are limitless. This is the foundation of uncommon learning (Sheninger, 2015b). Learning must always be relevant, meaningful, and applicable. Student engagement is a bedrock necessity of attentive and deep learning. Excitement about academic growth, in turn, drives increased student achievement,

Figure 5.10 Moving From the Right Answer to the Right Question

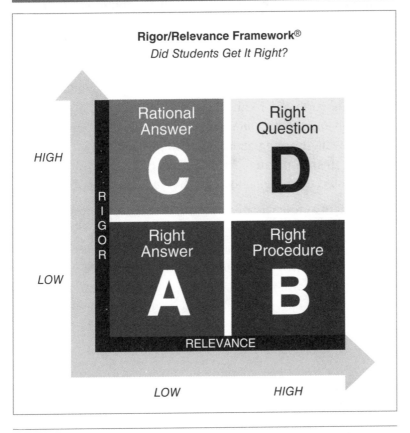

Rigor/Relevance Framework®
Did Students Get It Right?

Source: Copyright © 2018 by International Center for Leadership in Education, a division of Houghton Mifflin Harcourt. Used with permission.

not only in terms of meeting and exceeding standards, but also in terms of learning that extends into all realms of life. With the solid pedagogical foundation that the Rigor/Relevance Framework provides, digital tools and social media afford students the opportunity to take more ownership of their growth and development. Allowing students choice over which tools they will use to create artifacts of their learning that demonstrate conceptual mastery builds a greater appreciation for learning while simultaneously preparing them for the real world.

With advanced digital tools under their belts, students grow to develop their own learning tasks—such as podcasting, blogging, or digital storytelling—that stretch their creativity, originality, design, or adaptation. These students think and act critically to curate content and apply information to address a range of cross-disciplinary tasks that are both creative and original. This could include collaborating with others using social media, networking, or reviewing. Their work requires their ability to select, organize, and present content through relevant digital tools, which provide multiple solutions.

Education and digital technology have become intertwined. Learners and teachers alike are immersed in digital life and need more effective, specific ways to best use digital tools in rigorous and relevant ways to support and/or enhance learning. Educators must be able to develop and enact rigorous, relevant instructional methods and formats, while learning about and using effective digital tools to underpin their instruction. As long as educators are clear about the learning objectives, digital tools can be a powerful supporting tool.

As important as teachers are to the purposeful integration of digital tools to support rigorous and relevant learning, ultimate success at scale lies with leadership. Leaders must begin to transform school culture in ways where there are actually fundamental changes in teaching and learning so that technology is not just a gimmick or tool used to engage students. The Rigor/Relevance Framework (Figure 5.11, Technology Use by Quadrant) serves as a powerful

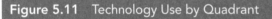

Figure 5.11   Technology Use by Quadrant

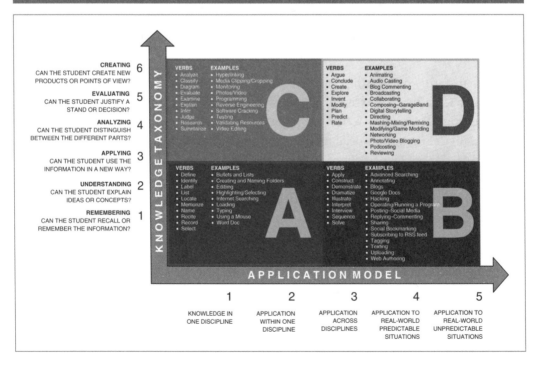

instructional leadership tool to ensure learning is at the forefront with technology initiatives. It assists leaders in the following ways:

- Provides a common language for all
- Constitutes the lens through which to examine curriculum, instruction, and assessment
- Creates a culture around a common vision

Improving instruction in a digital world can only happen with fundamental changes to teaching and leadership. Pedagogy first, technology second when appropriate. With a firm instructional foundation in place, technology can take our students places never before imaginable while meeting diverse learning needs like never before.

DIGITAL LEARNING IN ACTION

What should learning in schools look like in the twenty-first century? Are schools preparing students for success in a global society? These are two questions that quickly come to mind when reading the quote from Peter Senge at the beginning of this chapter. More than ever, it is essential that schools veer away from methodologies that worked for many years when we were educating a different type of student for a different role in society. Key to this transformation is the integration of authentic learning experiences and technology that engage students of all levels and make learning meaningful.

When I arrived at New Milford High School (NMHS) in 2004, there were many amazing programs in place. One was the Holocaust Study Tour. This global learning endeavor provides some students with the opportunity to travel to Europe for at least ten days and study the Holocaust in depth. This authentic learning experience cannot be reproduced in the classroom. For detailed information on the program, please visit the New Milford Holocaust Study Tour blog (http://hst10.blogspot.com/).

Technology allows the students and staff remaining at NMHS to share in the authentic learning experiences taking place in Europe (Germany, Poland, Czech Republic). We launched a blog where the students in Europe chronicle and reflect on essential questions, focusing on a dark time in human history. Meanwhile, students and staff back on the campus of NMHS use the blog as a catalyst for a variety of other learning experiences. Some teachers even have their students respond to the posts each day.

Skype has brought a whole new element to the program. Prior to each trip, students Skype numerous times with their guide, who resides in Israel. Throughout the year, students also Skype with Holocaust survivors in the elective course on the topic. As a leader, I used Skype to keep in contact with my teacher while on the trip and sometimes to converse with the students about what they were learning. We also encourage our history teachers to Skype with the study tour if the times can be worked out. At our district open house each year, we Skype with the group in Europe to kick off the event. The revolving theme for these events is always centered on what it is like to be a learner in the digital age.

English teacher Joanna Westbrook was always on the cutting edge when it came to the purposeful use of technology in the class-room. She never shied away from integrating tools like Twitter and Instagram as means to empower learners in ways like never before while making the experience both rigorous and relevant. Her focus was always on sound instructional design, which then allowed for the seamless integration of almost any tool.

One example that stands out was how she had her learners use Instagram as a means to dive deeper into the curriculum. The aim of this particular project was to challenge her learners to communicate a concept from *A Raisin in the Sun* through the use of visual images. They chose a theme/concept statement from the statements that were generated or addressed during their Socratic seminar at the end of the play. Here are the statements the kids came up with:

1. If you work hard enough, you can achieve your dreams.
2. Discrimination is a reality in our world.
3. Men and women have equal opportunities.
4. Success is having a lot of money.
5. It is honorable to sacrifice for the sake of someone else.
6. Sometimes we have to make a morally questionable choice to do what is right.
7. A family not having extra money is more difficult on a man than on a woman.
8. Poverty level has little impact on quality of life.
9. Family obligations are more important than individual desires.
10. People should be willing to do jobs they hate to provide for their families.

Once a statement was chosen, the students had to produce a series of photos and post them to Instagram in the form of a photo essay. Below are some more specifics on the task:

- **Identify the concept in the play:** The first two photos will portray the concept as it is expressed in at least two specific lines from the play. In your comment for both photos, you will quote the lines accurately and include the parenthetical documentation for the act, scene, and page number. The group members will be the "characters" in the photos, and the image you create must be true to both the stage directions and visual "spectacle" of Hansberry's play.

- **Connect the concept from the play to your world/life:** The next three photos will portray the concept as it is demonstrated in the world around you. In your comment for these photos, you must articulate how the concept is connected to the play *and* to contemporary society. Note you can *either* agree *or* disagree with the statement.

- **Portray Hansberry's spectacle:** On the day we take the photos, you must have assembled and planned the props you will use to convey both the details of the play and the ideas you want to communicate. *You must be prepared for the photos.*

- **Divide responsibilities:** You will work in a group of three. Each group must have at least one student with a smartphone. Each group member must be responsible for the planning/staging/arrangement/comment of at least one photo in the collection you submit. Divide tasks and be fair. *Do your bit!*

Online Resource 5.1 provides access to the standards-aligned rubric to see how the students were assessed.

The task above is a great example of Quad D learning as described in the Rigor/Relevance Framework. Following a "pedagogy first, technology second if appropriate" mantra really helped to ensure that technology either supported or enhanced learning aligned to the curriculum and standards. The task outlined above is solid, but what makes it effective in terms of learning is the assessment that went along with it. Once of the critical areas we focused on during our digital transformation was how our learners would be assessed and provided feedback. As technology changes, so must these two areas of pedagogy if the goal is to improve learning outcomes.

The Weehawken Township School District in New Jersey connected with OCEARCH (www.ocearch.org) shark trackers using digital learning tools as part of their STEM curriculum. OCEARCH is the world leader in tracking marine species such as great white and tiger sharks. The unique partnership kicked off when Weehawken students met online with OCEARCH founding chairman and expedition leader Chris Fischer via Skype. Fischer discussed OCEARCH's global shark tracker and taught students how to be stewards of the ocean. Fischer also discussed his 26 worldwide shark-tracking expeditions. He also recalled how the OCEARCH team tagged and released the now infamous Mary Lee the Shark, who frequents New Jersey waters (R. Zywicki, personal communication, 2018).

Weehawken fifth- and sixth-grade teachers were trained in how to bring the OCEARCH shark tracker into their classrooms and leverage the district's 1:1 Chromebook program. After the interactive online session with Fischer, Weehawken students continued to utilize the OCEARCH shark tracker on their Chromebooks during standards-based lessons in the fields of anatomy, statistics, cartography, and physics.

Eventually 30 Weehawken students, teachers, and parents travelled to Montauk, New York, to tour the shark research vessel *M/V OCEARCH*. Students were treated to a tour of the entire ship, including the science lab and shark-tagging platform. The *M/V OCEARCH* is an at-sea laboratory powered by Caterpillar engines, and it carries a hydraulic platform with a capacity of 75,000 pounds that can safely lift mature sharks out of the ocean for access by a multidisciplined research team (Zywicki, 2018). The crew can conduct 12 studies in 15 minutes when a shark is caught. OCEARCH has generated data for more than 50 research papers. The scientists and crew of OCEARCH were anchored off of the tip of Long Island, making final preparations for their second expedition to tag and track great white sharks who have a nursery off the New York coast, when the students joined them. In 2016, the OCEARCH team tagged 16 juvenile great white sharks off the coast of Montauk.

"Learning about math topics such as fractions and graphing percent change, is so much more relevant to students when they are using data from the Shark Tracker. It is a tremendous example of Quad D learning" (Zywicki, 2018).

A FOCUS ON CRITICAL COMPETENCIES

The examples provided focus on developing and enhancing essential competencies that learners need to succeed in today's world. To succeed in the new global economy, students need to be able to think like entrepreneurs; be resourceful, flexible, and creative; and think globally (Zhao, 2012). This is what employers are desperately looking for in new employees. Essential competencies also pave the way for our learners to be prepared to succeed in jobs that have not even been created yet. The only way schools can place learners into positions to seize opportunities present now and in the future is to authentically engage them in learning experiences that are relevant and meaningful, and that allow them to apply what has been learned through a variety of means, including the use of digital tools. Essential competencies align with all standards across the globe as well as the International Society for Technology in Education's (ISTE's) standards for students and teachers (www .iste.org/standards) and include the following:

- **Creativity:** Technology has the power to unleash the creativity of our students. It not only allows students to demonstrate conceptual mastery through learning artifacts, but also affords them the opportunity to create their own form of art as described by Seth Godin (2010). By doing so, a culture of learning is established that will make our students indispensable as they move onward into college and careers.

- **Collaboration:** Digital tools allow students to collaborate on projects and other activities regardless of time and location. This competency provides a competitive advantage to students, as they no longer have to rely on strictly meeting face to face to complete learning tasks together. More and more career paths rely on teamwork to complete projects through the use of technology.

- **Communication:** Effective communication is one of the most important skills needed to succeed in today's society. Digital tools expose students to a variety of means to communicate in the real world, thanks to ubiquitous connectivity.

- **Critical thinking and problem solving:** Digital tools provide learners with an evolved means to reason effectively through both induction and deduction; use systems thinking; solve problems in innovative ways; and make judgments and decisions through analysis, reflection, synthesis, and evaluation. They can also be used to solve complete problems and develop unique solutions that traditional means cannot.

- **Entrepreneurism:** An often overlooked or undervalued competency, entrepreneurism can be developed and enhanced through the use of digital tools to solve problems and create artifacts of learning. It instills a sense of taking risks and dealing with failure along the road to success when constructing new knowledge and applying skills to demonstrate learning. Allowing students to create apps, games, websites, business plans, virtual worlds, and videos can play a role in developing and enhancing this competency.

- **Global awareness:** Web-based tools and other forms of technology empower students to connect with peers across the globe and develop a better understanding of issues, customs, cultures, architecture, and economics. In a globally connected world, this competency has become sought after by employers whose professions know no geographical bounds.

- **Technological proficiency:** The importance of this competency goes without saying. The more reliant society becomes on technology, the more we must effectively embed it into the teaching and learning culture to adequately prepare students for the real world. Kids might know how to use tech, but they need more guidance on how it can be used to support their learning.

- **Digital media literacy:** Students today need to be given opportunities to create and critically consume digital content in order to develop essential literacies. They need to learn how to interpret an array of new messages conveyed through digital media. Research has shown that integrating media literacy into modern education can cultivate stronger relationships among educators, schools, and learners through the use of technology (Yildiz & Keengwe, 2016).

- **Digital responsibility, citizenship, and footprints:** When schools routinely integrate technology for learning, they in turn teach their students how to use it appropriately. They also empower students to develop positive digital footprints when they create content online or share it through social media. These experiences then develop skills that students can and will use to their advantage well beyond their school years.

The integration of technology for learning allows students to use real-world tools to solve real-world problems. Digital leadership places a strategic focus on developing a teaching and learning culture that not only is student centered, but also empowers learners to construct their own meanings and essential understandings of concepts by nontraditional means. It is ever so important to make sure learning outcomes are associated with the use of these tools. Figure 5.12, created by Bill Ferriter (2013), hammers home this point.

Figure 5.12 Using Technology as a Tool to Facilitate Deeper Learning

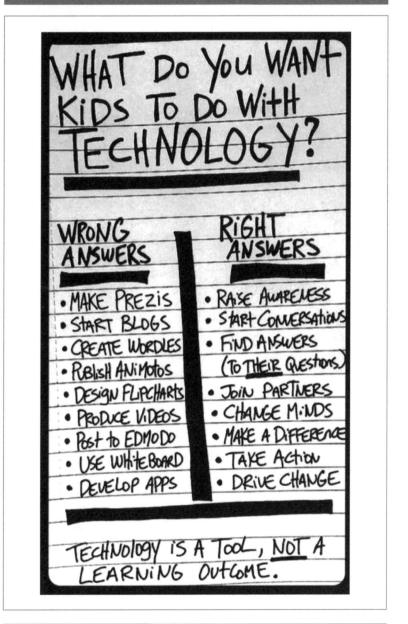

Source: Ferriter (2013). Used with permission.

This type of learning can be, and most often is, messy at first, as this shift requires leaders to give up control. In addition to giving up a certain level of control, administrators must grant teachers autonomy to take calculated risks in order to discover ways to develop innovative practices that combine digital tools with sound pedagogy. This shift leading to change and eventual transformation is a difficult process.

It is so important to look beyond just student engagement when it comes to technology. If the emphasis is on digital learning, we must not get caught up in the bells and whistles or smoke and mirrors that are commonly associated with the digital aspect alone. Engagement should always translate into deeper learning opportunities, where technology provides students the means to think critically and solve problems while demonstrating what they know and can do in a variety of ways. Technology should be implemented to increase engagement, but that engagement must lead to support, enhancement, or an improvement in student learning. It should not be used as a digital pacifier or gimmick to get students to be active participants in class. With technology there should be a focus on active learning where students are doing the work.

DIGITAL CITIZENSHIP AND RESPONSIBILITY

Just because today's students have grown up in a technology-rich world does not mean that they know how to effectively and responsibly utilize technology. It is a common misconception that today's learners can seamlessly transition from the routine use of devices for personal reasons to using them for learning, research, and enhanced productivity. We routinely hear how students use digital tools inappropriately for sexting, cyberbullying, cheating, video-recording teachers and fights with peers, and plagiarizing. Unfortunately, these behaviors have become quite common, as schools are not doing their part to educate students on digital responsibility, citizenship, and creating a positive footprint online. For the most part, students know how to use technology. However, many do not have a sense of the competencies to use it to support their learning or protect their identity.

At New Milford High School, we made it our responsibility to integrate digital responsibility across the curriculum. Our program began early in the school year with assemblies for every grade level.

During this time, we presented the root causes of cyberbullying as well as strategies and advice to prevent it. We then transitioned into online conduct in social media spaces and how that can impact college acceptances and employment. During this part of the presentation, I pointed out to students the fact that once they post something online (e.g., comments, pictures, videos, etc.), that information can be accessed, adapted, archived, and shared by anyone who has access to their accounts. Near the end of the presentation, we asked students to Google themselves and share with us any content they discovered during the search that they were not aware of. It was at this point that reality really set in.

In addition to a presentation early in the year, we consistently integrated digital tools throughout the school year to enhance learning, improve productivity, and conduct sound research. As students actively used these tools to connect, collaborate, contribute, and create, they were developing media literacy skills. Teachers also worked with students to properly cite resources pulled from the web, and to give proper credit when they used content that was governed by a Creative Commons license (creativecommons.org). As they published their own work in the form of learning artifacts, they began to create a positive digital footprint that they could be proud of. The systematic integration of technology, modeling of effective use by school staff, education programs for both students and parents, and an immersive culture (1:1 or Bring Your Own Device) all aid in educating students on digital citizenship. Common Sense Media offers a free digital literacy and citizenship curriculum that leaders can easily begin to implement in their schools. This can be accessed at www.commonsensemedia.org/educators/curriculum.

SUMMARY

The most important aspect of digital leadership is ensuring that changes to pedagogy are occurring so that technology and innovative ideas actually lead to improved student learning. An emphasis must first be placed on the instructional design in order to successfully integrate the wealth of digital tools. When students are allowed to use authentic resources to apply what they have learned to demonstrate conceptual mastery and solve real-world problems, their experiences in school become more relevant and meaningful. The Rigor/Relevance Framework can be used to develop a common language, vision, and expectations so that technology becomes more than a bells-and-whistles approach to education. It is extremely important for leaders to create a culture that not only supports the use of tools for learning, but also teaches students about digital citizenship.

GUIDING QUESTIONS

1. When looking at the first image in this chapter, where does your respective learning culture lie? What steps have to be taken to make it more reflective of the real world?

2. Is technology being integrated in a purposeful way grounded in sound pedagogy?

3. How has assessment and feedback changed?

4. Using the Rigor/Relevance Framework, identify the quad where the majority of the digital learning tasks in your classroom, school, or district reside. How might you begin to scale change to increase the level of thinking and application?

iStock.com/monkeybusinessimages

Transforming Learning Spaces and Environments

6

> We need to move away from classroom design that is "Pinterest pretty" and use research/design thinking to guide the work.
>
> —Eric Sheninger and Tom Murray

Research should be used to inform as well as influence the actions we take to implement sustainable change at scale. It is also a great way to move those who are resistant to change to embrace new ideas. In studying various pieces of literature on the effect of design,

Barrett and Zhang (2009) began with the understanding that a "bright, warm, quiet, safe, clean, comfortable, and healthy environment is an important component of successful teaching and learning" (p. 2). Their research suggested direct connections between the learning space and sensory stimuli among students. The evidence of such connections came from the medical understanding of how human sensory perception affects cognitive calculations. They identified three key design principles:

1. **Naturalness:** Hardwired into our brains, humans have the basic need for light, air, and safety. In this area, the impacts of lighting, sound, temperature, and air quality are prevalent.

2. **Individualization:** Each individual's brain is uniquely organized, and we perceive the world in different ways. Because of this, different people respond to environmental stimuli in various ways. Therefore, the opportunity for some level of choice affects success.

3. **Appropriate level of stimulation:** The learning space can offer the "silent curriculum" that affects student engagement levels. When designing the space, it's important for educators not to overstimulate and thus detract from students' ability to focus, but instead to provide enough stimuli to enhance the learning experience.

School leaders will often write off the notion of redesigning learning spaces due to financial constraints. However, research indicates that schools don't need to spend vast amounts of money to make instructional improvements (Sheninger & Murray, 2017). In fact, changes can be made that have little to no cost yet make a significant difference. Examples include altering the classroom layout, designing classroom displays differently, and choosing new wall colors (Barrett, Zhang, Moffat, & Kobbacy, 2013; Barrett, Zhang, Davies, & Barrett, 2015). These research-based factors are minimal financial commitments that can help boost student outcomes.

The effect of learning spaces on various behaviors—territoriality, crowding, situational and personal space—has been the focus of some sociological and environment behavioral research (Sheninger & Murray, 2017). The consensus of this research is that the space itself has physical, social, and psychological effects. One study measured the impact of classroom design on 12 active learning practices, including collaboration, focus, opportunity to engage, physical movement, and stimulation (Scott-Webber, Strickland, & Kapitula, 2014). The research indicated that intentionally designing spaces provides for more effective teaching and learning. In this particular study, all of the major findings supported a highly positive and statistically significant effect of active learning classrooms on student engagement.

In a research study on the link between standing desks and academic engagement, researchers observed nearly 300 children in second through fourth grade over the course of a school year (Dornhecker, Blake, Benden, Zhao, & Wendel, 2015). The study found that students who used standing desks, more formally known as stand-biased desks, exhibited higher rates of engagement in the classroom than did their counterparts seated in traditional desks. Standing desks are raised desks that have stools nearby, enabling students to choose whether to sit or stand during class. The initial studies showed 12% greater on-task engagement in classrooms with standing desks, which equated to an extra seven minutes per hour, on average, of engaged instruction time.

There's little disagreement that creating flexible spaces for physical activity positively supports student learning outcomes. However, it's important to note that it's not simply the physical layout of the room that affects achievement. One particular study investigated whether classroom displays that were irrelevant to ongoing instruction could affect students' ability to maintain focused attention during instruction and learn the lesson content. Researchers placed kindergarten children in a controlled classroom space for six introductory science lessons, and then they experimentally manipulated the visual environment in the room. The findings indicated that the students were more distracted when the walls were highly decorated and, in turn, spent more time off task. In these environments, students demonstrated smaller learning gains than in cases where the decorations were removed (Fisher, Godwin, & Seltman, 2014).

In addition to the physical and visual makeup of the learning space, a building's structural facilities profoundly influence learning. Extraneous noise, inadequate lighting, low air quality, and deficient heating in the learning space are significantly related to lower levels of student achievement (Cheryan, Ziegler, Plaut, & Meltzoff, 2014). Understanding how the learning space itself can affect the way students learn is key. Part of the issue facing school leaders today is that quite often the decision about learning space design is made by those without recent (or any) experience teaching or by those with little knowledge of classroom design. If learning is going to be transformed, then the spaces in which that learning takes place must also be transformed (Sheninger & Murray, 2017).

CLARK HALL—A CREATIVE LEARNING ENVIRONMENT

Gahanna is a middle- to upper-middle-class suburban community with more than 53,000 residents, including a little more than 7,000 students, located outside Columbus, Ohio. There are eleven schools that make up the Gahanna Jefferson Public School District: seven elementary schools, three middle schools, and one high school. Gahanna Lincoln High School (GLHS) is a sprawling building that gained a number of additions over the years to accommodate a growing student body. However, despite attempts to contain student growth within the current structure, student enrollment continued to climb. An audit by the Ohio School Facilities Commission revealed that the high school was over capacity, falling short 71,000 square feet by their code, and unable to accommodate all of their students. The challenge of finding more space for an overcrowded building presented a unique opportunity to do something different than building a second high school. This is where the Clark Hall story begins.

Shift 1—A Shared Vision for Success

Former Gahanna Jefferson Public Schools superintendents Gregg Morris and Mark White had the vision, the financial understanding, and the courage to launch the Clark Hall project as a way to reduce crowding in the current high school building. Instead of asking the community for a second high school—something that the community of Gahanna was adamantly against——they came up with the concept of a creative learning environment with the input from a number of stakeholders. They quickly realized that this could be the opportunity to do something creative to provide more space for students while meeting the needs of today's learner. In keeping with the vision and strategic plan of the district, they decided to build Clark Hall. Their district design team included several central office administrators as well as Dwight Carter, an award-winning former school principal who fully understood and operated by the Pillars of

Digital Leadership. He was the principal of GLHS when Clark Hall was devised and built.

Shift 2—Infrastructure Upgrades and Internet Access

To prepare for teaching and learning in Clark Hall, the transformative new building that was to be added to GLHS, the team first had to address problems with the network in the original GLHS building. The type or number of network-connected devices available to students and staff is insignificant if the school's wireless network is unable to handle the digital, technological, and creative needs of today's students and teachers. While GLHS was a wireless campus, users of its network experienced significant problems on a nearly daily basis. This problem was compounded when the decision was made to open the campus to allow students to use their own mobile devices, creating a BYOD environment.

As the year progressed, there were many problems with the network. It was not only slow; it also blocked access to many of the sites students wanted to access. Laptops were especially slow. It got to the point where teachers preferred planning lessons without technology to dealing with the network issues they were running into daily. The complaint was constant: "It takes the students forever to log on!" Dwight and other administrators went around placing blame on the technology team, the "old computers," and whatever else they could think of. It wasn't until much later, however, that Dwight realized it was his own fault! He didn't talk with the technology coordinator about opening up his campus to mobile devices prior to doing so, and the increased use had quickly clogged the network.

While this was a major problem, it forced the team to focus on the fact that before any more devices could be added—school purchased or BYOD—they had to upgrade the existing wireless network. Morris and White, with the assistance of technology coordinator Joe Schiska, negotiated a deal with Cisco Systems to drive down the pricing to upgrade their wireless network across the district. This was the most important component of the technology integration plan. In the words of Joe Schiska, "We went from a two-lane highway to a two-thousand-lane highway" in terms of the speed and accessibility of the network. With this hurdle out of the way, the Gahanna team began to prepare teachers for what it would mean to teach and learn in such a unique environment.

Shift 3—A Choice to Teach and Learn a Different Way

Teachers assigned to Clark Hall in Year 1 were placed there of their own accord. All teachers were told that, while the focus would be on student learning, a large expectation for the purposeful use of technology aligned to sound pedagogy was placed on this group. Thus, in preparation for moving into Clark Hall, about 40 teachers and administrators participated in a digital learning boot camp. It was during this professional learning experience that Dwight learned how other educators were using digital tools to engage and empower learners.

As additional preparation for teaching in such a different environment, the Gahanna team did a book study with teachers and administrators using Ian Jukes's book, *Teaching the Digital Generation: No More Cookie-Cutter High Schools* (Kelly, McCain, & Jukes, 2009).This stretched their thinking and provided a framework for them to move forward. Through this study, they focused on

- **Time management:** How are we going to help students manage their time to optimize learning?

- **Collaboration:** How are we going to provide opportunities for students to collaborate with one another to solve problems and create content?

- **Technology integration:** How are we going to get the technology into the hands of the students, so they own their learning?

- **Pedagogical change:** How can we transition from a teacher-centered classroom to a student-centered learning environment?

The culmination of this book study was a visit from Ian Jukes, who shared his knowledge of digital learning with the staff. Much of his focus centered on technology not just for the sake of having technology, but technology in the hands of students on a daily basis to be used as a tool for learning. With this concept in mind, Dwight then sent four of the teachers who wanted to teach at Clark Hall to a project-based learning (PBL) conference, with the understanding that it would be their responsibility to share their learning with others upon their return. PBL was chosen because the principles of PBL complemented the team's established objectives, including a focus on the importance of technology integration and student voice/choice (D. Carter, personal communication, 2018).

Shift 4—A New Normal

After two years of planning, Clark Hall opened. Clark Hall is a 51,000-square-foot, three-story work of art. It doesn't resemble a typical American high school at all, but rather an innovative office building. The team's objectives for Clark Hall were to

- Provide an open, bright, and flexible space for learning.
- Provide student choice.
- Integrate technology to engage students.
- Be flexible with time to focus on learning.
- Provide students with opportunities to express their natural creativity.
- Utilize teachers as facilitators.
- Promote interdisciplinary and interconnected projects.
- Make learning fun!

With flexibility built into the daily schedule, teachers have more time to interact with students on an individual basis, students feel more relaxed and more compelled to engage in the learning process, and collaboration among students just seems natural. The entire building has become a learning environment, not just the classrooms. There is soft seating throughout the building: in the two common areas, in seven of the fourteen classrooms, in several small conference rooms, and in the hallways. At any time during the day, visitors will see pockets of students working individually or collaboratively on their laptops completing assignments, while the teachers are in the classrooms working with individual students. There are also soft-seating nooks in the hallways that resemble a modern university student commons: Students are lounging on the chairs within the classroom and hallway spaces diligently using their laptops to write blogs, research, complete projects, or complete assignments posted on the teacher portals.

Dwight and the Gahanna team got away from the traditional beige walls and standard furniture, because they wanted a space that was comfortable and less formal or institutional, and that evoked creativity. They returned to the days of elementary school, where there are bright colors like lime green, bright orange, red, gold, and royal blue. They chose splashes of color on the walls and bright, colorful modular furniture. Half of the classrooms don't have traditional desks or chairs, but instead have couches, soft armless chairs, ottomans on wheels, café-style tables, and exercise balls for students to sit on. There are also brightly colored area rugs in classrooms to soften up the spaces a bit. When students are asked what they think about Clark Hall, their responses are uniformly positive:

- "It's so comfortable over here. I can think and do my work."
- "It feels like I'm in college because I have freedom, but there is also a lot of responsibility to get my work done."
- "I love the bright, open spaces! It's not like main campus."
- "I love all the technology! The laptops work and the wireless is so fast. It makes it a lot easier to use it to complete projects."

Each classroom and small conference room has a short throw LCD projector connected to a desktop computer, so teachers' lessons can be interactive, and students can use these projectors as well. Each room is also wired for surround sound with a microphone to help project the teacher's voice. Dwight found that lessons become more interactive, engaging, and visual with the effective integration of technology. The modular furniture adds to the flexibility.

Clark Hall inspired change on GLHS's main campus as well. One of the main hubs of most schools and universities is the library. They wanted their library to have the same feel as Clark Hall, so their librarian, Ann Gleek, dreamed big and made some significant changes: removing some of the book shelves, painting the walls, and changing some of the furniture to reflect the informal style of Clark Hall. These changes made for a more inviting environment for students and were a huge hit.

Shift 5—Real-World Space to Reflect Real-World Learning

Clark Hall houses 14 classrooms, each with its own conference room attached for small-group work or breakout sessions. In addition, the building contains high-powered wireless internet connections, natural light, a laptop for every student, and collaborative spaces in the hallways, so students are able to make the best use of the space for learning. Some spaces on the first floor are leased out, and the revenue from these leases helps to pay off the mortgage for this property. It was accomplished through the vision of former superintendents Morris and White, along with District Treasurer Julio Valledaras, who worked with legislators to change the laws to allow the district to lease out space on the first floor of Clark Hall. Additionally, a strategic partnership has been formed with a land developer who built 9,000- and 14,000-square-foot buildings at the front of the property to lease to retailers. The retail space is at 100% capacity, with businesses like Panera, Chipotle, AT&T, and the Rusty Bucket serving students and the community at large. The Clark Hall building is a thriving economic model that benefits the community, the students, and the schools. All of this was accomplished without raising property taxes.

Shift 6—Strategic Partnerships

Dwight and the Gahanna team also formed a strategic partnership with the YMCA. The YMCA provided more than $55,000 of exercise equipment to outfit one room in Clark Hall and now uses it as an annex to provide evening classes for its members. Some of the high school's physical education classes use it during the day, and it has led to the creation of a fitness club that meets twice a week after school.

The school had already had a partnership with the Eastland-Fairfield Career Center, and GLHS was the satellite location for the Center's Architecture Technology program. This program moved to the first floor of Clark Hall with two new programs: Teacher Professions, which prepares students for careers in education, and the Bioscience Technology program, which prepares students for one of the fastest-growing fields in the world. These programs are cutting edge and provide relevant opportunities for students. The students in the architecture program actually helped to design their room and were able to walk through the site as it was being constructed.

Clark Hall has been one of the most exciting additions to the Gahanna District. It has given teachers the freedom to explore and take calculated risks in the classroom, and has provided a unique learning experience for students. It is helping them not only to reform what they do, but transform how they do it. Besides curriculum and assessment, educational reform must include reforming or transforming the physical learning environment. According to Daniel Pink (2011), design is one of the elements of the right brain that we must tap into. We have to look differently at the space we have now and spruce things up . . . a lot . . . for the sake of learning.

DESIGNING SCHOOLS TO ENGAGE AND DRIVE LEARNING

The story of Clark Hall represents a research-based approach and a much-needed shift in school design. It offers a glimpse of how learning environments can be restructured to better meet the diverse and unique needs of today's learners. Digital leadership looks at societal trends as inspirational elements and potential catalysts for change in the structure of the schools themselves as well as the designs of programs. The environment of Google presents many of these elements for leaders to reflect upon when looking to move toward change in this area.

On a trip to Google's offices in New York City, I noticed many features that made the office stand out, such as the use of scooters as a means of transportation. There were even racks throughout each floor where Google employees could park their scooters. One could not miss the Lego wall in a lounge area. The wall was lined with bins of different sized and colored Legos. It was clear that employees were encouraged to unleash their creativity whenever it suited them. Specialized areas and rooms were located throughout the building. These included gaming, nap, and massage rooms, which catered to the diverse interests of Google employees. A great deal of emphasis was placed on food, as there were minikitchens galore. It was obvious that appetite contentment was a priority at Google. Some of these kitchens were decorated in particular themes. One of the most elaborate minikitchens was decorated as a jungle, complete with hammock-like chairs, small waterfalls, decorated trees, and live frogs. Equally impressive were the massive espresso, cappuccino, and coffee machines in each kitchen, as well as the overwhelming selection of foods and beverages and a bistro dining area that provided employees with an unparalleled lunch. Lunch was truly a dining experience, and there was an immense selection of choices.

Google-themed artwork was visible throughout the building. Company pride was apparent everywhere. Clever reminders not to do certain things were located throughout the space. One sign posted throughout the building was a picture of an alligator with its tail propping the door open with this reminder: "Beware the Tailgator!" Obviously, Google doesn't want some doors propped open for security reasons. Office spaces contained entire walls that were transformed into whiteboards, perfect for brainstorming and outlining creative ideas. Many of these offices even had a large table that could seat 12 to 16 people. Open spaces with comfortable furniture that invited collaboration (leather couches, plush lounge chairs, etc.), not to mention more coffee stations, were also readily apparent.

The atmosphere described above really inspires and motivates employees to perform at a consistently high level. Who wouldn't want to work in this type of environment? Now, imagine what would happen if schools adopted a similar thought process and designed learning and common spaces using the principles described above. Our learners deserve spaces like the ones highlighted above. Digital leadership anticipates the potential this could have on increasing achievement and motivation, and developing a passion for the learning process. Such a transition—along with the integration of the other Six Pillars of Digital Leadership—creates schools that students can't wait to get to and are reluctant to leave at the end of the day. School redesign influences the education reform conversation to include addressing students' needs. Digital leadership makes this a reality.

MAKERSPACES

Depending on who you talk to or what you read, you will see varying definitions of what educational makerspaces are. While at first that can seem confusing and overwhelming, the good news is that probably none of them is incorrect. Makerspaces are deeply personal to those involved, both the teachers and the students. Laura Fleming defines an educational makerspace as *a unique learning environment that allows for tinkering, play and open-ended exploration for ALL* (Fleming, 2015). This definition has guided all of the work that she has done in the library makerspace at New Milford High School, and also the work that she facilitates in schools around the world.

When we created our makerspace at New Milford High School many years ago, we never anticipated the positive impact it would have on our learners. In a time where wood shop, metal shop, and agriculture were cut for the mere reason that the content was deemed nonessential or could not be tested, something had to change. This was the reality for many schools across the globe. In our particular case, not having trade-based courses was devastating, as one-third of our population was classified as having special needs. For all intents and purposes, most of these students could care less about the curriculum, standards, or standardized tests. The creation and evolution of our makerspace solved this problem.

The premise was simple: Allow students to utilize guided inquiry in an informal learning environment that was facilitated by the use of real-world tools to do real-world work. We wanted our learners to identify a problem and then develop a workable solution through tinkering, inventing, prototyping, and creating. Students were not only able to actively explore their passions, but also learn from failure as well as trial and error. Our students thrived in an environment where the word *fail* really stood for first attempt in learning. There was no clearer evidence of this than when students were using old computer parts to design and create an entirely new operating system from scratch.

The makerspace was less about the latest technological gadget and more about the process of tinkering, inventing, creating, and making to learn. This is probably the single most important lesson I learned from Laura Fleming, the teacher-librarian extraordinaire who was the original architect of our makerspace. I say original architect, as after the space was initially established, she empowered the students to chart its course going forward. Success rested in her ability to focus on her role as a facilitator or coach as opposed to someone who knew how to use all the stuff. She was the quintessential guide to possibilities who unlocked the learning potential of our students.

We meticulously planned with our students a vision for how the space would foster powerful learning experiences grounded in rigor, relevance, and relationships using tools such as 3D printers, Arduinos, snap circuits, LEGOS, and Raspberry Pi. Maker activities naturally align themselves to Quad D work as outlined by the Rigor/Relevance Framework presented in Chapter 5. It is through these hands-on activities that students employ a range of higher-order thinking skills to solve real-world, unpredictable problems that have more than one solution. Through this engaging process, students also readily make connections to a range of other disciplines.

Online Resource 6.1 provides access to a collection of makerspace resources curated using Pinterest.

Makerspaces in education have grown at an exponential rate; however, we certainly do not want to see them become just another passing trend. They are not just rooms with high tech equipment in them; they are at their core an educational philosophy and approach that is rooted in firm research and a wealth of evidence-based best practices. Sylvia Martinez and Gary Stager (2013) credit Seymour Papert as "the father of the maker movement" (p. 17). The maker movement in education is built upon the foundation of constructionism, Papert's philosophy of hands-on learning through building things. Makerspaces are a mindset, a culture. It's about the pedagogy. A *great* makerspace has seven key attributes: It is personalized, deep (allowing deeper learning), empowering, equitable, differentiated, intentional, and inspiring (Fleming, 2017). Have all of that, and you can call your space a makerspace, maybe even a *great* makerspace.

The sustainability of makerspaces lies in the proper planning of these unique learning environments. No two school makerspaces should be exactly alike, because no two school communities are exactly alike. Properly planning your makerspace will help to ensure that your makerspace is one that is not just vibrant and meaningful for now, but also will help to ensure that your makerspace is sustainable into the future. Makerspace planning should be rooted in data that you have collected about your students, your school community, and the wider world that we are living in. Figure 6.1 outlines the key areas to focus on when planning a makerspace.

Makerspaces are always a work in progress. The moment you say you are done, because you have created a makerspace, is the same moment you are doomed. It is critical to take time to reflect on your makerspace: What worked? What didn't? How can I refine my space so that it continues to grow and evolve with my students, the school community, and the wider world that we're living in? The real power of makerspaces is that they democratize learning. They make materials, supplies, resources, and concepts available and accessible to *all,* giving learners the opportunity to become creators and innovators and to turn their knowledge into action. Now, with the tools available at a makerspace, anyone can change the world (Hatch, 2014).

Figure 6.1 Makerspace Planning

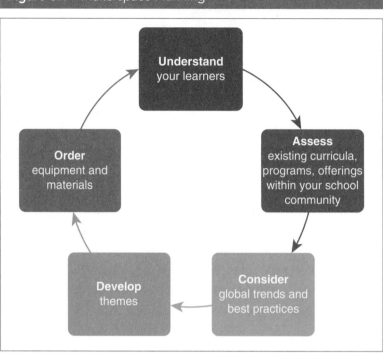

DEVICES FOR ALL (1:1)

When looking around the Burlington School District in Burlington, Massachusetts, it is hard for Patrick Larkin, the assistant superintendent for learning, to believe how quickly they made the transition from a district that banned devices in classrooms to one that went out and purchased over 2,000 mobile devices so that staff and students could have access to more educational resources throughout the school day. They used to deny the changes that were happening outside of their school doors, because they could not deal with what they thought might happen if they were to allow students to have the internet at their fingertips while sitting in classrooms. However, when they made an honest assessment of their mission statement—which charged them with preparing all students for the "real world"—and coupled that with the amazing things happening with technology in the world outside of their doors, Patrick and other administrators knew it was time to take off their blinders and make some changes.

In reality, the thing that was holding them back was their own past experiences. Yes, the adults in the school were handicapped by their own pasts. As students, they experienced little to no technology in the classroom and a great degree of micromanagement for each move they made. In turn, they were prepared to pass on this same degree of rigidity to their own students. There was also the lack of trust shown by administrators who would not allow staff to utilize mobile devices, even when concrete educational tasks were tied to the lessons where students were empowered to use their devices in support of learning goals.

However, somewhere along the line, something changed. The starting point may have been when the administrators looked at some data that told them that, despite the fact that they did not allow mobile devices in school, more than 95% of their students were sending and receiving multiple text messages each day. Or maybe it was when they began to look more closely at the district's mission statement, which contained phrases like *lifelong learning* and *responsible citizenship,* and came to the realization that they could not do either to the fullest extent if they had the most modern learning resources on lockdown.

After a great deal of discussion among staff members, Burlington High School staff, under the leadership of then-principal Patrick Larkin, decided to take a small step outside of their comfort zone and modify the existing policy regarding the use of digital devices in school. Many years before, the district had made a change to its policy and allowed devices to be utilized in the classroom "at the teacher's discretion." Ultimately, it was agreed that staff and students needed more access to resources in their classrooms, not less.

Amazingly enough, a year later, the leaders were so comfortable with the decision that they formed a planning team to devise a way to get a device in the hands of every student throughout the school day and become a 1:1 school. Teachers realized that putting devices in the hands of all students opened up more possibilities than problems, and they were on their way. The school administrative team encouraged staff members to try new things and share successes, and not to worry about failures. At the same time, a new classroom walk-through protocol called "learning walks" initiated conversations about learning and increased discussions about effective strategies and resources that could help create higher levels of student engagement.

Speaking of student engagement in learning, one of the most important aspects of the school's 1:1 planning team was the inclusion of students as equal members at the table helping to chart the path. After a bit of discussion with students about this initiative, it became clear that they were not just typical members of the planning team. Their thoughtful insights and suggestions made it clear early on that they were equal partners in this endeavor who would need to have significant roles in this change if it was to be successful. This gave rise to the idea of the BHS Student Help Desk, a semester course for students who were interested in technology and/or problem solving.

While Patrick and other Burlington leaders knew that the Student Help Desk was a good idea, they never imagined how successful it would become. Administratively, the idea was conceived in part because the district IT staff, composed of three individuals, could never handle all of the issues that the addition of a thousand new iPad devices would bring. They wanted to ensure that when there were questions or problems with the devices, staff and students could get a quick response. Not only did students at the Student Help Desk handle each question that came their way, they also started a blog on which they posted information on the iOS updates and video tutorials for various digital resources and apps. On top of the day-to-day support of Burlington staff and students, the students have spoken to hundreds of visiting educators who have come through the school looking to implement similar programs. They also have spoken at local and regional conferences about their experiences, providing honest answers and advice to educators from all over New England, just as they did for us at the start of the journey.

While the basic goal at the start of this journey was to bring more resources into the school by providing teachers and students access to digital tools, something much more significant transpired. There was a clear movement away from teacher-led learning environments and a transition to learner-led environments, where teachers and students were learning together. Because the voices of students were included in this undertaking, worlds have collided, and a very interesting phenomenon has taken place: technology-experienced students joining forces with pedagogically experienced educators to bring about some amazing changes.

The truth of the matter is that it has nothing to do with devices and has everything to do with rethinking what our students need to prepare them for the rapidly changing real world beyond the school walls. A word of caution though. You can't just place a device in the hands of students and think that learning miracles will happen. The key to success relies on ensuring the pedagogical change detailed in Chapter 5 takes place as well as ongoing, job-embedded professional learning. Devices need to support or enhance learning, not drive instruction. It is always important to remember that we don't build schools, curriculum, or assessment around technology. Every decision and investment digital leaders make is all about improving the learning experience and outcomes for kids.

IMPROVING ACCESS WITH BYOD

As we continue to move even further into the century, technology becomes more embedded in all aspects of society. I see this firsthand with my son. When he was in second grade, the gift he wanted most at Christmas was an iPod Touch, which Santa was kind enough to bring him. Then there was his younger sister, who regularly asked to use my iPad so she could either care for her virtual horse or dress Barbies in creative ways. After I downloaded all of the apps my children requested on these devices, the majority of their time was spent engaged in games that required thought, creativity, and sometimes collaboration. My point here is that many children across the world have access to and are using technology outside of school in a variety of ways. Not only do many have access, but also older children possess their own devices—that is, smartphones, laptops, tablets, e-readers, et cetera.

As society continues to move forward in terms of innovation, technology, and global connectivity, schools have been stymied by relentless cuts to education funding. This has resulted in reductions in staffing, larger class sizes, deferred repair of aging buildings, and the inability to keep up with purchasing and replacing educational technology. It is essential that we rectify all of the above-mentioned impacts of budget cuts and place an emphasis on what we can do to provide our learners with experiences that will adequately prepare them to survive and thrive in a digital world. If finances are an obstacle, then the time is now for districts and schools to seriously consider developing a Bring Your Own Device (BYOD) culture to further engage students in the teaching and learning process in a cost-effective fashion.

The world of education is often defined by the "haves" and "have-nots." It is this separation that ultimately drives decisions when it comes to educational technology. Why should students in less affluent districts not be afforded the same opportunity as those in districts with large budgets to utilize tools to create, collaborate, connect, communicate, and develop essential media literacies?

BYOD makes sense, as we can now leverage a variety of devices that many of our students already possess. It is how we utilize these student-owned devices in schools that is the key to a successful implementation.

There are many well-respected educators that I also greatly admire who feel that BYOD has no place in schools. Their main reasons for this are equity in terms of students who do not have devices and the belief that it is each district's or school's responsibility to provide all technology to be used by students in schools. I wholeheartedly agree with their positions, but those of us who have been or are currently in the trenches must play with the cards that we have been dealt. As educators, it is our duty to do everything in our power to provide our students with the best learning opportunities possible. In many cases, allowing students to bring their own devices to school assists in meeting this lofty goal.

We launched our BYOD program at New Milford High School in September of 2010. There were many lessons learned from this journey, the most important being that the students greatly appreciated this shift. Policies were developed for students to bring in their own computing devices; a ban on cell phone use during noninstructional times was lifted; and educational programs were put in place to teach our students about digital citizenship, responsibility, identity, and footprints. We did not let excuses like equity issues stop us from moving forward with a decision that turned out to have real value to our students and teachers. Key components of a BYOD (or 1:1 for that matter) learning culture include the following (Sheninger, 2015b).

1. **Infrastructure:** Herein lies a common pitfall for many schools/districts that implement BYOD. Before going any further, it is pivotal to ensure that the plumbing can withstand the stress of mobile technologies accessing the Wi-Fi network. You need to expect that there will be more devices connected to the network on a given day than there are students. Not only will some students bring in more than one device, but you have to account for staff member access as well. There is nothing worse than developing and implementing a lesson that integrates mobile learning devices than to have the internet slowed down to a snail's pace. Or even worse, the network crashes or begins to negatively impact teachers and students using school-owned mobile technology. Charging stations or bars should also be located throughout the building.

2. **Shared vision:** This is extremely important, as you will have staff and community members on both sides of the fence. Before going full steam ahead with BYOD, gather key stakeholders, especially students, to establish a shared vision that includes rationale, goals, expected outcomes, expectations, and means to assess the effectiveness of the initiative. Central to a BYOD vision is a consistent focus on student learning.

3. **Strategic plan:** The shared vision that is created by all stakeholder representatives, including students, will drive a plan for action. As is the case in any successful implementation, sound planning and sustainability is imperative. During the planning process, you must consider community outreach, budget allocations to improve existing infrastructure, policies, professional development (teacher and administrator), student trainings, and evaluation procedures (e.g., how do you know that this is impacting student learning?). Sound pedagogy must be at the heart of any BYOD initiative.

4. **Policy development:** Part of the strategic planning process will be to align current policies and develop procedures relating to BYOD. It is important that the resulting artifacts are not too overbearing and afford students the opportunity to be trusted and empowered to take ownership of their learning. A sound policy addresses Wi-Fi login procedures, a focus on learning, acceptable use, equity, and absolving the school of any liability for lost, stolen, or broken devices.

5. **Professional learning:** As I work with schools and districts across the country on BYOD and 1:1 implementations, I can honestly say that this is one area where mistakes are made. Teachers need proper support in terms of developing pedagogically sound lessons, designing assessments aligned to higher standards, exposure to web-based tools and apps that cater to BYOD, ensuring equity, and developing classroom procedures. Prior to rolling out BYOD, teachers should know full well what the outcomes are as articulated in the shared vision and have a set of tools and instructional strategies that can be used on the first day. Another key to success is ongoing professional learning to provide teachers with additional strategies and ideas so that devices are used to support pedagogy. In addition to teachers needing learning support, leaders also need professional learning in regard to the observation and evaluation process. They are the ones after all that have to make sure that devices are being used properly to support learning while addressing higher standards. Before implementing BYOD as a school or district, make sure professional learning has been provided to teachers and administrators.

6.   **Student programs:** Students themselves need a form of professional development on the expectations and outcomes of device use. Successful initiatives contain an embedded component that includes educational programs for students before a BYOD initiative is rolled out and programs that are continued each year. These programs, which can be held once in the beginning of the school year, focus on how devices should be used to support learning as well as digital responsibility. As principal, I held annual assemblies in the early fall for each grade level that focused on cyberbullying, creating positive digital footprints, and the tenets of our BYOD program. I also visited the middle school and worked with every student starting in Grade 6 on all of the above. The end result was that our students embraced the shared vision, and device use was more focused on learning than off-task behavior. We were also in a better position to give up control and trust our kids.

7.   **Budget allocations:** Although BYOD initiatives are a cost-effective means to increase student access to technology, school money has to be put aside to fund specific apps and devices for students who might not have them. We put money aside to purchase Chromebooks that were signed out like library books to our disadvantaged students. We also used these funds to increase the availability of laptops in school in the form of mobile carts, which teachers could sign out.

Instead of bashing BYOD and coming up with ideas on how and why it won't work or is unfair, we would best be served by brainstorming ways in which it can become an educational component of our schools. The excuses to write off BYOD only serve to undermine the students we are tasked with educating. BYOD will be unique to each district and should be carefully constructed based on socioeconomics and community dynamics. To begin the process, students should be asked for their input. Digital leadership looks beyond the excuses for why it can't work and looks toward possible solutions to better engage learners now and in the future. It's time to focus on the "what ifs" instead of the "yeah buts."

BLENDED LEARNING VERSUS BLENDED INSTRUCTION

As I continue to think through the use of technology in schools, I am always drawn back to this guiding question: How can students learn by using technology in ways that they couldn't without it?

To improve the learning experience for kids, we must continue to develop ways that technology becomes a ubiquitous component of our work, but also leads to a demonstrated improvement in practice. Here is where the tool supports or enhances the pedagogical technique to aid in conceptual mastery, construct new knowledge, or demonstrate learning through the creation of a learning artifact. One such method is blended learning.

Blended learning is one of many strategies that can add a level of personalization while also making the experience a bit more personal with the right conditions. However, there seems to be a bit of confusion as to what blended learning is or the conditions that have to be established for it to improve feedback, differentiate instruction, and empower learners. Based on what I have seen during my work in schools and through sharing on social media, the majority of what educators are calling blended learning is blended instruction. Here is the difference:

> Blended instruction is what the teacher does with technology. Blended learning is where students use tech to have control over path, place, and pace.

For me at least, the distinction above brings a great deal of context to the discussion of how technology can improve learning for our students. Now I am not saying it is bad practice when educators integrate tools into their instruction. As long as the level of questioning focuses on higher levels of thinking, students can use technology to show that they understand, and that's a good thing. However, this is not blended learning. If students genuinely own their learning, then they have to have some level of control over path, place, and pace while receiving more personalized feedback regarding standard and concept attainment. Herein lies the key to the practical use of flex learning spaces in education. The dynamic combination of pedagogically sound blended learning and choice in either seating or moving around in flex spaces results in an environment where all kids can flourish and want to learn. Figure 6.2 outlines the key elements of rigorous blended learning environments.

I have been very impressed by how Kirk Elementary and Wells Elementary in the Cypress-Fairbanks Independent School District have been implementing blended learning on their campuses. In each case, the station rotation model has been the preferred strategy. I have observed students rotating through various stations that

Figure 6.2   Elements of Rigorous Blended Learning Environments

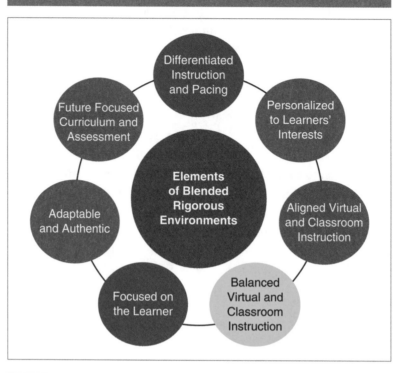

Source: Copyright © 2018 by International Center for Leadership in Education, a division of Houghton Mifflin Harcourt. Used with permission.

include teacher-directed instruction, independent reading or practice using technology, formative assessment, flipped activity, and collaborative problem solving. In some cases, students have individual learning playlists to work through. Students rotate through the various stations, and the rotations are typically triggered by music. The use of mobile technology and flexible seating provides students choices as to where they will learn. In the example above, technology is blended into their learning experience so that students have some control over path, pace, and place.

Kanchan Chellani, a New Milford High School mathematics educator, has managed to successfully create this desired positive and energetic blended learning environment using the flipped approach. She created and assigned short videos as homework so that students were able to develop a foundational or working knowledge of the relevant mathematical concept that would foster discussion in class and promote a collaborative working environment. Additionally, this approach provided ample class time to dive deeper into key mathematical topics and for students to engage in projects, case studies, cooperative activities, virtual manipulatives, and content review games to reinforce the learning. Although enabling the flipped approach to instruction transformed the way material was taught and comprehended by students, it had been difficult for her to find resources that combined curriculum delivery, real-world examples, and assessments in a cohesive manner. As a result, she started to create her own online learning modules, using the software Adobe Captivate.

Adobe Captivate is a type of digital content creation software that fosters interactive e-learning content. She made use of the tool by creating learning modules that taught the basic mathematical concepts as well as provided practice problems, real-world examples, and assessments that allowed for better comprehension of the material in an organized fashion. In these learning modules, instruction was provided using digital content, simulations, videos, screen captures, voiceovers, et cetera, to meet the visual, auditory, and tactile needs of the diverse student population. Once the instruction had been provided, guided practice problems and real-world examples were then discussed to reinforce the learning of the mathematical concept and to illustrate its significance. A variety of prompts and formal assessments were also embedded within the project in order to ensure that learning took place.

All in all, the significant shift that we should focus on is what the student is purposefully doing with the technology. Student agency is at the heart of effective blended learning. It is also important that it supports high-level learning, provides better means of assessment, and improves feedback. Blended instruction is a start, but blended learning is where our practice should move.

INDIVIDUALIZED AND PERSONALIZED LEARNING

Possibly one of the most important shifts needed in schools is to provide individualized and personalized learning experiences to students. Learning has fundamentally changed with the evolution of the internet and other technologies that allow for ubiquitous access to information and knowledge. Adaptive learning tools can be a part of this, but as Chapter 5 outlined, there has to be an emphasis on making learning personal for kids. Digital leadership focuses on transforming learning environments through online course offerings (synchronous and asynchronous), independent studies, and use of OpenCourseWare (OCW) to provide students with continuous options to learn anytime, anywhere, and about anything. Infusing online learning opportunities should be a given in a digital world. Online Resource 6.2 provides links to numerous OCW sites that can be used to support all learners.

One of the most cost-effective means to create a more personalized and individualized learning experience for older students is through the use of OCW and massive open online courses (MOOCs). Pioneers in open learning like Wikipedia have harnessed the collective intellect of the planet "to collect and develop educational content under a free license or in the public domain, and to disseminate it effectively and globally" (https://wikimediafoundation.org/about/mission/). Prestigious centers of learning are also making good use of the internet's power to share knowledge in the form of OCW. OCW can best be defined as high-quality digital publications created by leading universities that are organized as courses of study, offered free of charge, and delivered via the internet. OCW courses are available under open licenses, such as Creative Commons. These courses allow for personalization of studies as students explore topics of their choosing.

The independent open courseware study (IOCS) program developed by Tenafly Middle School teacher Juliana Meehan and me and pioneered at New Milford High School represented a bold, authentic learning experience for secondary students that allows them to fully utilize open courseware (OCW) to pursue learning that focuses on their passions, interests, and career aspirations. IOCS is aligned to the Common Core, ISTE Standards for Students, and state technology curriculum standards, as well as the Partnership for 21st Century Skills Framework for 21st Century Skills. IOCS students were able to choose from an array of OCW offerings from such schools as the Massachusetts Institute of Technology (MIT), Harvard, Yale, the University of California at Berkeley, Stanford, and many others, and apply their learning to earn high school credit.

The IOCS experience can be accessed through the IOCS website (Online Resource 6.3), which contains links to OCW offerings that were constantly updated for our students. The site also provides an overview of the program, the IOCS rubric, frequently asked questions (FAQs), and a Google form through which students register for courses. Other documents, like periodic check-in forms, are also available on the site.

Students chose an OCW course (or part of a course) from an approved, accredited university through the IOCS website. Using the IOCS Google registration form embedded in the site, they registered for their course by identifying the institution, course number, and title. Sometimes, if the course was extensive or very advanced, students could decide to complete only certain parts of that course, in which case they identified what part(s) they agreed to complete at the outset.

Once they had chosen their OCW course, students engaged in the activities provided by that particular unit of study. Learning activities vary widely from institution to institution and within disciplines, but coursework usually consists of one or more of the following: course lectures, which can be video presentations or texts; learning activities like experiments or open-ended questions; demonstrations; and interim and final assessments. Students apply themselves to these activities over the course of a high school marking period.

Students received individualized mentoring as they progressed through their OCW course. Highly motivated students who have found their "perfect" course may need little guidance, while others may benefit from varying degrees of structuring and advice along the way. IOCS mentors checked in with students on a regular basis to gauge the level of mentoring intervention needed. In all cases, the advanced content and high expectations inherent in the coursework provided students with a glimpse into the demands that college poses and helped them prepare for their higher education.

Students combined their creativity with their newfound knowledge to synthesize a unique product that demonstrated and applied the new knowledge and skills they gained from the OCW course. The aim was for students to go beyond a static PowerPoint presentation laden with mere text and pictures and produce an actual product—whether it was demonstration of a new skill, creation of a physical model, design and conduct of an experiment, formulation of a theory, or some other creative product—to show what they had learned (see the IOCS Rubric in Online Resource 6.3).

The culminating IOCS experience was a five- to seven-minute student exposition of learning in front of faculty and IOCS peers. The work was assessed according to the IOCS rubric, which is aligned to national and state standards. By developing a framework for the advanced learning opportunities that OCW promises, schools can enable motivated students to progress beyond the scope of their traditional secondary curriculum.

As more universities begin to make their courses available in the form of OCW and MOOCs, opportunities to individualize and personalize learning will be endless. Bold leaders will view these resources as key components to district-approved independent study programs for credit. One fantastic resource for digital leaders that contains all of the necessary support structures is OCW Scholar from MIT (Online Resource 6.4). These courses are actually designed for independent learners who have limited additional resources available to them. The courses are substantially more complete than typical OCW courses and include custom-created content as well as materials repurposed from actual MIT classrooms. The materials are arranged in logical sequences and include multimedia such as video and simulations.

What makes OCW Scholar perfect for an independent study is that everything a student, teacher, and leader needs is available here. Virtually every MIT course on this site has video lectures, assignments and solutions, recitation videos, and exams and solutions. There is also a detailed description of the course, an outline of the format, and a syllabus. For the student, there is structure, a defined path, and opportunities to practice and apply what has been learned. For the teacher or independent study advisor, there are course descriptions and assessments to justify credit. For the leader, there is a legitimate means to provide a world-class learning opportunity to any student who wishes to pursue it.

Dr. Robert Zywicki, the superintendent of the Mount Olive School District in New Jersey, has always been ahead of the curve when it comes to providing personalized pathways to learners. Third-through sixth-graders at Theodore Roosevelt School in Weehawken School District, his former school district, were introduced to a cutting-edge and research-based method for learning math— playing video games. Called ST Math, the approach was meant to get students solving problems by thinking them through, instead of following steps in a rote fashion. "ST" stands for "spatial/temporal." Math questions were posed in graphics on a screen instead of in words on a board or worksheet. The key to the ST program was that it encouraged children to engage in strong mathematical thinking, whether they have developed those language skills or not. According to Dr. Zywicki, "The students have to think about the problem visually and spatially, and then try something they think is appropriate" (R. Zywicki, personal communication, 2018).

Students got four chances to solve each problem, such as using the place values of 10,000 and 1,000 to move bricks together to build steps for a penguin to climb, or determining how many flower petals a bee visited. The ST philosophy is less about getting the right answer than it is about the process of problem solving itself. The idea is, by learning from their mistakes, students can soon grasp the concepts behind the problems.

Students who are unsuccessful at solving an ST math problem, or have skipped it altogether, automatically are presented with similar problems until they have grasped the concept well enough to solve the problem. "The program intuitively provides personalized remediation," says Zywicki. Similarly, students who excel at solving the math problems are automatically confronted with more-challenging math problems. According to Dr. Zywicki, ST Math helps students in two ways:

> First, the kids are developing a growth mindset in which they set goals for finishing levels of the game by mastering new skills. Second, research from Stanford University has shown that "number sense" rather than memorization and rote procedure is the essential element for students' math success. ST Math forces kids to develop their number sense. (Boaler & Zoido, 2016)

SUMMARY

Digital leadership is a call to action. It is a calling to leaders to critically reflect on the learning spaces and environments that embody a school or system and begin to enact pivotal changes to empower learners. If students are to engage in meaningful, real-world learning, a concerted effort has to be made to create classrooms and a culture that better reflect the conditions where kids will work and learn in the present as well as the future. Digital leadership drives school leaders to look past traditional constructs and incorporate trends embraced by Fortune 500 companies.

Investments in digital tools and changes to pedagogy must be accompanied by transformed spaces and environments to truly create a relevant learning culture. When energy and time are spent in this area, schools will not only authentically engage students, but also better prepare them for success in today's dynamic society. The end result will be opening the door to learning while creating global scholars, thinkers, and creators.

GUIDING QUESTIONS

1. Would you want to learn in the same classrooms and spaces as well as under the same conditions as all your learners? Why or why not?

2. How might you change the structure and function of your buildings to better support learning? Where are areas of opportunity?

3. Shifting spaces requires changing pedagogy. Do the spaces in your school or district match your desired pedagogy?

4. How are devices being used in your school(s)? What needs to change or be improved?

5. Where are we with implementing personalized and blended learning opportunities with fidelity for our students? What has to be done to begin or improve this process?

iStock.com/Nastasic

Professional Growth and Learning

7

A SHIFT IN PROFESSIONAL LEARNING

Serving as an educational administrator is an exceptionally rewarding profession; however, it can also be an extraordinarily challenging one. Administrators will be the first to admit, "It's lonely at the top." Principals and central office administrators often feel isolated in their roles. As both leaders and managers of their organizations, they are expected to be everything to everyone. From teacher supervision to student discipline to curriculum development to change management, principals and other school leaders need to continually develop themselves professionally in numerous areas. The same can be said for all educators.

Traditional professional development offerings for administrators in particular are often lacking in their approach to developing comprehensive leaders, and they offer little to no opportunity for school leaders to work collaboratively and network with one another. Let's face it, in many cases traditional professional development has been done to us. We all have at least a story or two, maybe even more, where we have been forced to sit through mandated trainings that are a mix of "sit and get," or material that truly isn't very relevant to the diverse needs of educators today. To top it all off there was little to no follow-up after we had all been "developed." The needed shift in education is to move from professional development to professional learning. The big difference here with the latter is being engaged in an experience that we want to be a part of and find useful to improving professional practice. Figure 7.1 identifies what educators expect from professional learning.

Research supports this shift. The following elements have been found to be associated with effective professional learning in over 30

Figure 7.1   10 Things Educators Want for Professional Learning

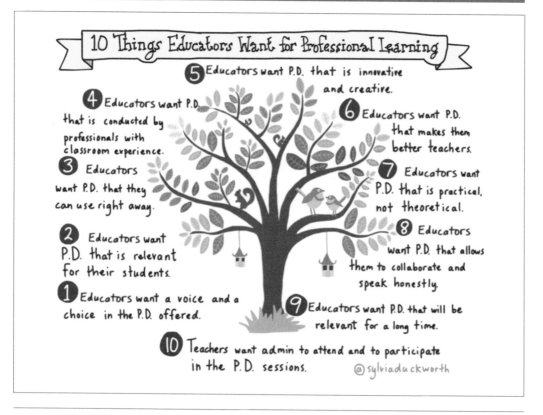

Source: Sylvia Duckworth

different studies (Darling-Hammond, Hyler, Gardner, & Espinoza, 2017; Rock 2002):

1. Is content or practice focused

2. Incorporates active learning utilizing adult learning theory

3. Supports collaboration, typically in job-embedded contexts

4. Uses models and modeling of effective practice

5. Provides coaching and expert support

6. Offers opportunities for feedback and reflection

7. Is of sustained duration

Digital leaders work to improve professional learning in their respective districts, schools, classrooms, or organizations based on what is known to actually work. Professional learning is characterized by sustained, collaborative, coherent, and job-embedded learning that leverages both traditional and digital pathways. It is essential for school leaders to develop professional learning networks both within and beyond their local organizations. With today's technologies able to connect people around the world more efficiently than ever, school leaders can easily amass ideas and support structures in order to better themselves and bring a wealth of resources to their schools. They can also work with their teachers to do the same.

As a first-year principal, Lyn Hilt quickly recognized the need to reach out to other administrators for support, ideas, and feedback. Though her administrative colleagues at the local level were generous in their offerings of support, Lyn's desire to lead her elementary school and support her teachers and students in modern teaching and learning required that she reach beyond the walls of her school building to access the expertise of school administrators and teachers from around the world.

It started simply enough. Lyn turned to the internet to explore topics of interest, including professional learning communities (PLCs), classroom management, home/school communications, educational technology, and teacher supervision and evaluation. While Lyn found relevant information in educational journals and formal publications, she soon realized that many educators chose to share their personal, real-world educational experiences with others through blogging. Lyn recognized the value of writing as a means of reflection in order to better her practice and appreciated that others did the same. To organize the growing list of blogs she enjoyed, she utilized a feed aggregator to make reading a streamlined effort. Now she had all of the blogs she enjoyed reading in one place.

Lyn decided she would like to begin blogging to share her ideas with the global education community. Initially, her blog contained no information identifying her or her school. Like many educators who first contemplate sharing their ideas online, she was fearful of receiving negative or critical feedback. She wrote simple summaries of topics of interest to her as an administrator, posing questions about how to approach problem solving or program implementation. Lyn's earliest blog posts served their purpose in helping her reflect upon her practice, but her audience was limited. Most of the questions posed in her posts remained unanswered, unlike questions in other blogs she read, where meaningful conversations erupted in the comments sections. She needed a way to efficiently share her posts and grow her readership in order to deepen the conversations and her learning.

THE RISE OF SOCIAL MEDIA AS A TOOL FOR GROWTH IN PROFESSIONAL PRACTICE

At an educational technology conference many years ago, Lyn was first introduced to the social networking tool Twitter. She created an account initially but did not interact with other educators, instead convincing herself Twitter was a tool best used for following celebrity happenings and for people who thought it was fun to share what they ate for breakfast that day with the world. Through her reading of educational blogs, however, Lyn noticed that many of her favorite bloggers shared their posts via Twitter. She began to become more active on Twitter, following other principals and teachers whose voices were prevalent in conversations about the topics she cared so much about. She discovered a weekly Twitter chat for educators, #edchat, and through her participation, she began to develop professional relationships with educators from around the world. She tweeted links to her blog posts and soon discovered that more comments and enriched conversations about teaching and learning emerged.

While she was at first fearful of putting herself "out there," Lyn now understood the importance of transparency in learning in online networks. Lyn's blog at the time, The Principal's Posts (now rebranded Learning in Technicolor at lynhilt.com), was becoming well read, and she was gaining access to the resources, ideas, and feedback that she needed to grow professionally. Through her blogging and tweeting efforts, she connected with other administrators such as Amber Teamann (@8amber8) and Patrick Larkin (@patrick mlarkin), and she became a contributor on Connected Principals (connectedprincipals.com), a blog featuring posts from principals and school leaders around the world. She was grateful to find a community of administrators who viewed themselves as "learners first" (L. Hilt, personal communication, 2013).

PERSONAL LEARNING NETWORKS (PLNs)

Lyn's use of Twitter was one of the integral steps in her developing a Personal Learning Network (PLN). PLNs can be defined as collections of like-minded people with whom one exchanges information and engages in conversation. These conversations focus on mutual interests and goals, with the main objective of professional growth and improvement. They have been around for centuries and originally consisted of friends, family, coworkers, et cetera. The evolution of the internet and social media has changed the dynamics of PLN formation, but they still serve the same centuries-old purpose. Free social networking tools and seemingly ubiquitous access to them provide leaders with the ability to connect and learn like never before. What used to be boundaries to PLN formation—time, location, access to people—are no longer issues.

Educators have always understood the value of collaboration, and, as a result, professional communities of practice arose. The research of Alec Couros (2006) illustrates the differences between educators that are and are not connected through social networks and identifies the shift needed to move from a traditional educator to a networked approach. He describes how networks found in our traditional schools are more closed than open. An educator may have professional and social contacts that span the globe, but these are likely rare. Teacher practice and content knowledge are more likely shaped by geography than by digital connectedness. This is how learning communities have been structured for many, many years. The flow of information and resources also tends to be more one-dimensional (Figure 7.2).

Technology has changed everything when it comes to professional learning. A connected leader is still supported by traditional networks but now has the ability to tap into other professional learning

Figure 7.2 Traditionally Networked Educator

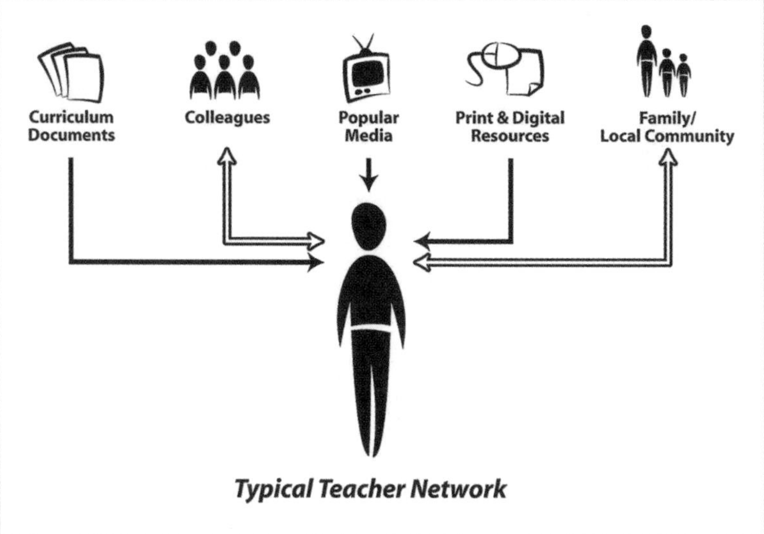

Curriculum Documents | Colleagues | Popular Media | Print & Digital Resources | Family/ Local Community

Typical Teacher Network

Source: Couros (2006). Used with permission.

resources using digital tools. Beyond the usual localized relations, those who are connected to a greater social network are more informed about their practice, beliefs, and perceptions regarding education. Perhaps more important, these educators engage in both *consumption* and *publication.* Knowledge is shared and exchanged, not simply taken.

The driving force in a connected learning model is each individual leader. Each member of a PLN transitions between the physical and virtual networks to communicate, collaborate, acquire resources, elicit feedback, get support, and share ideas, data, strategies, and information. It is the consistent give and take at the individual level that makes a collective PLN exponentially stronger, more knowledgeable, and wiser. Why would any leader refuse the opportunity to tap into this human-generated portal of information and to improve? The essence of the PLN is that the *who* of potential members and collaborators is increased exponentially because of individual members networking through collaborative technology platforms, the *what* (Jacobs, 2009).

This dynamic model of learning not only supports the diverse needs of leaders, but also emphasizes a two-way flow of information (Figure 7.3).

Figure 7.3 Digital Leaders

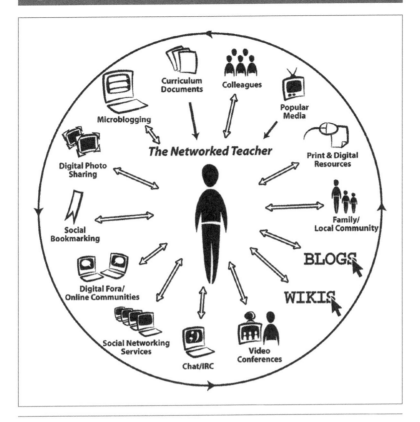

Source: Couros (2006). Used with permission.

Lyn Hilt was now able to quickly acquire quality resources to support her leadership efforts. She was able to reach out to members of her network when in need of feedback, encouragement, and inspiration. In addition to having the principalship, Lyn served as the elementary technology integrator in her small district and was charged with leading educational technology initiatives at the elementary level. This required her to become more informed about innovative teaching and learning. She was asked to write elementary student blogging guidelines in order to proceed with the district's new blogging initiative. Rather than begin from scratch, potentially spending hours of time on the task, Lyn tweeted a request for examples of current student blogging guidelines that other educators were using. Within minutes, she received a tweet with the link to a quality set of guidelines developed by a fellow educator. Within a short time, Lyn modified the contents to meet her district's needs, credited the teacher who created the original guidelines, and the task was complete.

Another challenge for any principal is supporting teachers of various grade levels and content areas. Lyn used Twitter and her PLN's knowledge base to acquire resources for her teachers at all levels, including lesson ideas, research studies and articles, and tech tools for use in the classroom. She encouraged her teachers to develop their own PLNs, and she supported her teachers in that effort by modeling her use of social media to form connections with other educators. She also held workshops for teachers to help them learn more about social media and the power of the PLN. Soon her teachers were reaching out and forming their own PLNs via Twitter, connecting with grade-level colleagues from around the world. They were leading technology initiatives in the district, forming global classroom partnerships through the use of programs such as Skype and Edmodo, sharing their ideas with one another more freely, and ultimately enhancing student learning experiences in their classrooms.

Through the support of her PLN, Lyn became more knowledgeable about digital pedagogy and instructional design. She was able to enhance communication and collaborative opportunities in her school. The use of Google Docs and blogs streamlined the way she communicated with her teachers, and many of her staff embraced the use of these tools to plan more collaboratively in teams. To strengthen home/school connections, she began communicating with parents frequently through the use of a school blog and Facebook page, replacing traditional paper newsletters that did not allow for two-way communication. Her community was given access to the school's happenings with one click.

Parents had the option to engage with the content she shared, such as commenting on posts and viewing photos from school events. She transformed the way she approached professional learning at her school, thanks to the philosophies and ideas shared by those in her PLN. Through her engagement with online learning networks, Lyn received opportunities to present "the power of the PLN" to other educators at local, state, and national education conferences. She became involved with organizations and enjoyed being challenged each day to transform teaching and learning not only at her school, but by influencing other educators around the world.

"It's hard to describe how great the impact of my PLN has been," Lyn states.

> I am definitely a changed leader because of the connections and relationships I've formed. There's nothing like needing support or an idea and reaching out to hundreds, even thousands, of other educators for feedback. I've been introduced to ideas and content I never would have learned through traditional professional development. Forming a PLN is a necessity for any school leader who wishes to grow professionally.

CONNECTEDNESS AS THE STANDARD

Digital leadership requires connectedness as an essential component to cultivate innovative practices and lead sustainable change. It is not an option, but a standard and professional obligation in a digital world. The power and value of a connected learning model are tough to ignore. Leaders become the epicenter of their learning and determine *what, where, how,* and *when* they want to learn. This makes the learning process meaningful, relevant, applicable, and convenient. With these structures in place, the foundation is established to unleash passion, creativity, and a pursuit of innovation to do what we do better. Connectedness and control of learning provide leaders with the ability to determine their own path and to differentiate to meet their diverse learning needs.

This type of learning is fueled by intrinsic motivation, which is the most pivotal ingredient essential to lifelong learning, growth, innovation, and sustainable change. Passion and interest drive this model of learning, which in itself becomes a self-sustaining entity. Connectedness provides unparalleled access to a wealth of free resources. Using tools to share and acquire resources expands each leader's horizons. Many educators don't even know what tools exist, let alone how they can enhance the teaching and learning process. Leaders in this area typically know even less.

Where traditional models of professional growth and development fall short, a PLN driven by connections and conversations fills in the gaps with a focus on purposeful learning. It represents a two-way mechanism for constructive feedback, support, and advice. This feature alone is priceless. No longer do leaders need to feel like they inhabit isolated islands in their respective positions. Distance boundaries and budgetary challenges are overcome with just a device, internet connection, and a desire to improve. Stand-alone silos of information, the cultural components of many schools and leaders, dissipate. There need no longer be a quest to reinvent the wheel and constantly develop new, fresh ideas, because some of the best ideas and proven strategies for school and leadership improvement are readily available and accessible through a PLN.

There is no monetary cost for this powerful opportunity to grow. All it costs is an investment of time, which we ultimately determine. Leaders who embrace a digital style understand that this investment is necessary to create the types of schools needed to prepare students for a digital world. To accomplish this lofty goal, leaders must put in the time to learn in a way that drives them. This will then set the stage to build capacity in others through knowledge gained from a global network.

The internet provides the means to connect with the best minds in the field of education. One of the most amazing attributes associated with social media is that they make the world a much smaller place. You can now connect with world-renowned educational researchers or experts from your living room. Possibly even more powerful is the ability to learn from actual practitioners doing the same job as you. Access to the ideas, strategies, and collective knowledge of both of these groups will ultimately make you a better educator. Silos of information become a thing of the past.

A connected learning model is also extremely transparent. A quote attributed to over one hundred people sums it up nicely: "If you are the smartest person in the room, then you are in the wrong room." With a PLN, all educators have a human-generated search engine to power learning to unprecedented levels.

A PLN will provide leaders with the seeds of change, but it is up to each respective leader to plant and cultivate his or her network in order to witness its growth and development into transformative culture elements. If leaders do this, it will not be long before these seeds of change mature and begin to bear fruit by becoming embedded, sustainable components of the school culture and professional growth. With the tools that are now available, connectedness should be the standard, not just an option in education. When reflecting upon the many benefits of becoming connected, digital leaders understand that they cannot afford not to become connected.

Developing a PLN

No one can argue that the evolution of the real-time web has dramatically altered how we communicate, gather information, and reflect. The construction of a PLN enables leaders to harness the power inherent in innovative technologies in order to create a professional growth tool that is accessible whenever and wherever necessary. In particular, a PLN will provide any leader with a constant supply of resources, thought-provoking discussions, knowledge, leadership strategies, and ways to successfully integrate technology.

Most leaders have no idea where to begin when attempting to create a PLN that meets their learning and leadership needs. The vast majority don't even possess a working knowledge of basic digital tools and how they can be utilized for teaching and learning. The following list (Ferriter, Ramsden, & Sheninger, 2011), which has been updated to reflect more recent changes in technology, provides some good PLN starting points and resources to assist any leader in a digital world who desires to take his or her professional growth to new levels.

- **Twitter (twitter.com):** This microblogging platform allows educators from all corners of the globe to communicate in 280 characters or less and allows for the sharing of resources, discussion of best practices, and collaboration. Twitter chats are a fantastic way to connect with and learn from practicing administrators. One great example is #Satchat. Founded by Brad Currie (@bcurrie5) and Scott Rocco (@scottrrocco), #Satchat takes place every Saturday morning on Twitter and enables educators from around the world to connect and share best practices that will inevitably promote the success of all students. The inspiration for this Twitter discussion directly relates to my work and that of others who promote what is possible when social media and web tools are effectively utilized. The charge of improving every day as a lead learner and having substantial influence on a child's education is the enduring goal of #Satchat. All willing and able educators who see what is possible for their students are welcome to join.

- **LinkedIn (www.linkedin.com):** This is a professional networking site that allows educators to connect, exchange ideas, and find opportunities. Educators can join a variety of groups that cater to their individual learning interests and engage in discussions as well as submit, read, and comment on articles.

- **Blogs:** These are incredible sources of information that allow educators to reflect, share opinions, and discuss various topics. This is a common medium with which to discover best practices, examples of innovation, and professional experiences of both novice and veteran educators. Common blogging applications include Blogger (www.blogger.com), WordPress (wordpress.org), and Medium (www.medium.com). Connected Principals (connectedprincipals.com) is a great example of a collaborative school leader blog that consistently generates great ideas and strategies that can be assimilated into professional practice.

- **RSS Readers:** RSS stands for "real simple syndication." An RSS reader is a tool that allows leaders to keep up with educational blogs, news, videos, and podcasts all in one convenient location. By subscribing to various RSS feeds, leaders create a customized flow of information that is continually updated and accessible through the use of mobile devices or the internet. Leaders can even create their own RSS feeds! Popular RSS readers include Feedly (www.feedly.com) and RSSOwl (www.rssowl.org).

- **Tablet and smartphone apps:** Free apps for iOS (Apple) and Android devices tap into existing RSS feeds and social networks to create customized sources of educational information. The Flipboard app (flipboard.com) will turn any leader's social networks and other RSS feeds into a digital magazine that can be navigated with the flip of a finger. It allows leaders to establish their own categories, and then the app does all of the work. It aggregates all relevant news, blog posts, and video feeds into each customized category, providing digital leaders with only the information that they find most valuable to their growth and development.

- **Digital discussion forums:** These are communities of educators interested in similar topics. One of the more popular platforms is Ning, where educators can create or join specific communities. Ning sites offer a range of learning and growth options such as discussion forums, event postings, messaging, news articles, chat features, groups, and videos. Popular educational Ning sites for leaders include Classroom 2.0 (www.classroom20.com) and School Leadership 2.0 (www.schoolleadership20.com). Another fantastic digital discussion forum is edWeb.net. In addition to numerous communities that leaders can tap into here, there is one specific to those interested in the principles of digital leadership (www.edweb.net/leadership).

- **Social bookmarking:** This is a method for storing, organizing, curating, and sharing bookmarks online. There are no better tools out there than social bookmarking tools, which allow busy leaders to make order out of the chaos that initially emerges with access to the amazing resources made available through PLNs. Social bookmarking tools allow leaders to use the cloud to store all of their resources, which are then accessible from an internet-connected device. The popular site Diigo (www .diigo.com) allows leaders to add descriptions as well as categorize each site using tags. Leaders can even join groups and receive e-mail updates when new bookmarks are added. Diigo's expanded features allow users to highlight and annotate the websites that they bookmark.

- **Facebook:** This social networking site allows people to not only keep up with family and friends, but also to connect and engage with professionals. Many national and state educational organizations have created Facebook pages as places for leaders to congregate online, engage in conversations on professional practice, and share resources. Each customizable page or group provides a variety of learning opportunities and growth options for educators. Some examples include the National Association of Secondary School Principals (www.facebook.com/principals), National Association of Elementary School Principals (www.facebook.com/naesp), American Association of School Administrators (www .facebook.com/AASApage), and International Center for Leadership in Education (www.facebook.com/RigorRelevance/)

- **Pinterest (pinterest.com):** The best way to describe this tool is as an electronic bulletin board where users can "pin" images from around the web. For visual learners, it is a great way to curate resources and other information. Images that are pinned are categorized into various user-defined boards on one's profile. Images are linked to websites, and pins can be shared and searched for. To see an example, visit www.pinterest.com/esheninger.

- **Voxer (voxer.com):** This simple-to-use push-to-talk app can function like a walkie-talkie. With Voxer, educators can engage in both synchronous and asynchronous conversations about professional practice. A "vox" can be voice, text, GIF, or even a video. Many educators use Voxer to engage in virtual book studies. You can also use it as a tool to support professional learning communities (PLCs) in lieu of face-to-face meetings.

Beginning the process of creating and maintaining a PLN can be confusing and at times frustrating. To aid in this transition, leaders can visit a specially designed Google site that will walk them through the process while providing detailed notes, video tutorials, downloadable documents, and examples of the tools mentioned above in practice (sites.google.com/site/anytimepd).

edWeb.net

One of the best learning resources for school leaders is edWeb.net. This previously mentioned digital discussion forum is a professional social and learning network that helps educators connect with colleagues, share expertise and resources, join PLCs, and host individual online communities—all for free. edWeb has grown to over 500,000 educators who are at the forefront of innovative ideas and especially forward thinking about integrating technology into teaching and learning. Members are from all over the world and all levels of education, but conversations and programs are mainly focused on K–12 education.

edWeb hosts online PLCs—with free webinars—to create a model for personalized professional learning. edWeb PLCs make it easy for any educator to join a community, watch live or previously recorded webinars, and earn CE certificates for participation. All resources are archived on edWeb, creating an open and free resource for any educator. In 2018, edWeb won the SIIA CODiEb Award for Best Overall Education Solution and was selected by the American Association of School Libraries as one of the Best Websites for Teaching & Learning.

edWeb is a great professional learning resource for you as an educator or school leader, as well as for your teachers, school librarians, and staff. Many schools and districts are embedding edWeb in their professional development programs. You can also use edWeb to create your own PLCs—at no cost. Your communities can be public or private, so they are ideal for professional collaboration. As an added bonus, edWeb provides personal support for members. Help is just an e-mail or phone call away, which is so important for helping educators to learn how to use the latest collaborative technologies. Leaders can join the digital leadership community at www.edweb.net/leadership. This PLC helps school leaders use web-based tools to be innovative, help teachers grow professionally, enhance student learning, and improve communications with all stakeholders.

THE PROFESSIONAL GROWTH PERIOD

The Professional Growth Period (PGP) is a job-embedded growth model created at New Milford High School. It arose out of the need for teachers to be able to follow their learning passions as well as form their own PLNs with support from colleagues and administrators. In order to establish the PGP, administrators at New Milford High School had to look at areas of opportunity to free teachers in the eight-period schedule. The solution came in the form of the noninstructional duties that each teacher was assigned as per the contract—one duty period per day. To make the PGP a reality, all noninstructional teacher duties were cut in half, thus freeing each teacher for two or three 48-minute periods per week, depending on the semester. This resulted in giving my staff the time and flexibility to learn how to integrate the tools that they were interested in, as well as to form their own PLNs.

The key to this model was the autonomy granted to teachers to learn about anything that motivated or interested them as long as it had the potential to impact student learning. PGP time was dedicated to engaging in professional learning opportunities in order to become a better educator and learner. Teachers were empowered to follow their passions and work to define a purpose. They were expected to spend this time learning, innovating, and pursuing ways to become master educators. Think of it as a differentiated and personalized learning opportunity that caters to each teacher's specific needs and interests.

In order to give teachers the autonomy that they deserved, each staff member was expected to submit a learning portfolio at their end-of-year evaluation conference. This learning portfolio had to demonstrate how PGP time was used to improve professional practice, enhance learning, and ultimately increase student achievement. The learning portfolio became a showcase of innovative practices and made the entire PGP model transparent. To make this possible my admin team and I assumed the duties that we freed up our teachers from.

WHY EVERY LEADER NEEDS A PLN

Educators who have embraced this concept have experienced first-hand the positive impact on professional practice that being a connected educator brings. The premise is relatively simple. Carve out a little time each day (15–30 minutes), and use one of many available free tools to learn. It is less about the specific tool that is used for the foundation of a PLN and more about the relationships, engagement, and new knowledge that result.

Leadership is a choice and not one that should be made lightly. With this choice comes a great deal of responsibility to initiate and sustain change that will lead to a transformed school culture. Learning has been, and always will be, a pivotal component of this process. With time always being in short supply, leaders must be on the forefront of leading the learning themselves if that is what they expect of others. Basically, we get what we model. Outside of instruction there is not a more important leadership quality that successful and effective administrators must focus on. Quite simply, the best leaders are always learning. Learning is the fuel of leadership.

With budget crunches and lack of time, it is often a challenge to participate consistently in invaluable, formal learning opportunities. Nothing beats quality, face-to-face professional learning. It is through these opportunities that time, applicability, and relationships intersect, resulting in a powerful experience. However, leaders today now have the means to supplement formal learning opportunities with a PLN. This is equivalent to a human-generated search engine that never shuts down and is powered by the knowledge of world-renowned experts and practitioners alike.

PLNs can be a tough sell at times, especially when they are being pitched to administrators who are either against or not on social media. I can relate, as this is where I was years ago. I swore I would never be on social media, as I didn't have the time for it and it would not help me professionally. Boy was I wrong. Now, like many others, I preach the many benefits connected learning brings to all educators. Administrators, though, are at times tough nuts to crack. Figure 7.4 lists 10 reasons why every leader should have a PLN.

Figure 7.4 Why Every Leader Needs a PLN

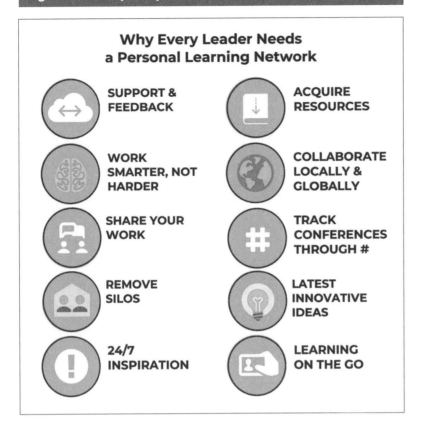

SUMMARY

At the heart of digital leadership is a connected model of learning and professional growth. Connectedness becomes the standard, not just an option or a blatantly discredited method of professional development. Leaders in a digital world embrace and leverage social media to learn any time, from anywhere, and with anyone who might help them do what they do better. The PLNs that they form become invaluable tools that are always at their disposal to help them acquire knowledge, resources, ideas, strategies, advice, and feedback as well as to learn from world-renowned experts and practitioners in the field of education. You don't have to have a PLN to be a great leader, but why would you close the door on the chance to be even better? Learning becomes much more relevant and meaningful as the leader calls the shots and becomes the center of the process. With the empowerment of digital leadership, leaders no longer *attempt* to find the time to learn and get better, but *make* the time to learn and get better.

GUIDING QUESTIONS

1. How are we creating personalized and contextualized experiences for educators in order to move from professional development to professional learning?

2. How is my learning path adapting to the changing needs and interests of learners in order to improve school culture?

3. How are we motivating and inspiring educators to seek out more on their own in digital spaces and share it with others?

4. Where am I currently at with the development of my Personal Learning Network (PLN)? What steps must I take to get more from it, and how will I encourage others to do the same?

iStock.com/oatawa

Communication

8

Just as teachers differentiate for a variety of learning styles in the classroom, it is important for schools to differentiate their communication efforts if we want true stakeholder partnerships between home, school, and the greater community. For school leaders, communication and community relations have been identified as one of the nine most important skills to master (Hoyle, English, & Steffy, 1998). It is difficult for any school leader to be successful if he or she cannot communicate effectively (Arnold, Perry, Watson, Minatra, & Schwartz, 2006). Bottom line is that you will not find an effective leader who is not an effective communicator. Sound communication strategies assist leaders to

- Accomplish tasks and get things done.
- Pass on important information.

It's Tuesday night at 7:00 PM, and the monthly Home and School meeting is about to begin in the library at Knapp Elementary School in suburban Philadelphia. The Home and School president begins by greeting the 14 parents in attendance and then looks up at the big projector screen to welcome the 44 parents logged in from home who are also participating via a live video feed. Parents "virtually" sign in and acknowledge their name and their child's grade, and provide a simple greeting.

The Home and School president begins the meeting by asking the principal to deliver a monthly report, which includes updates, new ideas, and other important announcements to engage families who are both in the room and tuning in from home via live video feed. The meeting continues over the next 60 minutes with conversations happening both physically and virtually. Parents without cars, without a babysitter, and without good mobility for whatever reason participate virtually without the need to physically be in the room where the meeting takes place. The school meets the parents "where they are" thanks to the digital leadership of Joe Mazza.

- Acquire information.
- Develop a shared vision.
- Reach decisions through consensus.
- Build relationships.
- Move people to embrace change.

Communication is an art to some extent and takes work. In order to grow in this area, it is important to understand the foundation for successful communication regardless of your role or audience. As you will learn later in this chapter, technology can certainly support and enhance the ability of leaders to disseminate information and authentically engage with stakeholders. However, before we get to this point, it is incumbent upon all of us to remember the critical elements that all great communicators understand. Leaders who effectively communicate listen intently, facilitate dialogue (hear, respond, add thoughts), ask questions, get to the point clearly and concisely, create an open environment for discussion, and employ a multifaceted approach. The best communicators focus on being present, consistent, and engaged to get the right people the right information at the right time.

Joe Mazza, the former principal of Knapp Elementary who is currently at the helm of Seven Bridges Middle School in Chappaqua, New York, took the lead in this area, and his school benefitted from his efforts. Like our students, today's parents are also evolving in the tools they use each day as moms and dads. Technology is here to stay, even though the tools and specific ways to engage will continue to evolve. Parents as well as teachers have identified parent–school communication as a critical factor to promote children's school success (Buchanan & Clark, 2017). As such, it is our job to keep current with the astronomical increase in technology use by our stakeholders.

When many school leaders hear the words *Twitter, Facebook,* and *Snapchat,* they cringe. Immediately, visions of excessive socialization, cyberbullying, sexting, time wasted, and meaningless conversations in the form of updates come to mind. Does this happen? Of course, it does, but that does not mean leaders should shut the door on the opportunity that social media provides to engage an array of stakeholders while building powerful relationships in the process. There are many ways in which schools and leaders can harness the power of these free resources to improve communications and ultimately enhance their overall effectiveness and efficiency. Societal shifts have made traditional forms of communication such as snail mail, newsletters, website updates, and even e-mail less relevant, as many stakeholders no longer rely on or value these communication mediums. Certain parents and guardians still rely on these, so no one is saying that you must dump them if you still find value in their use. Digital leadership compels us to meet our stakeholders where they are at, as they have become accustomed to and dependent upon 24/7 access to information and engagement. It calls for a hybrid construct of communication techniques that blends the traditional methods mentioned above with the systematic use of social media tools to create a dynamic, two-way system that will increase engagement with all stakeholders.

NO BETTER TIME THAN NOW

Social media provide a treasure of resources that leaders can incorporate into their communications plan. Billions of people are active on Twitter, Facebook, Instagram, and YouTube. LinkedIn, Snapchat, and blogs are also very popular tools being used today for personal and professional reasons. Digital leaders have learned that the easiest way to showcase social media for families and other community members is linking their accounts so that each tweet sent from the school is automatically embedded onto the school's website homepage.

Many years ago, as principal at New Milford High School in New Jersey, I made a small change that ultimately transformed my leadership style and my school. I shifted from using traditional forms of communication with families and community members—newsletters and e-mail—to using social media. With a click of a mouse, I set up my Twitter account and changed the course of my instructional leadership.

Twitter was my first step in a social media communication strategy that expanded to include a range of tools and approaches. What made these tools different from any I'd used before was their power to reach in all directions. Whether sending updates on school cancellations or tweeting about great student projects, with a few keystrokes, I could share ideas and information with students, students' families, community members, and the larger world—while inviting everyone's responses.

This transformation involved more than new tools. My colleagues and I had to make pedagogical and philosophical shifts, which had a deep impact on New Milford's students and our community. Each of these transformations was powerful for me personally. Watching my colleagues and me learn new things, reach out across geographic divides, and take risks offered a powerful model for students. As I leveraged social media to enhance our school's impact on learning and our image, I discovered key principles for effectively communicating through digital tools: *transparency, flexibility*, and *accessibility* (Sheninger, 2015a).

The power of using social media rests in the ability to engage stakeholders in two-way communications. Tools let me share information about New Milford more frequently and accurately and provide updates in real time—which engaged more stakeholders than traditional methods had. Teachers, parents, and even outsiders began contributing ideas to New Milford's work. This shift required me to commit to a new level of transparency and openness. This sometimes meant sharing challenges as well as successes and opening myself to feedback from anyone. One important aspect of our approach was involving students, parents, teachers, and community members in shaping the tools and processes we would use to communicate. This required a great deal of flexibility, as we invited many stakeholders into our leadership and decision-making process. The accessible nature of social media thanks to mobile technology makes it a breeze to get out accurate and positive information regardless of time and location.

Using social media tools that complement one another is extremely important, but to get to this point, it is important to understand the major social media tools available to school leaders and how they can be used to enhance communications. Always know that over time tools will change, which is why it is extremely important to always focus on your communication goals first and foremost. Never forget that the most important quality of communication is the humanistic element.

Twitter

Twitter is a microblogging platform that allows users to send free messages called *tweets* in 280 characters or less. Tweets can be text, images, links, videos, or even a combination of these, making it a dynamic communications tool. The brevity and succinctness of tweets allow leaders to communicate real-time information that not only is impactful, but also saves precious time. Character limits and the ability of people to receive tweets as SMS text messages make this a powerful communications tool. Instead of spending money on expensive information delivery systems, digital leaders can use Twitter for free. One of the benefits of using Twitter is that you can communicate information whenever and wherever you want, making it extremely convenient.

Parents today are extremely busy, and it is often difficult to keep track of all of their children's events. Twitter provides a great medium for leaders to send out routine reminders of school functions such as concerts, art shows, athletic contests and scores, scholastic competitions, and Back-to-School Night. This not only keeps all stakeholders in the know, but also provides access to this information through a variety of mobile devices where traditional means of communication fall short.

There are many meetings that occur at schools, and they involve a variety of stakeholder groups. Leaders can use Twitter to send out meeting reminders (parent-teacher organization/association, athletic boosters, etc.); notify attendees of a room and/or time change;

distribute agendas beforehand; create a video recap; and make the minutes of the meetings available to all, even if they were unable to attend the meeting. Of course, all of this information can be posted on a website, but chances are stakeholders are not frequenting these as much as they did in the past. The key again is to use social media tools not only to get the information quickly and easily to stakeholders, but also to redirect them to other sources of information that provide more depth. When communicating successes about my former school, I was always on the lookout for favorable media coverage to amplify, such as the evidence we had that our innovative practices were improving student learning outcomes.

Then there is the weather. Snow in particular drives superintendents crazy. The second schools close due to weather or other issues, stakeholders want to know. Digital leadership calls for leaders to anticipate where current notification systems might fail and have backup plans or strategies in place. During Superstorm Sandy, New Milford High School and the town of New Milford were without power for days. This resulted in many parents and staff members not receiving the message sent out through the automated call system each night. Twitter and Facebook became invaluable communications tools in the storm's aftermath, as school-closing information was still pushed out and accessible through mobile devices.

Athletics are the hub of many schools, and it is near impossible to attend each and every event due to the number of teams and competition levels. With Twitter, school leaders can keep the avid sports fan in the community abreast of this information through either a school account or a separate one for the athletic department. New Milford High School did just this, because sports were a vital component of the school culture (Online Resource 8.1).

The success of our students should be celebrated at every opportunity. Twitter makes it easy for school leaders to capture, curate, and share student achievements and successes as they happen in a way that can be accessed by stakeholders no matter where they are. Tweets that celebrate and commend the work done by students are possibly the most influential type of communication today. These messages can be descriptions, pictures, links to press releases, or even videos that capture the moment. Think about the impact of communicating pictures from the art show, video (live or archived) from the winter concert, real-time athletic scores, or updates on who is attending a college fair in your building.

Teachers are the backbones of our schools and, unfortunately, their innovative work is not shared and celebrated as much as it should be. Twitter allows school leaders to create more of a transparent culture by tweeting out lessons, ideas, and innovative learning activities that are observed during classroom walk-throughs, formal observations, or just a daily stroll through the building.

In this day and age, a much greater emphasis has been placed on school security and communicating information to parents during times of crisis. School leaders must always be on the cutting edge and anticipate how they might dispense precious information if traditional means (radios, e-mail, P.A. system, landline phones, etc.) are unavailable or inoperable. Twitter, as well as a host of other tools and apps, on a mobile device solves this potential problem and can be used to keep all stakeholders informed during and after emergencies.

Effective communication is not just about making the news, but making sure that all stakeholders hear it. Whether in the form of a school newsletter or articles that appear in mainstream media outlets, Twitter can be used to send links to more detailed information about the school, recently adopted policies, scholarship opportunities, referendums, and construction projects. Social media have made it easier than ever for leaders to collect and curate resources for parents, teachers, and students. Integrating the use of Twitter to communicate to stakeholders the available internet resources that can extend learning beyond the school day builds support and appreciation for the work being done by educators.

While at New Milford High School, I created an official Twitter account (Online Resource 8.2) to send out the above information. I developed a simple instruction sheet and disseminated it annually to all of my parents, because although many people know what Twitter is, they may not know how it can be used for professional communications. It explained to parents how to sign up, how to activate updates on their cell phones, and what types of information would be sent out. To get started with using Twitter as a school and professional communications tool, follow these simple steps:

1. Create a free account at twitter.com. For set-up tips and assistance, visit support.twitter.com.

2. Develop a username that reflects the use of the tool for school communications.

3. When establishing your account, make sure to include a biographical sketch, the link to the school or professional website, and an avatar (i.e., a picture of you or the school).

4. Add a background that showcases school pride, such as pictures of the building, your mascot, or your school colors.

5. Notify key stakeholders of the Twitter account and how it will be used for communications.

Online Resource 8.3 (Template: Twitter for School Communications and Engagement) provides a template you can use to notify parents how to sign up for Twitter.

Facebook

As I learned years ago as a principal, many more people use the social media tool Facebook than Twitter. Billions of people across the world are on this social media site, including students, parents, grandparents, community members, and local businesses. The sheer numbers alone compelled me to create a Facebook page for New Milford High School. This communications tool became the hub for everything we did at our school. It evolved into a conduit for school pride and connecting to graduates as a two-way communications medium. Schools and leaders that have introduced Facebook as a communications tool understand that stakeholders are no longer visiting static, boring websites that rely on one-way communication efforts. Digital leadership is driven by the desire to meet our stakeholders where they are, even if it is not comfortable at first. It is also about anticipating the risks of having an open Facebook page for two-way communication efforts and knowing how to deal with issues as they arise.

All stakeholder groups routinely comment on and like informational updates that are communicated using this social media tool. The same information sent out using Twitter was placed on our New Milford High School Facebook page. The ultimate power of Facebook as a communications tool lies in its ability to foster community engagement through two-way communication. It is important for leaders in a digital world to understand the value and merit of allowing this engagement and interactivity. If a school Facebook page is just used as a tool to communicate information while not allowing comments and likes, then it is no different than a school website. It is a form of "social" media after all. Don't forget that.

Getting started with Facebook as a communications tool is relatively easy, but you do need to have a personal account in order to create a page for your school or institution. Even though a personal account is needed, no one can access any of your information from any page that is created. To begin the process of creating a Facebook page for your school, visit www.facebook.com/pages/creation. Once there, follow these simple steps:

1. Select Business or Brand.

2. On the next page, add the name of your district, school, or organization. Below that, add Education for the category. Add a profile and cover picture of your school or mascot. Your page is now ready to go.

3. Select Settings on the top right. You will now see a range of options on the left. Select Edit Page, and completely fill out the About section by including a description of your school, website, mission statement, operating hours, map of location, and any other important links (e.g., Twitter feeds, athletic calendar, etc.).

4. Create a unique Facebook web address.

5. Once the page is created, click Edit Page on the admin panel to manage the permissions for the page. It is important to select settings that support two-way communication.

With a new Facebook page as part of a communications plan, leaders can begin to further engage stakeholders. In addition to status updates, leaders can communicate information through the uploading of pictures and videos (live or prerecorded). Events can easily be created that will keep all stakeholders in the know. There is even the ability to create polling questions to further engage stakeholders that visit the site. Engagement can be measured by determining the number of "likes" and "impressions" on individual status updates on the page wall. "Impressions" refer to how many times a specific post was displayed within news feeds. Leaders can easily see the impact of communicating through a Facebook page with integrated analytic features on the admin page. When you click on the "insights" graph, a much more detailed graph appears providing analytic data on each day and post.

Using Facebook and Twitter together allows leaders to deliver positive information into the hands of stakeholders. Where leaders once relied on the news media, press releases, and websites, they now have the ability to get out links to media articles and website updates as well as pictures and video that highlight school programs. By doing so, they ultimately enhance public relations (Chapter 9) and create a brand presence (Chapter 10) for their building, one that conveys a message of success, organization, innovation, and achievement. Figure 8.1 lists K–12 schools that use both Twitter and Facebook as part of their communications plan.

TRAILBLAZERS MODELING THE WAY

If you're part of a growing Personal Learning Network (PLN) on Twitter, you have instant access to cutting-edge communication strategies used by many of today's most highly regarded leaders. Schools are beginning to respond to the increasing digital parent audience. However, for reasons such as policy restrictions, fear, lack of trust, lack of supporting research, and lack of resources, only a

Figure 8.1   Schools Using Social Media for Communications

School	Twitter	Facebook
New Milford High School, New Milford, NJ	twitter.com/ NewMilfordHS	www.facebook.com/ NewMilfordHS
Waldwick High School, Waldwick, NJ	twitter.com/ WaldwickWHS	on.fb.me/WyS5rn
Arapahoe High School, Centennial, CO	twitter.com/ahswarriors	www.facebook.com/ ahswarriors
Coppell High School, Coppell, TX	twitter.com/CoppellHigh	on.fb.me/YeJsQ8
Black River Middle School, Chester, NJ	twitter.com/ BlackRiverMS	on.fb.me/14M8ADP
Harry H. Herndon Intermediate School, Royse City, TX	twitter.com/herndonheros	on.fb.me/12ij8aX
Utica Junior High School, Utica, OH	twitter.com/ EJHSBulldogCtry	www.facebook.com/ fayettecountypublicschoolstn/
Wells Elementary School, Cypress, TX	twitter.com/ CFISDWells	www.facebook.com/ CFISDWells
Hermosa Schools, Hermosa, SD	twitter.com/ hermosaschools	www.facebook.com/ HermosaSchools
Cypress-Fairbanks Independent School District, Cypress, TX	twitter.com/CyFairISD	www.facebook.com/ CyFairISD

small population is truly providing social media tools to connect families. Aside from my New Milford High School Facebook and Twitter accounts, some inspiring school examples to check out are Chris Lehmann's Science Leadership Academy High School (Facebook and Twitter) and Cheryl Fisher's Wells Elementary (Facebook, Twitter, Instagram). Consider hosting ongoing trainings for staff, administration, and parents throughout the school year to showcase the menu of communication offerings your school provides. Don't assume that all of your stakeholders already know how to use the tools you are using or that they want to at first.

ENGAGE STAKEHOLDERS USING A MULTIFACETED APPROACH

Educators must be experts in effective communication techniques, especially when it comes to parents and other key stakeholders. As the times and tools have changed, we now have a variety of means to disseminate information in a more efficient and cost-effective fashion. There are four key principles that lay a foundation for communicating effectively with parents: transparency, honesty, accessibility, and flexibility. As you will see, these four principles can be applied to the following strategies that are listed below.

1. Make your professional e-mail and Twitter accounts available. This way, parents can contact you at their convenience. If you have not created such an account for your school, I highly recommend that you do so. During the beginning of each school year, I always sent home a letter to all parents that provided detailed information on what Twitter is, how to create an account, and configuring the settings to receive SMS text messages. This versatility allowed parents to receive updates on their own terms, making Twitter unlike any traditional communication tool that I ever used as a principal. As far as transparency goes, there might not be an application more effective than Twitter. In response to parent feedback, I created an "official" school account (@NewMilfordHS). The New Milford High School Twitter page included a link to the school's main website as well as our school's colors, mascot, and logo. This made our page stand out to viewers and helped to establish a brand presence. Information tweeted out from this account in real time included sports scores, special schedules, school news, student achievements, staff accomplishments, campus weather, and emergency information.

2.   Create your own website and include contact information, your availability to meet with or speak to parents, extra help hours, student assignments, press coverage, et cetera. This is also a great way to convey to parents your philosophy on education, professional accomplishments, and vision for helping learners succeed. My website can be viewed at ericsheninger.com.

3.   Hold training workshops for parents. Many of them use social media tools on a personal level, but hands-on trainings provide a detailed look at both *why* and *how* they will be used to communicate better with stakeholders.

4.   Call home on both positive and negative issues. Combining this traditional method of communication with that of social media will continue to build and maintain strong relationships. Leaders must never forget how powerful this type of communication is even in the digital age.

5.   Share as many student and teacher accomplishments and success stories as possible. Parents want and need to hear the great things happening in our buildings and classrooms. If you don't tell your story, then someone else will. Consider creating a monthly report or blog post that captures these moments. I created the *Principal's Report* at New Milford High School that was communicated to our parents using our school website as well as Twitter, Facebook, and a slew of other social media accounts as well as push notifications through the school mobile app. Online Resource 8.4 shows a sample report. The premise was simple. Send out a blank template to my staff once a month, and ask them to share all the amazing work they were doing with our learners as well as professionally. All I then did was curate what they sent me, create a PDF, place it on the website, and then used that link to share online using eight different tools. Online Resource 8.5 (Principal's Report Template) provides a blank template.

6.   Set up a separate phone number for parents using Google Voice. Google Voice is a free, web-based phone service that leaders can use to set up a phone number for parents and other stakeholders to call and leave messages. This number is totally separate from personal and/or school cell numbers and never actually "rings." Once a phone message is received, an e-mail containing a text transcript will be sent for the leader to follow up on.

7.   Make resources readily available for parents using a social bookmarking or curation service such as Diigo or Pinterest. Once these

are curated, they can be categorized with a description that can be communicated to parents using Twitter, Facebook, or e-mail. Leaders can even create separate resources for students and staff.

8. *Always* return parent phone calls and e-mails in a timely fashion! It is also extremely important to respond to tweets and Facebook comments to foster two-way communications while increasing stakeholder engagement.

9. Invite parents into your classrooms and schools. If parents cannot physically attend, leaders can now set up live video streams over the internet using an array of free tools such as Periscope, Facebook Live, Ustream, or Google Hangouts.

10. Develop a school Facebook page to advertise events and provide up-to-date school information. As mentioned previously in this chapter, the New Milford High School Facebook page became our informational hub on which parents came to rely.

11. Institute a positive referral policy and make parents aware when their child is recognized. This can be done traditionally with a phone call or e-mail, but can also be done publicly using social media tools such as Twitter or Facebook.

12. Start a blog, let parents know about it, and encourage them to comment on your posts. Blogs are fantastic communication tools where parents can glimpse into your educational life and become more familiar with the culture of your school.

13. Create a hashtag (#) and add it to all social media messages that relate to your school, district, or organization. Hashtags categorize messages on main social media sites (Twitter, Facebook, LinkedIn, Instagram) in a way that makes it easy for other users to find and follow updates or conversations about a specific topic or theme. The key is to create a unique hashtag. For example, Wells Elementary in Cypress, Texas, uses #ExploreWells and adds it to all their messaging on social media. If you click on the hashtag, a separate web page will load showing anyone a curated conversation.

14. Look for other means to reach stakeholders. In my quest to create a paperless environment at New Milford High, I discovered ZippSlip (Online Resource 8.6). ZippSlip enables schools and parents to fully process paper forms online from any smartphone, tablet, or computer. All results are tracked and displayed by their cloud-based app, which is 100% compliant with the Health Insurance Portability and Accountability Act (HIPAA) and the Family Educational Rights

and Privacy Act (FERPA), ensuring privacy. There's no training, and virtually no IT support is required. Leaders can leverage this two-way, fully secure channel for media-rich interactions with parents and the community. This solution not only allowed my parents to sign and submit all school forms electronically, but it also provided me with a portal to send e-mail and video messages to them.

If we're going to succeed as a school, we've got to get several different stakeholder groups—parents, students, community leaders, and businesses—to embrace a set of core beliefs. That means that digital leaders need to constantly try to craft messages that have resonance and to deliver those messages in ways that are likely to be heard. In many ways, communication is the most important thing we do every day.

Adding the "e" to FACE

Family and Community Engagement (FACE) has been well researched over multiple decades. Researchers like Dr. Joyce Epstein, Dr. Anne Henderson, and Dr. Karen Mapp have published a great deal on the importance of meeting parents where they are in terms of building home/school partnerships. Joe Mazza coined the term *eFACE*, or electronic Family and Community Engagement. It uses technology tools to bridge home and school while creating and maintaining partnerships. According to Epstein (2011), true home/school partnerships call for communication to include plenty of two-way options, not just one-way sharing. The use of technology to support a comprehensive eFACE plan opens new doors by providing access to conversations already happening in virtual spaces such as Facebook, Twitter, LinkedIn, Instagram, YouTube, blogs, and Snapchat.

Joe insists that technology cannot be the magic bullet for home/school partnerships, but it can certainly complement the overall efforts. In an increasingly digital age, it is even more important to take the extra time necessary to maintain face-to-face communication with eye contact, respect, body language, tone, and empathy as the ideal relationship builder whenever possible. Face-to-face, two-way communication should continue to be at the root of our communications efforts. Growing and fine-tuning these efforts along the way is vital. The feedback may or may not come while using technology; however, not offering these tools as a means of two-way communication limits those parents who *are* already comfortable with these tools. As much as students need us to differentiate in the classroom, parents need us to differentiate for their needs. Leaders should read *Beyond the Bake Sale* (Henderson, Mapp, Johnson, & Davies, 2007), with particular attention to the four core beliefs of partnership with schools. Whichever communications (FACE and/or eFACE) you choose, the core beliefs you have in place should not change, and face-to-face communications should remain the foundation of your efforts.

eFACE—Electronic Family and Community Engagement Offerings

It is important to note that technology cannot replace face-to-face communications and the eye contact, tone, empathy, and mutual respect that speaking with someone face to face provides us as humans. Video conference tools like Skype and Facetime create opportunities for these discussions when physical meetings are not possible; however, Joe found that while technology can complement our FACE efforts, it cannot replace them.

Through two-minute technology surveys, he found that 93% of his families were either on mobile phones or computers with internet access each day. With this data in mind, he crafted a menu of options for two-way communications. For those who did not have a computer and did not understand English, he sent home a translated hard copy of what was communicated, as it is imperative to understand and commit to equal access for all families.

The Evolution of eFACE

Knapp Elementary School began its eFACE efforts with a mass Google account set up to broadcast e-mails out to parents. After the first six years, it had over 500 e-mail addresses included on this list. It used this tool to link parents to various resources without sending large files, et cetera. While this was a nice first step to identify electronic addresses, it only served as a one-way offering, and it didn't provide much opportunity for two-way, back-and-forth communications.

Fast-forward the tape. It eventually evolved into using technology as a means to solicit information directly from families, which was the best way to communicate with them. Joe built a solid partnership with the Home and School president, and they shared many of the tools used to engage families, including a family engagement wiki. On that wiki (which means *quick* in Hawaiian), parents and teachers added and archived resources and events for families. Instead of sending out large PDFs or Word documents and flyers, information was housed in the wiki, and parents were sent a link to the content.

Knapp Elementary chose to use a wiki because it was quick and easy to update content, and the wiki served as a two-way tool much like a blog. In staff members' busy roles, it had become increasingly important to spend more time with the students and staff and less struggling with the formatting of a website. Feedback from their families suggested that the wiki option provided a user-friendly interface with a great deal of information for new and veteran families to digest throughout the school year. Many wiki sites have shut down over the years, but there are many great alternatives available. The same can be accomplished by creating and using a free Google Site.

One of Knapp's family engagement goals had been to find ways to get more parents involved in the leadership of its Home and School Association. During its monthly meetings, only 15 to 20 parents were coming out to participate in the discussion. At one particular Home and School meeting, a dialogue was held around how they needed to double their attendance at these meetings, draw from a greater cross-section of their school's population, respect parents' limited vehicle access, and understand the need for babysitting services—all this with no funds lying around to pay for whatever it was that would make this happen.

The following month they tried "Home & School 2.0," and broadcasted a *live* audio and video feed of the meeting. Through this effort, they grew their monthly participation to over 50 participants, as referenced earlier. Student clubs began presenting at the heart of each of these broadcasted meetings, which kept the focus on students. Knapp Elementary School has a high population of working moms and dads, and many of them work two or more jobs. The feedback provided to Joe was that this new way of communicating was a better option for the busy parents in that they could now tune in from either home or work for free. One of the best parts of these meetings was that several teachers also tuned in and shared during the meetings from the comfort of their own homes. Knapp Elementary School's full menu of family engagement offerings includes all of the following:

- Twitter (@KnappElementary)—Daily classroom messages are tweeted out by Knapp Elementary staff and parents highlighting the learning that is taking place

- Facebook—Facilitated by the Home and School Association at www.facebook.com/knappelementary

- The family engagement wiki

- The Knapp Elementary family engagement app

- An eBully reporting system, eBucket filler, eVolunteer

- Home & School 2.0—Monthly meetings broadcast from school and local community gathering places to encourage maximum participation from stakeholders

- ZippSlip—Private electronic mail interface, paperless forms, two-way feedback

- Google Text line—Texting options that come in and out of Joe's iPad

- Remind (www.remind.com)—Text alert system for emergency cancellations

- Poll Everywhere (www.polleverywhere.com)—Real-time polls for getting feedback during meetings

- Backchannel tools that work much like Twitter without the need to log in (Padlet or Mentimeter are great options for this)

- KnappModo—Edmodo (www.edmodo.com) setup for students in Grades 4–6 with parent access

- Google Photos account for Knapp Elementary

- Google Translate—Located on each wiki page for parents who do not speak English fluently

- Language Line—A conference call interpreting service offered for every family

- KnappTV—YouTube channel for student broadcasts

- Audioboom—Knapp audio channel for quick school announcements

- Kidblog.org—Blogs through which students can share life at Knapp Elementary

SUMMARY

The internet represents a promising opportunity for promoting family–school communication (Bouffard, 2008). If we are serious about keeping children and public education in focus, schools can no longer afford to turn a blind eye to social media tools in their overall communication efforts and, specifically, in meeting the needs of all families. The same can be said for all leaders at the individual level. Educators can take advantage of a multitude of ideas and resources, using the very social media tools mentioned here as well as those not listed to communicate with families. With many leaders being forced to "do more with less," utilizing free tools to enhance communications has never been more vital. Digital leadership compels all educators to meet their stakeholders where they are at using a multifaceted approach. By using tools, digital leaders can foster a culture that supports and promotes two-way communication. Tools will change, but the need to effectively communicate will not.

GUIDING QUESTIONS

1. How effective are you as a communicator? What about your school or district? Identify areas where improvement is needed and action steps to get there.

2. How has communication with all your stakeholders changed? What have you found to be successful strategies?

3. What new tools do you plan to utilize and why?

4. Do you employ a multifaceted approach that encourages two-way communication and engagement? How might you improve in this area?

iStock.com/ipopba

Public Relations

9

Since we cannot change reality, let us change the eyes which see reality.

—Nikos Kazantzakis

Having served as superintendent of the Van Meter and Howard-Winneshiek community school districts in Iowa, John Carver understands the importance of creating a brand. By his utilizing social media, a voice was created, stakeholders were engaged, thinking was shared, and consensus had been be built for facilitating change.

John feels that we are at a "printing press moment" in the history of humanity. The invention of the printing press amplified and shared thinking, eventually turning every system of its day upside down. The printed word empowered all who could read to explore and share knowledge and experiences. The Bible was made available to the masses, the Catholic Church fractured, governments were toppled, and new systems of social class and economics emerged. Humanity is again at the tipping point. Like the printing press, digital devices connected to the internet are unequivocal game changers.

A DISTRICT FORGES A NEW PATH

Van Meter Community School District began utilizing social media tools to create a global footprint, becoming leaders in transforming teaching and learning.

The Van Meter Community School District is located in Central Iowa, just outside the capital city of Des Moines. It is a small district of about 630 students in kindergarten through 12th grade. North of Van Meter, growing at a rate of almost 600 students a year, is the Waukee Community School District. The West Des Moines School District—boasting an Olympic gold medalist and *Dancing With the Stars* champion, Shawn Johnson, as a graduate, as well as a Grammy-winning music program and state championship athletic teams among its assets—lies to the east. To the west and south are several "county seat" school districts, which are three times larger than Van Meter.

Thus, surrounded by prosperous communities with growing school districts, Van Meter was facing an identity crisis. The real fear was that Van Meter would experience either rapid uncontrollable growth like that happening in Waukee or no growth at all, that it would cease to exist and be swallowed up by one of the neighboring districts. In both cases, the fear was that the district was not in control of its own destiny. With that fear came a sense of urgency and a realization of the need for change. To ensure survival and viability, new thinking was needed.

The need for change came from the realization that the current system of education needs to improve. At present, education in many countries is modeled after a century-old design, as outlined in Chapter 2. At the beginning of the Industrial Revolution, the United States moved away from "rugged individualism" to interdependent global consumerism. System thinking at that time was applied to learning design, and the United States moved from the one-room schoolhouse to the consolidated factory model school system. That model served us well for more than one hundred years, but the world has since changed. The crucial need for the United States today, as well as other countries across the globe, is an educational system that empowers learners and develops creativity and imagination, not one focused on standardization, conformity, and compliance. A new system of learning that is differentiated and personalized, and that connects to student interests and strengths, must be made a reality. Teaching, learning, and leadership need to transform to something yet undefined. The lesson here is simple. Don't prepare learners for something. Prepare them for anything!

New Thinking Emerges

John recognized that the educational system was flawed and failing, and that its failures had ramifications. Bringing this recognition to local patrons was a challenge. In many instances, elements of the school community did not see the need, and in some instances, resisted change. Information electronically provided to patrons and stakeholders in real time quickened the realization that change was needed and was inevitable. Crucial to the transformation was a focus on learning and an acknowledgment of the world our children live in, including its technology and social media.

Many years ago, all students in grades 6–12 were issued laptop computers in Van Meter, making Van Meter a 6th–12th-grade "1:1" laptop district. For teachers, this meant developing pedagogy to use technology to enhance and amplify learning. This change led to significant shifts not only in teaching and learning, but also in how Van Meter would begin to leverage social media tools to tell its story and form a new standard for public relations.

John acknowledged the fact that the transformation of the Van Meter School District required some significant changes. Van Meter's direction going forward was to embrace change and build capacity within the organization to make transformation possible. Using traditional tools such as e-mail to send out weekly administrative updates kept stakeholders informed of the progress being made. YouTube videos, blogs, and weekly updates on Twitter responded to and addressed the conditions and emotions generated from change. Without the systematic use of social media as part of a greater public relations effort, stakeholder embracement of these dramatic changes might not have materialized, and this, in turn, might have derailed the transformation of this school district.

Change was a collaborative effort. All leaders across the district used social media to connect and tell the Van Meter story. They shared their thinking and progress in designing a new modality of learning using technology. Utilizing blogs, Google Sites, YouTube, and Twitter, the team built Personal Learning Networks in order to share and grow, as well as to model that behavior for staff. Through social media, synchronicity occurred. Others shared in the findings Van Meter unearthed. In creating the #vanmeter brand, thousands connected through Twitter. As ideas and concepts were shared virtually, they affirmed that the present education system was primed for growth and improvement.

Get Connected, Tell the Story, and Do Not Walk Alone

Because of its size and proximity to Des Moines, Van Meter had little access or coverage by the media. With the exception of monthly *Bulldog Brief* school newsletters and the school web page, Van Meter was isolated. Social media would become the means by which Van Meter would share information with patrons in real time and connect regionally, nationally, and globally. Social media, specifically Twitter, gave Van Meter schools a voice and connections not only to stakeholders but also to educators, politicians, inventors, and business leaders regionally and nationally. Through social media and web-based tools, classrooms moved from being silos of learning to global learning centers. The Van Meter School District's future now had unlimited potential (J. Carver, personal communication, 2018).

TELL YOUR STORY

The Van Meter story teaches us a powerful lesson: If you don't tell your story, someone else will. More often than not, when someone else tells your story, it is one that you don't want told. This is the reality for virtually every school leader. In the past I feared and dreaded the role of public relations as the typical situation played out time and time again. No matter how much progress we made or success we experienced, it was always that one negative story that would dominate the media coverage and sway public opinion. I can vividly remember each news situation that completely blew things out of proportion and greatly distracted from the meaningful and significant work that was occurring on a daily basis.

There is a fundamental problem with the mainstream media when it comes to public relations. That problem is that they are a business. In order to generate business, they must create and promote stories that capture the attentions of their intended audience. Make no mistake about it, the news media wants and needs to make money. When it comes to education, the stories that most often help the media improve their bottom line are those with a negative spin. The more controversial and negative stories are the ones that attract viewers and in turn generate revenue. I don't know about you, but I grew quite resentful of the media in the past as they would be so quick to call my office to get a comment on a negative situation, but would not give me the time of day when I had a positive story for them to cover. Sound familiar? The goal of mainstream media is to increase viewers, ratings, and circulation. In a time of unprecedented education reform efforts and relentless attacks on the profession, leaders regardless of title no longer have to stand by and take the relentless onslaught of a negative press. It's time to change the narrative.

Thankfully this all changed when I discovered the power and value of using social media as a public relations tool. I began to generate our own news related to New Milford High School and quickly learned of the many tools available that could be used at any time from anywhere to tell our story. In essence, I became the storyteller-in-chief. As a result of the innovative work my students and teachers were engaged in, I discovered that there was an abundance of newsworthy content that my stakeholders craved. Instead of reaching out to the news media to cover these stories, we in essence became the news media, using mainstream tools such as Twitter, Facebook, and YouTube. As social media evolved, so too did our public relations strategy to tell our story.

The end result is that the news media began to come to us and/or followed our social media channels to capture our story. After we took control of our public relations, major New York City news outlets such as CBS and NBC—as well as *USA Today, USA Weekend, Education Week,* and *Scholastic Administrator*—all reported positive news stories about us. I literally lost count of additional media coverage, as it became the norm. It also led to the establishment of professional relationships with reporters who wanted to tell accurate and positive stories about innovative schools.

Stories by far are the best way to begin the process of shifting the way stakeholders perceive schools. Even though technology has greatly reduced the attention span of adults and kids alike, a powerful story can captivate an audience regardless of age. The act of storytelling is uniquely human and hardwired into our DNA. Throughout history, stories have been shared through cave drawings, paper, books, audio recordings, and video. Numerous research studies have shown that a well-told story activates the emotional part of the brain, which in turn aids in memory (Murphy Paul, 2012). Figure 9.1 details how storytelling affects specific areas of the brain. The best storytellers are our learners, followed by teachers. As a principal my main job in the area of public relations was to amplify their great work, which was happening on a daily basis just like in every school around the world. Great stories focus on innovative practices that have resulted in evidence of improved learning outcomes.

Digital leadership is about building the capacity to create a solid foundation for positive public relations using social media that complements communication efforts, as described in Chapter 8. It empowers all educators to become the storyteller-in-chief and, in turn, creates a constant flow of information that highlights and focuses on schoolwide success and positive culture. This makes total sense as not only a cost-saving pathway to sharing positive news, but also a practical means to get this information into the hands of stakeholders who frequently rely on and use tools such as Twitter, Facebook, YouTube, and many others.

Figure 9.1   How Storytelling Affects the Brain

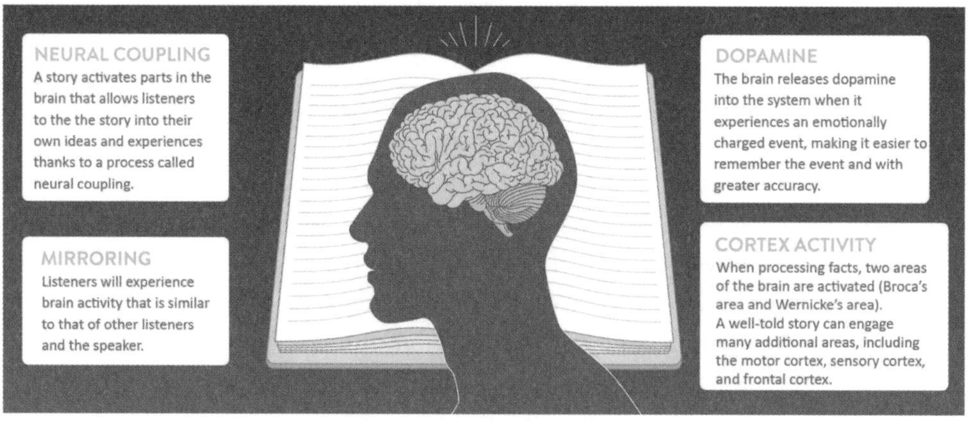

NEURAL COUPLING
A story activates parts in the brain that allows listeners to the the story into their own ideas and experiences thanks to a process called neural coupling.

MIRRORING
Listeners will experience brain activity that is similar to that of other listeners and the speaker.

DOPAMINE
The brain releases dopamine into the system when it experiences an emotionally charged event, making it easier to remember the event and with greater accuracy.

CORTEX ACTIVITY
When processing facts, two areas of the brain are activated (Broca's area and Wernicke's area). A well-told story can engage many additional areas, including the motor cortex, sensory cortex, and frontal cortex.

It is important to note that traditional media outlets still have immense value in terms of reach and influence, especially with those stakeholders who have yet to fully embrace social media as a way to access information. Digital leaders fully understand this and work to build relationships with local, national, and global reporters in an effort to flood the airways with as much positive news as possible to create a more accurate narrative. A successful public relations strategy focuses on stories being spread across a wide range of media, including television, radio, print (newspapers and magazines), and digital devices.

Social media integration for public relations should no longer be optional for schools. Whereas its use for communication provides basic information in a timely fashion, digital leaders take it to another level by crafting specific, positive messages. Social media allow leaders to create unique communities for their schools/districts, establish a digital presence, construct feedback mechanisms on websites and other spaces, and welcome stakeholders into a conversation. Here are six reasons why a public relations strategy through the consistent use of social media matters:

1. Build and enhance relationships.

2. Engage people near and far in conversations about awesome work in your schools.

3. Give everyone a voice, from learners to teachers to administrators to community members.

4. Learn from each other. The best ideas are those being shared by practitioners in the field who have experienced success amidst an array of challenges.

5. Share ownership. Now everyone can be a storyteller, which helps to increase motivation while building greater capacity for change.

6. Catalyze further change. The more we share, the greater the chances of moving innovative and successful practices from isolated pockets of excellence to systemic components of school culture.

Upon becoming principal of New Milford High School, I made it one of my primary goals to work hard at sharing all of the accomplishments centered around teaching and learning occurring with my stakeholders on a routine basis. As principal, I was aware of these things, but I was pretty sure that the majority of the educational community was not. Combined with the fact that the local media were finicky when it came to reporting on the many positive things occurring at my school (or any school, for that matter), I decided that it was up to me to take control of our public relations.

It was at this point that I created the monthly *Principal's Report* that could be viewed on the main page of our high school website. Even though it was simplistic from an aesthetic standpoint, this document was a powerhouse when it came to the depth of information that it contained, as detailed in Chapter 8. Then social media came into my life. My immersion in Twitter made me realize that I could take my public relations plan to a whole new level. As I continuously learned about other social media tools, I began to diversify the types of information shared and how it was disseminated. This necessitated the creation of a media waiver (Online Resource 9.1) in order to share information related to students.

Here is what your digital public relations strategy could look like:

- **Principal's report or district newsletter:** A monthly summary of achievements and advancements that have a positive impact on teaching, learning, and school culture. This can be a stand-alone document on a school website or something more dynamic, such as a blog. The benefits of having this information in a blog format are that it encourages stakeholder engagement, since readers can comment on the posts.

- **Twitter:** Daily updates on news, events, student achievements, staff innovations, et cetera. It is also another medium for distribution of the detailed report explained above or mainstream news articles using links. Capturing moments through pictures, video, and text as they happen has proven to be a powerful method of improving a school's public relations plan, as stakeholders receive this information at home or on the go through mobile devices.

- **Facebook page:** This serves the same purpose as a school Twitter account, but this tool has much more influence, as many more stakeholders, including graduates, utilize Facebook on a daily basis. In addition to school-generated material, public relations efforts are maximized when links to mainstream news articles are added to a school's page. Once established, a link to the Facebook page can be placed on the school website.

- **Picture tools:** A picture is worth approximately a thousand words. Instagram is the most powerful picture sharing tool available. It provides leaders with the ability to share and showcase students, staff, and events through pictures. Separate accounts can be set up just for the school. A link to pictures from Instagram can easily be shared across other social networks.

- **Video tools:** Well-known tools such as YouTube and Vimeo allow leaders to share and showcase students, staff, and events through video. A one-minute video equates to about 1.8 million written words. YouTube is great for video clips of around 15 minutes or less, but this can be extended by visiting www.youtube.com/verify. Vimeo will support larger video uploads. Separate accounts can be created just for schools to post entire events such as concerts, student announcements, or athletic competitions, or to highlight montages created using popular technology tools such as iMovie. Many schools across the country are now creating promotional videos and trailers using iMovie as a part of their public relations plans. The ability to shoot video from smartphones and tablets and easily create short videos using available templates has become a hallmark for digital leaders anticipating how to better engage their stakeholders. Live videos can be streamed using a variety of tools such as Facebook Live, Periscope, IGTV (Instagram TV), and Ustream. These free services allow leaders to stream live video and archive it to share at a later time. They can be used to make events such as graduation, guest speakers, athletics, musical productions, and concerts available to a greater audience.

- **Blogs:** There is no better tool for sharing detailed student and staff accomplishments. They allow for detailed descriptions of classroom innovations, summaries of school events, descriptions of large construction projects, student guest posts, and state-of-the-school/district messages. Most important, they allow leaders to tell their powerful stories using a mash-up of multimedia content. Video, images, audio, and links to supporting content can be seamlessly integrated to create a more engaging experience for stakeholders. As leaders become more tech savvy, each blogging tool offers specialized widgets to customize the blog. Widgets enable bloggers to modify the design and content of their blogs without any HTML knowledge. The three most popular platforms are Google Blogger, WordPress, and Medium.

Let me add some context to the above strategies. After putting an action plan in place to improve our Advanced Placement (AP) scores, we saw a 20% increase on average from historical lows over three straight years. I blogged about how we accomplished this feat, explaining how we accomplished these gains. Four years into our digital transformation, we saw some impressive gains in student achievement and were acknowledged not just in New Jersey, but also nationally. I bought plaques for the sole reason of being able to take pictures of them on Instagram. Once I had the picture, I shared it using an e-mail blast, Twitter, LinkedIn, Remind, Facebook, and our school app. During walks-throughs and observations, I always took pictures and videos of innovative practices in action. These were then amplified the same way as the plaques (Figure 9.2).

WE NEED MORE STORIES OF SUCCESS

Educational transformation is occurring throughout the world, with rural areas facing many of the same challenges as urban areas. Population shifts, shrinking populations, how to prepare youth for the bold new world, and jobs are all common themes. Rural Iowa

Figure 9.2   Amplifying Success

also faced the challenge of connectivity and providing course offerings. The Howard-Winneshiek Community School District is a community of 1,300 students located in rural northeastern Iowa and was fortunate to have John Carver at the helm there as well. With elementary campuses located in Elma, Lime Springs, and Cresco, and junior high and high school campuses also in Cresco, the district spread out over 462 square miles. The district's mission statement, "To prepare and empower our students to think creatively, serve, contribute, and succeed locally and globally," illustrated the community's commitment.

Howard-Winneshiek Community School District established a hashtag on Twitter to enhance its public relations. The purpose of this public relations strategy was to showcase how the district was going to prepare their fifth grade for the new world of work. The goal of the district was that, years into the future, a new educational system would be in place. This new system of learning would identify student passions and strengths, and then utilize social media and digital tools to differentiate instruction, connect learners, and allow creative ways to demonstrate understanding. A strategic outcome for students was to develop their imagination. Supports and protocols were established to support young entrepreneurs.

At the time, iPads were issued to sixth, seventh, and eighth graders, and interactive whiteboards were placed in all classrooms. Digital devices were placed in the hands of high school students. Twitter, e-mail, and text messages were used to notify stakeholders of school delays and closings due to weather. The Howard-Winneshiek Board of Education established a Twitter presence and followed district happenings. Former Iowa lieutenant governor Kim Reynolds shared that she followed tweets shared by Howard-Winneshiek School District. Skype and iChat were used to provide real-time video connections. This, in turn, helped to facilitate differentiated instruction and learning projects between Howard-Winneshiek elementary classrooms and the world. *The Weekly Administrative Update* was sent out electronically to stakeholders, and the district created its own YouTube channel.

All of these social media efforts connected a small, rural community with the rest of Iowa and beyond. For rural communities like this one, social media is the best tool for public relations. These communities finally have a voice and are telling their stories. Howard-Winneshiek participated in and provided leadership at the regional and state level for the Governor's Science, Technology, Engineering and Math (STEM) initiative. Partnering with Northeast Iowa Community College and with support from the Keystone Area Education Association, the district moved rapidly to build a K–12 STEM talent pipeline. The Howard-Winneshiek Board of Education's desire was to "position the Howard-Winneshiek schools as the educational destination for the region," and in doing so embraced a belief that "it's all about quality service." Because of this thinking, the rate of change at Howard-Winneshiek accelerated exponentially. The biggest challenge facing Howard-Winneshiek and rural Iowa continues to be obtaining broadband connectivity. There are large gaps in coverage across Iowa and many other parts across the world, and this must be addressed in order to continue to move forward.

As leaders begin to integrate social media tools into their public relations plans, they will begin the process of making their schools more transparent, and they will evolve into the role of storyteller-in-chief. This transparency will give stakeholders a clearer picture of all of the many positive things taking place each and every day. Each tool listed above should be linked to current school websites. URLs should be added to all print materials and e-mail signatures in order to maximize exposure to these sources of information. In time, a greater sense of pride will develop, as stakeholders will be more knowledgeable about the great work being done.

SUMMARY

Historically, the ability to share thinking and perspective has been limited to those who had money and was subject to filters and "editors." These "screens" determined what ideas and thoughts went forward. Digital devices connected to the internet and utilizing social network tools have leveled the playing field. Today, any person, any age, anywhere, at any time can connect with any person, any age, anywhere, at any time to share thinking and create, and the outcomes are "going viral." We are truly no longer "I" but "we." The tools to take ownership over public relations will surely change, but the need to disseminate powerful stories will not. Leverage the tools available aligned to the strategies presented in this chapter to move your stakeholders from a state of perception to reality. Greatness is a part of all schools. Make sure people know this fact.

GUIDING QUESTIONS

1. How many times has the mainstream media covered a positive story about your school or district this past year? What steps can you take to increase this number?

2. What does your current public relations strategy look like? How can this be improved?

3. Explain what tools are used for public relations and how. What other tools can be embraced, and where are there opportunities for growth?

4. Discuss successes in your school, district, or at an individual level. How will you commit to sharing these on a consistent basis?

iStock.com/cnythzl

Branding

10

> People will forget what you said, people will forget what you did, but people will never forget how you made them feel.
>
> —Maya Angelou

Communication and public relations can be treated either as two different entities or as two essential leadership strategies that work in concert with one another. Digital leaders seize on the latter while building a powerful brand presence for their institutions and/or leadership style. Trish Rubin knows branding matters in a changing world of learning fueled by powerful digital resources. She presents one simple definition of brand that connects with your innovative role as an educational leader in a digital world: *Brand is a distinctive sum experience people have with a product, service, or experience* (T. Rubin, personal communication, 2018). Whether they know it or not, leaders who have integrated social media as a component of their communications and public relations strategies have already begun the process of establishing a brand presence. Those who are not leveraging digital tools run the risk of having their brand presence created for them by others, which might not be a good thing. We all have a choice now. Define or be defined. Digital leadership focuses on behaviors and specific strategies that will create a positive brand presence, which, in turn, will instill a greater sense of pride in the leaders' work and/or school function.

From her own journey, Trish knows school leaders are responsible for the sum experience people have with educational products and services. She believes professional conversations about developing, delivering, and maintaining excellence can be enriched with two discussion topics on *brandED*, an educationalist view of branding that fuses the brand concept with education. Trish Rubin stands at the intersection of a life in education with an encore career in business. Her résumé is one of a teacher, school administrator, and national literacy thought leader. Today, Trish's business calling card identifies her as a business brand strategist, but she has the heart of an educator and takes every chance to blend her experience in schools with her communication work in business.

A MOVE TO *brandED* THINKING

Trish's career path led me to wonder, "Can a smart school leader use a business concept to inform educational practice in a digital world?" The answer is yes. In our vision, *brandEd* school conversations are led not by a business executive but by a progressive school leader possessing digital tools and an interest in a brand's benefit to three educational outcomes: school *culture, performance,* and *resources* (Sheninger & Rubin, 2017). Trish has seen instructional managers quickly build and communicate distinctive educational "products and services" using elements of a *brandED* campaign, and forecasts that more educational leaders will choose this actionable path. The digital world empowers leaders across an expanding social media landscape to do so. Despite misguided reforms and the argument that educational change happens at a glacial pace, a digital school leader can create unique brand value to support excellence as seamlessly as the ad men and women of yesterday, and without the three-martini lunches! This can be accomplished at the district, school, and classroom levels and on the individual professional level.

From her office in New York City, Trish made her connection with me serendipitously as I was building my school's visibility on a nightly news broadcast, one of the benefits of exciting opportunities for my school through the business of my own *brandED* thinking. At the time I really had no concept of creating or leveraging a brand as part of a leadership strategy. Over time I realized that a positive brand presence materialized organically through the consistent creation and sharing of content as part of communication and public relations efforts. As they say, the proof is in the pudding. Over a period of five years, New York City news outlets composing the number one media market in the world covered positive stories at my school over 15 times. Our school brand also led to hundreds of thousands of dollars of free technology, professional development, trips for staff abroad, and invitations to present on our work at conferences near and far.

Why *brandED* Thinking?
A Look at Brand History

BrandED may be a new term, but branding isn't a new concept. Decanters of wine found in the ruins of Pompeii attest to early "labeling" of product. Today, brand impacts politics and purchasing. *Passion* is Spain's one-word "nation brand," according to UK brand theorist Wally Olins (2008). Nation branding is a science that sells, and it is similar to the science of branding the next popular children's toy. Big returns are at stake in both efforts. You think the word *brand* is overused? That's the power of a word on digital steroids. The brand conversation is everywhere. This pervasive *B* word is no longer restricted to corporate marketing meetings.

Early in the twentieth century, the Morton Salt girl and the Quaker Oats man heralded the birth of mass brand presence in the marketplace. In the 1960s, brand moved beyond packaging. *Mad Men* executives created product "personalities." The Marlboro Man and the Maytag Repair Man built relationships with the consumer through the "social media" driver of the day, the color television. In New York City, Madison Avenue's separate advertising teams and creative departments merged, giving birth to the science of brand building. You can argue that today's products and services are sold online in a blink, no creative team necessary, but the real science of knowing how to *successfully* brand remains a form of art. This is strategic, not magical, thinking.

In the digital age, brand building isn't limited to a business-oriented crowd. Brand thinking—building compelling missions and campaigns—is possible for millions who own computers or smart-phones. When digital parents in your school community develop web pages and social media accounts for the unborn, complete with naming campaigns, they are launching a personal brand. Despite some of the laughable misuses, the concept is still a serious com-ponent of business—and can be for education. Your community is plugged in digitally and is already impacting your institutional brand, for better or worse. Like Trish, digital leaders see the inherent value of establishing a brand presence in today's world.

Historically, brand is based on building relationships, and relation-ships are key to brand campaigning in education. Aren't educators always building, brokering, and sustaining relationships? With a *brandED* mindset, "initiating" relationships becomes a first step. Strategic brand is grown through mutual trust and good faith, as you strategically initiate new connections. You can grow your own professional brand personality as well as that of your insti-tution by purposefully creating relationships that lead to school improvement.

The shift from business to education brand is simple. *BrandED* is about *telling,* not *selling,* in order to build powerful relationships with all school stakeholders (Sheninger & Rubin, 2017). Trish and I go on to expand our thinking on this concept:

> *BrandED* tenets are about trust, loyalty, promise, and cre-ating better offerings and innovations that distinguish the educational brand experience for every user including kids, parents, teachers and community. A brand isn't a short-term fix or a fad, but a way to strategically build a school's assets in a transparent digital world. No more Ivory Towers. *BrandED* is about a genuine personality that can impact school culture, achievement and resources. (p. 3)

It is more important than ever to embrace the power of establish-ing a positive brand presence in education. In the field of educa-tion, schools are considered a brand whether you like it or not.

They promise value in terms of academic preparation to succeed in society. To disagree with this notion discounts the fact that digital identities are created for everything by the click of a button and various social media posts. Leaders must be cognizant of this fact and proactively work to create a digital presence that conveys all of the good that happens each and every day in schools across the world.

TWO CONVERSATIONS AROUND *brandED* THINKING

There are two *brandED* conversations to test the thinking about bringing the benefits of a business marketing concept to your school, district, or organization:

1. The one about your professional brand

2. The one about your school's brand

The first conversation is reflective. It's about developing your own brand, not to celebrity star level, but one that creates a leadership personality to spark new professional effectiveness. The second conversation is shared with the community where *brandED* thinking is introduced and the idea of delivering on a promise of excellence for educational "product and service." Once you have sorted out your professional personality and begin to live it across the digital landscape, teaching your own stakeholders makes you as creative as any top tier marketer.

Conversation One: Professional Brand

Ask yourself, Do I need a professional brand? With an eye on the growing digital world, Trish believes the answer is yes (T. Rubin, personal communication, 2018). You need what business guru Tom Peters (1999) calls a "Brand YOU"—one that is based on a core belief. It's what you stand for and who you are. As nations do in building their brands, reduce it to a word and run with it. CBS journalist Lee Woodruff, the wife of the nearly fatally injured reporter Bob Woodruff, has a personal brand of "Resilience," and all her work and relationships are informed by that one word. If you want to build a *brandED* conversation, start with your own brand-naming project.

Call it a personal brand; call it a professional brand or your brand personality. Live it. Become the purveyor of purposeful, visible behaviors that initiate and build relationships and connections, both face to face and on social media. This kind of professional brand does not have to be personally transparent. It should communicate, but it does not have to be intrusive. You don't have to share your favorite color or where you spent last summer as you build your brand on social media spaces such as LinkedIn, Facebook, Instagram, and Twitter.

Take a page from business. Think USP, *unique selling proposition.* Think Volvo, whose famous USP is "Safety." Volvo sells safety in a word. Your own brand is a genuine sell. You may already have a strong sense of personal brand if you are part of the digital landscape, but if you've shied away because social media seems to be an "all-about-me" effort, get beyond that. This isn't egocentric behavior; it's leadership survival in a digital world of messaging and a means to an educational end. Be the storyteller-in-chief of your brand effort. This effort creates loyalty and trust, the kind that made mega brands like Apple and Starbucks successfully develop with their markets.

If you don't intentionally claim your brand, some stakeholder on the other end of a computer will do it for you. Anyone with a smartphone today can define you and your school(s). Take charge of digital and real-time presence. You can build the institutional brand upon your solid foundation inherent in the learning culture where you work. Think about who can help you create a powerful brand presence. For me, it was Trish Rubin, and we have been engaged in dynamic conversations about the place of branding in my professional learning since 2009. She suggests starting your *brandED* mission by becoming a "*brandED* ace" (T. Rubin, personal communication, 2018). Digital leadership drives leaders to develop their own brand, which happens as they interact in online spaces through the use of social media. These interactions define one's thoughts, beliefs, and opinions on education and leadership. Digital leadership also reflects how research has been utilized to inform innovative change and provide evidence of actual improvement that validates efficacy. Digital leaders also provide examples of work, ideas, awards, and other types of recognition. All of these combined form an educational brand presence.

When you know your *why* and *how,* the stage is set to build a *brandED* presence. It is then time to associate, create, and engage.

Make yourself visible by choosing to associate with communities in real time and online as you initiate relationships. Create interest around what you do and say and the content you share with those communities. Finally, engage digitally and face to face with partners to acquire resources and discover opportunity in your effort. I try to advance some of the best minds in the field for leaders to study, such as Dan Pink, Sir Ken Robinson, Seth Godin, Jon Gordon, Michael Fullan, Adam Grant, and Lolly Daskal. Through the work of these individuals, leaders can mine subtle and not-so-subtle strategies that pertain to the personal branding conversation of thousands of people in the leadership and education space, and not just marketers and salespeople. Brand is a professional fit. Face it. Educators are in the business of building relationships to consistently move a learning culture forward. Trish speaks of how as a teacher she sold the value of education to kids, parents, bosses, other teachers, and businesses. How much easier would it be now with a clear personal brand in place?

Ask yourself, What's the return? Trish sees the *brandED* "collision" of business thinking and education as a powerful opportunity for leaders to create a new, more engaging presence. No more ivory towers. Thomas Friedman (2005), author of *The World Is Flat,* called this an "imagination mash-up"— that is, thinking that combines business and education in a dynamic way. A *brandED* leader expands relationships with business and education partners for better schools. A professional brand creates the ROI—what business calls a return on investment. This investment yields institutional return through improved school culture, school performance, and school resources.

Conversation Two: School Brand

Does leadership brand impact school culture? You've created your relational brand. Connect it to school improvement. Communicate a brand promise for improving your school's culture, achievement, and resourcing. These initial discussions should revolve around school culture. Ask your team how you are communicating your brand to the community. Your innovative thinking signals exciting change for your team. Encourage them to examine their own thinking. Ferriter, Ramsden, and Sheninger (2011) identified the following factors that go into a school's brand:

- **Student achievement:** Standardized test scores are most often used to evaluate the overall effectiveness of a school. Public relations and communication efforts focused on growth evidence in this area can be conveyed through social media. Doing so will help to create and strengthen a school's brand presence.

- **Quality of teachers and administrators:** Student achievement is directly linked to the quality of the staff at a school. Stakeholders are often more than willing to move to towns with higher taxes that attract the best and brightest educators. Utilizing social media to convey staff statistics can build the confidence of any community, which has a positive impact on a school's brand.

- **Innovative instructional practices and programs:** Course offerings, curricular decisions, unique programs, and innovative instructional practices play a key role in student engagement while having a positive impact on student outcomes (Whitehurst, 2009). Schools that have unique course offerings, curricula, and programs make a school or district stand out. The publication and dissemination of this information sends a powerful message related to college and career readiness and the ability of students to follow their passions.

- **Extracurricular activities:** Extracurricular activities are a valued component of any school community and help to develop well-rounded students. Leaders who use social media as part of a combined communications and public relations strategy will not only spotlight these activities, but also gain the attention of stakeholders.

Extend the conversation to include institutional brand and recruit an invested community. Private schools have long flourished under institutional branding. Today, social media, word-of-mouth, and conversational marketing using digital tools can quickly build identity that took private schools years to build. All K–12 schools, public and private, can use digital strategies to establish a brand to build a following just as private schools have done for years through traditional means. Your "market" is the entire community of stakeholders. Engage them in a strategy that creates a pervasive school culture to unify, create excellence, and attract followers who want to take part in the brand of your school. Figure 10.1 summarizes how *brandED* thinking can be amplified when digital leaders harness tech tools of today.

Ask your community members if they want to go beyond the logo to a brand of school improvement. Encourage thinking beyond a logo,

Figure 10.1 Amplifying *BrandED* Thinking With Social Media

a mascot, and a typical educator mission statement to build visible signals of *brandED*. Study your school's mission statement with a new eye on marketing. That's the first public signal of change. What makes your web-page mission statement different from that of any other school that offers value to stakeholders? Does it inspire trust? Suggest a deep belief in what the school is about? Microsoft's Bill Gates knew what he was about. His company's vision statement for 30 years was simple: "A computer on every desk."

Tie the threads of existing efforts for school achievement together. Anchor them as *"brandED* conversations" for improvement (Sheninger & Rubin, 2017). As you lead your community, look toward funding/resourcing possibilities. With a brand campaign, the words *student achievement and innovation* become authentic. Not achievement for the sake of a number on a test report, but achievement that is reflected by the authentic culture of learning that the school demonstrates every single day.

Digital leadership is about making your community a part of new school resourcing through brand building. Trish talks about the "thousand-people-who-know-you" rule in mass marketing as a guide for your campaign. As you begin, focus effort on serving a small part of the market and keep them happy. Your most loyal fans are already with you. As you begin to tell your own brand story through social media and digital contacts, these people will be your biggest supporters, and they will initiate more to the cause. Identify your core group. Create the movement with these cheerleaders.

Marketing isn't really a new concept for schools that have benefited from limited word of mouth and sporadic public relations in the local daily paper. In your *brandED* initiative, however, digital marketing—that is, communicating with wider audiences about school product or service—is innovative and sustaining. In the digital world, your supporters could be sitting down the street or eight thousand miles away. Engage them with the same marketing messages that keep them supportive. Promoting the school brand gets the word out about school culture and achievement. Your campaign can attract and retain people who care about education. Just think how many more budgets would be approved if the school brand were marketed more strongly and more personally every day.

When Trish Rubin gets excited about branding, it is because she sees its unique possibilities for school resourcing and funding. Imagine the intellect, talent, and means that your graduates hold and the marketing opportunities they present. Share the brand with graduates. Engage them with your current stakeholders. Most of your graduates live online, so virtually campaign to welcome them home and share the educational experience you are building with parents, students, and community. Bringing back graduates through a marketing campaign of social media and direct word of mouth can make a difference in getting financial and community resources of all kinds for your school.

Both school branding conversations are summarized in Figure 10.2.

Figure 10.2 *BrandED* School Leadership

BrandED Identity			
Build	**Positioning**	**Vision**	**Personality**
	Where do I stand as an educator? • My values • My unique perspective	How do I use my brand to benefit? • School culture • Student achievement • Funding • Resourcing	What's my unique selling proposition (USP)? • One word that illustrates my *BrandED* view for my community
BrandED Pillars of Action (ACE—Associate, Create, Engage)			
Share	**Associate**	**Create**	**Engage**
	• Become relational. • Join diverse communities. • Support groups. • Balance real-time with online connections. • Choose causes that reflect your brand.	• See yourself as a product. • Market your value across communities. • Develop real-time and online interests. • Create and share content. • Present yourself as a thought leader.	• Be transparent to your comfort level. • Join daily conversations online and in real time. • Be a connector of others. • Give before you get.

Source: Copyright © Trish Rubin (2013, March). Adapted with permission. www.trishnyc.com

WHY A *brandED* MINDSET MATTERS

> In the animal kingdom, the rule is, eat or be eaten; in the human kingdom, define or be defined.
>
> —Thomas Szasz

Here is a reality check for everyone that does not believe in the value of branding in education. Your brand is what stakeholders and others say about you as well as your district/school. Social media has changed the landscape and broadened the concept of branding to education as discussed previously in this chapter, whether you like it or not. Your digital footprint is crafted by not only what you create and post, but also what other people and organizations create and post about you. Just do a simple Google search and see for yourself. You might very well be surprised what's out there in regard to you and your school/district.

Now more than ever, educators, leaders, schools, and districts need to begin to think about a brand strategy. This is essential to not only control the narrative but to also be proactive in order to deal with negative content that can tarnish an image while influencing the perception of key stakeholders. It is important to always differentiate between a brand in the business sense and one in education. A brand in business is meant to sell. On the other hand, a brand in education is meant to build support, admiration, and respect for the honorable work you do each day for kids. By developing and enhancing our school and professional brand, we move past a developed perception of our admirable work by providing a necessary reality for all stakeholders to embrace and celebrate. Thus, a brand in education has nothing to do with selling, but showcasing work of students, staff, and leaders in an effort to become more transparent. Digital leaders understand the importance of branding in their work, and by leaders, I mean any and all educators who take action to improve learning opportunities for their students and themselves.

Here are some specific reasons why a *brandED* mindset matters (Sheninger & Rubin, 2017):

- Your brand will attract others to your work and that of your school. This can result in more qualified candidates applying for jobs, greater stakeholder support, or parents deciding to move to your district. It can also result in building a more vibrant learning network.

- It promotes recognition of amazing work that takes place in schools each and every day. With social media, anyone can now craft an accurate narrative of how our schools are preparing students for success.

- A positive brand presence motivates and inspires your staff/coworkers as well as colleagues across the globe in terms of what is truly possible. Success is amplified in a way that others can then replicate it.

- Your brand tells stakeholders about your school DNA. From logos, mascots, tweets, and hashtags, a positive brand presence helps you tell the real story.

- A positive *brandED* presence clearly articulates to stakeholders what to expect from your district, school, or you as a professional. This promise not only builds precious support but also invaluable relationships.

- A clear *brandED* strategy helps you stay focused on your mission, vision, and values related to your work to ensure the success of all students.

- By reaching people at an emotional level, a brand builds stronger relationships with key stakeholders. There is no better way to do this than consistently sharing ways that you are making a positive difference in the life of kids each day.

The foundation of a *brandED* mindset is focusing on sharing valuable content related to the mission, vision, and values of your school/ district or what you embrace as an educator. It requires a focus on strategies and ideas that are being successfully implemented to positively impact student learning. A positive brand presence will develop organically by using this simple equation:

Communications + Public Relations = *brandED*

The strategies and concepts presented in chapters 8 and 9 will help you to develop a powerful brand presence. It begins with improving communications. We must consistently meet stakeholders where they are at by employing a multifaceted approach to engage them in two-way communications. Digital and nondigital strategies are used to not only communicate important information but also become more transparent. It is also incumbent upon all leaders regardless of position to take control of their public relations. If you don't tell your story, someone else will. When you roll the dice and take this gamble, it typically results in a negative story being told. In education, we do not brag enough, and as a result, we pay the price dearly. By becoming the storyteller-in-chief you can turn this tide and take control of public relations for good. There is so much power in stories, and we must do a better job of sharing them.

Dr. Robert Zywicki, the superintendent of the Mount Olive School District, harnessed the power of branding when he was at the helm of the Weehawken Township School District in New Jersey. He utilized Twitter extensively to engage the community in districtwide reform, as well as showcase products of student work. Zywicki utilized Twitter and other social media tools to document the day-to-day transformation while simultaneously developing the district's brand of innovation and move to 1:1 learning. Evidence of this spread throughout the community, including a student-created district digital mission statement using creative hashtags that played on the district's name and verbs that related to student engagement and involvement. As part of his district branding efforts, he created a one-page document that outlined the three-year plan that could easily be displayed and shared everywhere. Figure 10.3 illustrates the image that was created as part of Dr. Zywicki's commitment to *brandED* strategy and thinking.

THE RIGHT HASHTAG

When it comes to branding, the hashtag (#) is everything. So why is it so important? A hashtag allows you to organize all of your messages on a variety of social media platforms (Twitter, Facebook, Instagram, and LinkedIn) together in one place. Think of it as a label for content. It assists educators who are interested in a certain topic or conversation to quickly find content on that topic. It represents a great way to curate everything you share so others can easily find or hear about what is happening in your district, school, or classroom. Once a hashtag is added to the end of a social media update on the above-mentioned sites, a hyperlink is created. When you or someone clicks on that link, it will take you to an entirely separate page that contains all of the updates that used that hashtag.

There are no specific rules for creating one. It can be as long or short as you'd like, but my advice is keep it as brief as possible, yet unique. Whatever you come up with should also align as much as possible to your vision or identifiable features of your learning culture. For example, Wells Elementary School in Cypress, Texas, created and exclusively uses #ExploreWells. Their mascot is the Explorers, and the rationale behind that hashtag is that all updates shared connect in some way or form to how students are exploring learning on a day-to-day basis. The Fall Creek School District in Fall Creek, Wisconsin, uses #GoCrickets. They have this hashtag on not only every social media post, but also on nondigital items such as t-shirts and spirit gear. In the case of both Wells and Fall Creek, the strategy is as simple as it is powerful. Rally stakeholders around the hashtag, where great information about students and the learning culture is consistently shared.

Figure 10.3 Weehawken School District Strategic Plan

WEEHAWKEN
SCHOOL DISTRICT

2016–19 STRATEGIC PLAN

Vision
Equity, Personalization, and Innovation

Mission
The Weehawken Township School District is a progressive, student-centered community of learners in pursuit of collective and individual excellence. To this end, we will implement systems and structures that ensure all students will achieve at their maximum academic potential, develop values that embrace civic responsibility, and hone skills to adapt to a dynamic global society.

2016–19 Strategic Goals
I.   Increase student achievement at all grade levels.
II. Enhance students' social, emotional, and and non-cognitive development.
III. Recruit, develop, and retain a high-performing and diverse workforce that utilizes research-based best practices.
IV. Engage families and the community-at-large in support of the District's Vision and Mission.
V.   Operate with integrity, effectiveness, compliance, transparency, and fiscal responsibility.

2016–2017 Strategies
- Map all standards-based curricula via teacher PLCs as per the NJQSAC District Improvement Plan.
- Implement and evaluate blended learning in all schools.
- Institutionalize a comprehensive Response to Intervention program.
- Increase stakeholder engagement by publicizing student achievement via social media, the web, and traditional print media.
- Develop faculty and institutionalize best practices via the 2016-18 District PD Goals.
- Establish school-wide social emotional and character education programs.
- Complete a long-range facilities plan.
- Engage stakeholders in a research-based evaluation of the Academically Talented Program.
- Continue recruiting efforts utilizing the Applitrack platform.

2016–17 SMART Goals
1. Map Stage One of all curricula by November 15, 2016 and Stage Two by June 1, 2017.
2. Maintain an adjusted cohort graduation rate of at least 90%.
3. Produce at least 10 press releases related to student achievement, curriculum, and instruction.
4. Increase faculty acquisition of professional development hours by at least 10% since 2015-16.
5. Reduce the suspension rate by 10% since 2015-16.
6. Reduce the instances of HIB by 5% since 2015-16.
7. Increase the number of PARCC "Met Expectations" scores in each tested level by at least 5% since 2015-16.
8. Increase AP Course Participation by 10% since 2015-16.
9. Increase SAT/ACT Participation by 10% since 2015-16.
10. Evaluate the reading level of 100% of the students in grades 1-6 utilizing the Diagnostic Reading Assessment at least four times during 2016-17.
11. Engage parents in at least four open forum meetings.
12. Publish a final report from the Academically Talented Program Committee by May 1, 2017.
13. Publish a long-range facilities plan by December 1, 2016.

Dr. Robert R. Zywicki, *Superintendent of Schools*
WeehawkenSchools.net | @WeehawkenTSD

SUMMARY

In a word, persevere. Let business-branding history inspire you to make your own *brandED* history. Creating a positive brand presence in the digital world takes patience, but the returns are there for you and your school stakeholders. The creation and maintenance of a *brandED* identity rely on the consistent and targeted use of social media for school communications and public relations. When combined with traditional methods, a leader's and school's brand will be established and resonate throughout the school and education community. The resulting message will inform and promote all the positive aspects of leadership, education, and established school culture. Leaders in a digital world understand and embrace lessons from the private sector to better connect and engage with all stakeholders in the twenty-first century. It's time to become the storyteller-in-chief.

GUIDING QUESTIONS

1. How are you consistently showing value to your community (current and prospective)?

2. What does it look like to authentically engage the community and build a positive brand presence to showcase your work with students? How can this be accomplished and sustained?

3. If you Google you or your school/district, what comes up? Does your digital identity align with reality?

4. How are you branding your school or district effectively? What action steps do you need to take to either begin or improve your branding efforts?

iStock.com/Urupong

Discovering Opportunity

11

If opportunity doesn't knock, build a door.

—Milton Berle

I love the quote above. It did not resonate with me early in my career as a school administrator, but later became sort of a personal mantra. For years I always looked at the world through a glass-half-empty lens. Challenges morphed into excuses, and in the end, nothing changed. In a sense, I wasn't pushed to be innovative or bring about substantive changes that genuinely impacted school culture in powerful ways. The same old thinking typically leads to the same old results. However, in disruptive times a traditionalist mindset can lead our schools and us further down a path of obscurity.

In these difficult and uncertain economic times, it is imperative that school leaders maintain and improve upon existing programs and initiatives focused on providing students with the tools for success in a digital world. Bold leadership is needed to continue to move schools forward while increasing engagement, enhancing learning, and improving student achievement. Digital leadership does not succumb to excuses imposed by the pressures of education reform or economic instability. Instead, it focuses on finding innovative solutions to deliver authentic learning experiences and support to continuously provide the best learning opportunities for students.

Opportunity presents itself in many ways and is defined as a set of circumstances that makes it possible to do something. I love this definition, as there are so many apparent connections to a growth mindset, entrepreneurship, and innovation. However, we must understand that opportunities will not just drop in our laps if a culture of possibility is not developed. You can always wish for something, and if you are lucky, it might come true. Unfortunately, this is not realistic or practical. On the other hand, you can act to create a different and better culture defined by actual outcomes aligned with improvement.

STRATEGIC PARTNERSHIPS

It is hard to imagine that years ago, parents, partnerships, and programs were running from the Maplewood Richmond Heights School District, Missouri, like it was infected with an educational virus. There was no sensible reason for outside resources to attach themselves to the district, because it was failing its community in many ways. Fast-forward to the present, and incredible opportunities for kids are spilling from every corner of the district. This would not be possible without the resources, programming, and people power that it received from its community, national, and global partners. Many of these initiatives were pursued and implemented as a result of the leadership of Robert Dillon, former principal of Maplewood Richmond Heights Middle School.

During this journey toward becoming an interconnected district with fluid learning partnerships, a tipping point occurred when community partners were energized by the mission and core drive of the organization. This energy created a desire for more and more partners to reach out to the district, so that they could be attached to the train of innovation that was moving at a rapid clip.

During this period, the staff and students of the district experienced another level of excitement, as it was now flush with new ideas and fresh ways to promote energized learning in kids. The Maplewood Richmond Heights School District was emboldened by this shift, and teachers and students leaned into the possibilities that emerged.

Throughout this period, some worried that this wave of opportunities would flood the system and blur the focus, causing mission drift. The theory was that exposing an organization to a myriad of community resources would drag the district toward the mission of the partners as opposed to the partners supporting the core work of the school. To combat this, it was essential for the school leaders at Maplewood Richmond Heights to remain steadfast to molding its portfolio of partnerships to surround its cornerstones of learning: leadership, scholarship, citizenship, and stewardship.

Another way that the Maplewood Richmond Heights School District was able to attract new opportunities was to craft a fresh vision that energized the community and beyond. Partners aren't looking for schools that have a mission that slips quietly into the mix of over 90% of schools doing education. It is key for innovative school and district leaders to brand their niche, their story, their unique space in the cacophony of educational conversation as detailed in Chapter 10. Only then will schools, districts, and organizations attract the best partners that can be sustained over time (R. Dillon, personal communication, 2013).

The Maplewood Richmond Heights School District took a systematic approach to building a robust set of resources and partnerships to support its students. These partnerships included university, mental health, interschool, experiential learning, corporate, and community partners. This vast network varies in its density of work with students, but each partnership provides time, talent, and treasured opportunities to enrich the educational experiences of the kids.

In a time when interconnectedness is easier than ever to achieve, finding these partnerships has been aided by the continuous flow of resources available through social media outlets, especially through educators using Twitter to mine the vast educational landscape for ideas and possibilities. The strategic use of social media spread throughout the district, from a few early adopters to teacher leaders to students. The following are some of the specific benefits that have been realized by staff and students from the opportunities and partnerships developed over the years.

University Partnerships

The Maplewood Richmond Heights partnership with Webster University allowed experts in the Reggio Emilia early childhood philosophy to be embedded in all aspects of its growth. Partnerships with Saint Louis University, Maryville University, and Washington University in St. Louis brought many students to college campuses with the hopes of opening additional hearts and minds to the possibility of college success. University partnerships also brought practicum students and adult resources into the classroom to partner with teachers in a variety of STEM (science, technology, engineering, and math) classes at the middle school and high school level. This is only a sampling of the ways that the district found synergy with universities in supporting its students. Maplewood Richmond Heights was careful to make sure that the partnerships were symbiotic relationships that allowed both sides to benefit. This meant that university classes were conducted in the schools, and a variety of university students visited district premises to experience how an aesthetically pleasing space supports student growth, how to integrate technology into classrooms, and how to build hope and promise in an urban school setting.

Experiential Learning Partnerships

Maplewood Richmond Heights Middle School is a school built on the metaphor of "school as expedition," which means that students are learning outside of the traditional classroom more than 20% of the school year. In order to make this possible, the need to foster and nurture partnerships was essential. Because of exceptional work by teachers and school leaders over the years, students have had opportunities to learn on site with partners at the Great Smoky Mountain Institute at Tremont in Tennessee and at the Dauphin Island Sea Lab in Alabama. These flagship partnerships are coupled to a variety of local and regional partnerships including The Audubon Center at Riverlands, Forest Park Forever, Missouri Botanical Garden, and the YMCA. Each of these experiences is designed to maximize student learning through experts in the field.

Interschool Partnerships

Excellent schools and excellent school leaders are awakening to the fact that student achievement cannot be successfully obtained solely through competitive endeavors. Instead, schools are focusing more resources on interschool partnerships to help them realize new levels of success for their students. This led the school leaders at Maplewood Richmond Heights to place a premium on building learning partnerships with schools throughout the country. It included a partnership with The College School in neighboring Webster Groves, Missouri. This collaboration had a fifth-grade class from The College School and eighth-grade science students from Maplewood Richmond Heights Middle School learning together about water quality, watersheds, and the sustainability of our practices surrounding water. The partnership provided students with the opportunity to build their skills of cooperation and communication. During National Novel Writing Month, one middle school teacher worked with a high school creative writing class in British Columbia, so that her students had writing mentors to support their commitment to writing every day throughout the month. Another group of middle school students learned about the power of student voice by presenting a number of "education for sustainability" topics to audiences filled with students and staff from other schools. Teachers throughout the district have embraced their role as stewards of the entire education system, meaning that they not only support the students in their classrooms, but they also support and partner with students and classes around the world to build leaders, scholars, citizens, and stewards.

Corporate/Community Partnerships

As the drive to have students enhance their empathy for their surroundings grew, additional community and corporate partnerships were necessary for the Maplewood Richmond Heights system learning. Partners like the Dana Brown Foundation, Novus International, and the Danforth Plant Science Center were all able to provide opportunities for the students to dig more deeply into the environmental justice issues surrounding food, water, and energy. Local businesses such as Schlafly Bottleworks and Kakao Chocolate became local case studies for how companies can use the triple bottom line of people, planet, and profits to be responsible members of the community. Partners like these also allowed students to explore and learn about the social justice and economic justice issues facing individuals in the community. Funding partners like Gateway Greening, Innovative Technology Education Fund, and the Sustainable Agriculture Research and Education Program have also provided supplemental revenue streams to support the vision and mission of the district. Each of these organizations has become a perennial partner with the district, meaning the roots between the organization and the school district go beyond a single moment or a stand-alone contribution. This depth of a partnership doesn't materialize with all partnerships, and schools and districts need to be ready to be nimble in holding or folding their partnership energy, so that a majority of time can be spent tending to and growing these excellent community and corporate partnerships.

Mental Health Partnerships

St. Louis County voters passed a one-quarter-cent sales tax measure that, in turn, created a community children's service fund to provide mental health and substance abuse services for children and youths ages 19 and under. As a result, Maplewood Richmond Heights built strategic partnerships with local agencies to support the students in the areas of mental and emotional health. Taking advantage of these opportunities required a willingness to share instructional time and spaces with these organizations, and it also required leadership to build awareness throughout the organization about the benefits that these services provide to the overall academic growth of the students. The school district has just more than half of its students living in poverty, and many other students struggle with mental health and substance abuse issues. Only through incredible agencies like Youth in Need, The National Council on Alcohol and Drug Abuse, Safe Connections, and Lutheran Family and Children's Services has the school district been able to tend to these foundational needs of the students and maintain the sustainable growth over time, leading the district to be recognized as accredited with distinction by the state of Missouri.

The future of Maplewood Richmond Heights School District remains incredibly bright, as a virtual village has been wrapped around each of the students to provide support, expert mentors, and a vision for the opportunities in life after high school. It took a deep commitment by school and district leaders to plant, nurture, weed, and harvest from this garden of partnerships. The beauty of planting rich soil, analyzing the nutritional needs to support the garden, and using sustainable practices surrounding partnerships is that they allow opportunities found to grow and opportunities that emerge to be realized. It is with this attitude that Maplewood Richmond Heights School District moves forward for each student that it cares for on a daily basis.

ACADEMIES

> In education, we spend too much time inside the box, which means we tweak our curriculum and teaching methods to raise test scores or meet other accountability measures. As educators, we must move to where there is no box, which means we must step far away from our traditional-looking schools and operating procedures and reimagine a system of school goals built around 21st-century disruptions.

> —Dwight Carter and Mark White (2017, p. 182)

In addition to school design, digital leadership anticipates the types of programs needed to authentically engage learners during their school experience while providing environments that focus on college and career readiness in a digital world. Even though more rigorous standards provide a framework to begin this process, it is incumbent upon leaders to develop holistic programs that allow students to follow their learning passions, engage in a cohort style of learning, and utilize constructivist theory to create their own essential understandings in academic areas. Here is where opportunities for kids arise on a daily basis.

Academy programs represent a bold new direction for education, one that considers student interests, national need, and global demand for highly qualified graduates capable of competing at the most challenging levels. They provide a defined framework for studies in well-defined, career-focused areas directly connected to university majors and workforce need. These programs cultivate emerging professionals who exhibit the knowledge, skill, character, and work ethic necessary for success in the global marketplace. To provide more learning opportunities for our students, the Academies @ New Milford High School were launched during my tenure as principal. Think of it as a school within a school. In addition to the array of career-focused curricula associated with each of the academies, there were special features that further define the academy experience:

- Professional mentorships

- Opportunities for dual credit

- Access to resources, field trips, and virtual courses outside school settings

- Book studies

- Relationships with partnering institutions and organizations, such as the Bergen Performing Arts Center (BergenPAC), St. Thomas Aquinas College, and Farleigh Dickinson University

- Master classes, workshops, and other related field studies

- Independent OpenCourseWare Study (IOCS), as detailed in Chapter 6

- A capstone project

- Specialized transcripts

- A special designation on diploma

We not only anticipated the needs of New Milford students that aligned with societal shifts, but demonstrated bold leadership to develop and successfully launch the academies. The entire program was designed using existing high school courses as well as adding new ones to complement the three academies—STEM (science, technology, engineering, and math), Arts & Letters, and Global Leadership—without costing the district precious financial resources. After the first year, funds were put aside to support extending learning opportunities for academy students, which mainly consisted of transportation for field trips. Online Resource 11.1 provides the entire philosophy as well as descriptions of the three academies and endorsements.

By creating our own academies and integrating them into the current structure, New Milford High School was able to dramatically change how students learn. This program was available to any student who wished to push himself or herself more, regardless of academic ability, while pursuing unique interests.

LEVERAGING SOCIAL MEDIA

The interconnectedness of the Pillars of Digital Leadership leads to continuous improvements in school culture and professional practice. As leaders begin to craft a strategy that incorporates social media and digital tools, the shifts and changes in behavior inherent in each of the six previously discussed pillars begin to take shape. Transparency through the use of social media breeds attention to programs, initiatives, and leadership style. Good news travels fast, and social media transmit the news to numerous stakeholders who are embedded in these spaces. This attention eventually leads to numerous opportunities in the form of strategic partnerships, authentic learning experiences for students, professional learning, school and professional recognition, and educational technology.

Numerous opportunities materialized for my school and me after we embraced social media and the Pillars of Digital Leadership. After learning about the work being done at New Milford High School through social media, AverMedia donated many document cameras and digital response systems to the school years ago. They also traveled to New Jersey from Arizona twice to train our teachers on how to use this technology. In addition to getting needed technology, NMHS teachers began regularly using these document cameras to record their lessons, which were then uploaded to YouTube and Google Sites to assist students with their learning of the concepts using the flipped approach detailed in Chapter 6.

Edscape evolved as a strategic partnership that was formed between New Milford High School and Teq (www.teq.com), an educational technology company in the northeast. This partnership resulted in the formation of the Edscape Conference that ran for six years and attracted thousands of educators from across the United States, Mexico, and Canada. This professional learning experience focused on transformational learning and provided educators with an internationally renowned keynote speaker, 60 concurrent sessions, an innovation lab, giveaways, and meals for a fraction of the price of a traditional conference. Held on the New Milford High School campus, this event not only brought further recognition to school programs and initiatives, but provided an exceptional learning experience for all New Milford District employees free of charge.

Unprecedented learning opportunities were also made available to our students. Connections through social media provided New Milford High School students with some incredible learning experiences that could not be replicated in the classroom. Some examples included Skyping with *New York Times* best-selling author Daniel Pink, testing out and providing feedback on the Chromebook to engineers at the Google offices in New York City during the initial launch stages, attending a Girls Leadership Summit at the United Nations, working on a case study with the Massachusetts Institute of Technology, traveling to the Newark Museum to provide advice on how it could bring its collection into the twenty-first century with the use of digital tools, and developing an app for the high school.

All of these amazing experiences cost the district nothing and would not have been possible without the Pillars of Digital Leadership.

School and professional recognition increased in step with our digital presence. The strategic use of social media as defined by the Pillars of Digital Leadership resulted in national and local media coverage highlighting innovative initiatives and student accomplishments. Mainstream media outlets such as CBS New York City, NBC New York City, *USA Today, Scholastic Administrator, eSchool News,* and *Education Week* have provided consistent coverage since the evolution of the Pillars of Digital Leadership. As I became a more transparent leader, an array of professional recognitions followed. These included numerous national awards, acceptance to the Google Teacher Academy, and becoming an Adobe Education Leader. Prior to using social media as outlined by the Pillars of Digital Leadership, I had not one single type of recognition for the work that I was doing as a principal.

I also had the opportunity to share my work and that of my teachers and students. Through the lens of social media, leaders make their work accessible to diverse audiences across the globe. As good ideas travel swiftly through social media channels, they will be embraced and implemented by others looking to initiate sustainable change. Over time, state, national, and global organizations will take notice and invite digital leaders to present and showcase their work for the betterment of all.

THE INTERCONNECTEDNESS OF THE PILLARS OF DIGITAL LEADERSHIP

Don't just discover opportunity, but also build doors to welcome it in. Herein lies the lesson I learned during my journey. The Pillars of Digital Leadership provided the circumstances and conditions to create the door for opportunity to knock on. The interconnectivity and symbiotic nature of each pillar led my school and me down a path that allowed us to reap the fruits of our labor. As you will see in Figure 11.1, each pillar lends itself to the next. Think of each as a way to build a better foundation and then scaffold from there. Here is a simple three-step approach to put this process into perspective:

1. Improve the work (Pillars 1–3).

2. Share the work (Pillars 4–6).

3. Follow up on opportunities that arise (Pillar 7).

| Figure 11.1 | The Interconnectedness of the Pillars of Digital Leadership |

Copyright © 2018 by International Center for Leadership in Education, a division of Houghton Mifflin Harcourt. Used with permission.

The work is learning for our kids. It requires taking a critical lens to our practice to build pedagogical capacity that will allow innovative ideas to thrive. After a better and stronger foundation is in place, the next step requires an evolution of the spaces and environments that influence the conditions impacting student learning. Finally, one cannot forget a commitment amongst all educators to pursue professional growth opportunities that lead to innovative changes in practice.

Once efforts have been undertaken to improve the work, the next step seems simple. In reality, it should be, but a focus on communications and public relations using a multifaceted approach to meet stakeholders where they are at requires a certain level of consistency. By getting information out there and telling your story, a brand presence organically forms as detailed in Chapter 10. It is here where opportunity arises.

SUMMARY

As leaders adopt and embrace the Pillars of Digital Leadership, numerous opportunities will arise in an array of areas that positively impact school culture and professional practice. By leveraging social media, leaders can share school and professional successes, build strategic partnerships, present work to a wide array of audiences, and discover authentic learning experiences for students and staff alike. All of this can be done in a relatively cost-effective fashion while improving all facets of education. These opportunities will build a greater sense of community pride in the innovative work being done in education. Once understood and embraced, the Pillars of Digital Leadership will continue to work in concert with one another to bring opportunities now and in the future.

GUIDING QUESTIONS

1. How have you successfully leveraged the power of digital to establish partnerships, acquire resources, and provide authentic learning experiences to your students? What more has to be done in this area?

2. What types of partnerships will you pursue in your community or location? Begin to develop a strategy for outreach and curriculum alignment.

3. Which Pillar do you think is the key to bringing about more opportunity in your classroom, school, organization, or district, and why?

iStock.com/LoveTheWind

Leading for Efficacy

12

As many people know, I am originally from the northeastern part of the United States. I was born and raised in New Jersey, where I also became a teacher and eventually a principal. After meeting my wife in 2002, I moved to Staten Island, New York, and resided there for 13 years. To be honest, I never thought I would leave that area of the country, as my wife and I had such strong roots there. Things change, however. The successful digital transformation at the school where I was principal attracted a great deal of attention from the mainstream media, schools locally and globally, and organizations, in part because we were able to show efficacy in our work. It was at this time that I decided to take a calculated risk and attempt to help other schools scale their digital and innovative change efforts. Online Resource 12.1 provides a synopsis of our transformation efforts.

As I transitioned from principal to senior fellow with the International Center for Leadership in Education (ICLE), my work began to take me all over the country and the world. I vividly remember the day when I was away working in Hawaii, and over a foot of snow got dumped on Staten Island. Shortly after I returned home, my wife sat me down and gave me an ultimatum. I either had to go back to being a principal so I could be home to shovel any and all snow in the future, or we had to move somewhere else in the country where it was warm and didn't snow at all. My wife knew full well how much I love the work that I do, so out came a map of the United States, and the discussions as to where we would raise our family for the foreseeable future began.

During our discussions, I had to set my nonnegotiables. She wanted warmth and no snow, while I needed a huge airport that was centrally located to cut my flight times and connections down. There were only two realistic choices at this point, Dallas and Houston. Since Houston was a bit farther south and we could get the exact home we wanted, the decision was made. One other factor that weighed heavily in our decision-making process was the school district that our children would attend. The icing on the cake for me was that when it was all said and done, taking into account our nonnegotiables, we decided to build our home within the Cypress-Fairbanks Independent School District (CFISD).

A SHINING EXAMPLE: WELLS ELEMENTARY SCHOOL

CFISD is an amazing school district that is not only one of the highest-achieving large districts in the state of Texas, but also firmly committed to scaling innovative practices to improve learning for all 120,000 students. For a year and a half, my team and I at ICLE had been assisting the district with implementing Bring Your Own Technology (BYOT) K–12, incorporating blended learning, and aligning sound pedagogy to the use of flex spaces. We also used our Digital Practice Assessment (DPA) process to help them determine where they were at, but more important, where they wanted to be for their learners. Online Resource 12.2 provides a detailed summary of the nuts and bolts of the DPA process. Now back to my story.

Shortly after arriving in the Houston area, I was contacted by Cheryl Fisher, a local CFISD elementary principal. She had been following me on Twitter and asked if I would be willing to visit her school and see how they were implementing blended learning across all grade levels. What I saw just warmed my heart, but more on this in a little bit. A little over a year later, Cheryl was named the principal of Wells Elementary, a brand-new school right smack in the middle of the community where I lived. I couldn't control my excitement, but there was a challenge ahead in the form of my daughter, Isabella.

Bella, who was in fourth grade at the time, had a big decision to make. Stay in the other community school where she had made friends for two years, or go to a brand-new school for her last year of elementary school. To be honest, she was leaning on staying put. I discussed this with Cheryl, and she said quite bluntly, "If your daughter decides to come to Wells, she will love learning every day." Well, I was already hooked, but Cheryl also made the time to meet with Bella and explain in detail the vision she had for the learning culture at Wells. What followed was the waiting in anticipation of what Bella would decide to do.

Thankfully, my daughter, on her own without much pressure from my wife and me, decided to attend Wells Elementary. Every day I asked her how school was and would literally tear up when she responded, as the answer was always the same: "It was great Daddy." My daughter was entirely in love with the school. As an educator and parent, this meant so much more to me than her consistently being advanced proficient every year on all standardized tests. Wells Elementary to me is a school of dreams because my daughter loved to learn there. Here are some specifics as to why:

- Schoolwide decision to have no homework.
- Students K–5 are empowered to use their technology to support their education as part of BYOT. In addition to this, technology is used to support and enhance learning while providing authentic opportunities to explore concepts.
- Strategic use of the station rotation blended-learning model, in addition to choice boards and playlists, to maximize learning time and increase student agency.
- Incorporation of flexible learning spaces throughout the building.
- Portfolio-based assessment using Seesaw and Google Classroom to provide better feedback to students aligned to standards.
- An entire staff that believes in the power of being connected and the importance of having a Personal Learning Network (PLN).

- Systemic use of a variety of social media tools to communicate with stakeholders to keep them in the know, tell their story, and develop a positive brand presence.

It is important to know I am not just making the casual statements above using only my parent lens. I am honored by the fact that I was the one who was engaged with Wells as part of a partnership with CFISD to support the district with research- and evidence-based digital leadership and learning solutions. As the job-embedded coach for the school, I worked with the teachers and administrators over the course of the first two years of the school's existence. As we embarked on creating and sustaining the vibrant learning culture described above, the goal was to impart a love of learning amongst all kids while also ensuring that they achieved. During the first-ever administration of standardized tests at this school, the results were amazing. Below are the percentages of students who were proficient or higher.

Overall Third through Fifth Grade, all students:

Math: 97%

Reading: 97%

Specific Grade Levels:

Fifth grade reading: 99%

Fifth grade math: 99%

Fifth grade science: 96%

Fourth grade writing: 93%

Even though they have fantastic initiatives in place and have experienced success, the Wells community knows that there is room for improvement. This is the case in any classroom, school, or district. We must always work on the pedagogical shifts needed to support a bold vision and plan for innovative learning. As you have read in this book, technology will continue to change as will a push to pursue innovative ideas.

A PUSH FOR EFFICACY

As a principal, the buck stopped with me. I was reminded of this by numerous superintendents during my tenure as a school leader. However, when we began moving forward with our digital transformation at New Milford High School, one particular superintendent asked me point blank what evidence I had that actually supported our claims that new equated to better. This not only stopped me in my tracks, but that moment in time provided the grounding that my school and I really needed. For change to really be embraced by all stakeholders, it is critical that we just don't tell and claim that improvement is occurring, but that we also show it.

Accountability matters and is a reality in our work. We are accountable first and foremost to our learners. As a supporter of the purposeful use of technology and innovative practices, I had to illustrate how effective these strategies were at improving learning. Statements and claims didn't cut it, and this was more than fair. It was at this time that the term *efficacy* kept finding its way into the conversation and my head. In the real world of education, efficacy matters, and it is important that this is part of the larger conversation when it comes to digital. It is a word that, in my opinion, has to be a part of our daily vocabulary and practice. Simply put, efficacy is the degree to which desired outcomes and goals are achieved. Applying this concept to teaching, learning, and leadership in the digital age can go a long way toward solidifying the use of technology and pursuit of innovative practices as established practices, not just frills or add-ons.

The journey to efficacy begins and ends with the intended goal in mind and a strong pedagogical foundation. Adding technology or new ideas without this in place will more than likely not result in achieving efficacy. The Rigor/Relevance Framework presented in Chapter 5 provides schools and educators with a check and balance system by providing a common language for all, creating a culture around a common vision, and establishing a critical lens through which to examine curriculum, instruction, and assessment. It represents a means to support innovative learning and digital practices.

Aligning a school's learning culture to this not only makes sense but also melds with a great deal of the conversation in digital and non-digital spaces as to why and how learning should change. A framework like this emphasizes the importance of a strong pedagogical foundation while helping to move practice from isolated pockets of excellence to systemic elements that are scaled throughout the learning culture. It also provides the means to evaluate and reflect in order to improve.

Once an overall vision for digital learning is firmly in place, you can begin to work on the structures and supports to ensure success. This brings me back to efficacy. The *why* is great, but the *how* and *what* have to be fleshed out. Determining whether technology or innovative practices, in general, are effective matters. Digital leaders focus on five key areas (essential questions, research, practicality, evidence/accountability, reflection) that can move any classroom, school, district, or organization on a path to digital efficacy.

Essential Questions

Questions provide context for where we want to go, how we'll get there, and whether or not success is achieved. Having more questions than answers is a natural part of the initial change process. Over time, however, concrete answers can illustrate that efficacy in digital learning has been achieved in some form or another. Consider how you might respond to the questions below:

- What evidence do we have to demonstrate the impact of technology on school culture?

- How are we making learning relevant for our students?

- How do we implement and support rigorous and relevant learning tasks that help students become Future Ready?

- What is required to create spaces that model real-world environments and learning opportunities?

- What observable evidence can be used to measure the effect technology is having on student learning and achievement?

- How can targeted feedback be provided to our teachers and students, so that technology can enhance learning?

Research

Research is prevalent in education for a reason as noted throughout this book. It provides us all with a baseline as to what has been found to really work when it comes to student learning. Now, there is good research and bad. I get that. It is up to us as educators to sift through and then align the best and most practical studies out there to support the need to transform learning in the digital age. We can look to the past in order to inform current practice. For example, so many of us are proponents of student ownership, project-based, and collaborative learning. Not only does digital support and enhance all of these, but research from Dewey, Vygotsky, Piaget, Papert, Bloom, and many others provides validation (see Figure 12.1). If efficacy is the goal, embracing a scholarly mindset to inform and influence our work, not drive it, is critical.

Figure 12.1   Authorship Learning

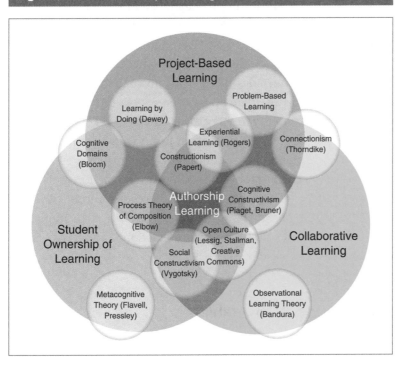

Practicality

All of what we do should align to the demands, and at times constraints, of the job. This includes preparing students for success on standardized tests. If it's not practical, the drive to implement new ideas and practices wanes or never materializes. For example, creation of rigorous digital performance tasks that are aligned to standards and the scope and sequence found in the curriculum is just good practice. All good performance tasks include some form of assessment, either formative or summative, that provides the learner and educator with valuable information on standard and outcome attainment. Again, this is just part of the job.

The Rigor/Relevance Framework assists in creating performance tasks that engage learners in critical thinking and problem solving while applying what they have learned in meaningful ways. There is also natural alignment to incorporating student agency. This is exactly what so many of us are championing.

Practicality implies working smarter, not harder, to achieve better results. The Pillars of Digital Leadership presented in this book provide a seamless framework to do what you are already doing better. Consciously think about each pillar from your perspective, and develop a strategy for improvement that makes sense. The job of the digital leader is not just to model the art of being connected, using technology, or changing spaces; it's also to model the art of human conversation and unplugging the devices. Connected educators can simply say that this is a world that their students are growing up in and they are always connected, but school leaders have some responsibility to show them other aspects of the world as well. It is important to remember that technology will not improve every aspect of what we do in education. Being practical means promoting a balance. Educators long for human interaction and have a need to take time to breathe and have real conversations with their colleagues. As important as technology is, and it is an important tool, so is our need to have human interaction, and digital leaders need to promote that too.

Evidence and Accountability

When integrating technology and innovative ideas there needs to be a return on instruction (ROI) that results in evidence of improved student learning outcomes (Sheninger & Murray, 2017). We cannot shy away from openly discussing how important this area is. Evidence and accountability are a part of every profession, and quite frankly we need more of both in education to not only show efficacy in our work but to also scale needed change. There needs to be a greater focus on instructional design, digital pedagogical techniques, and the development of better assessments aligned to higher standards.

For technology to be taken seriously as a tool to support and enhance teaching and learning, then, we must no longer accept assumptions and generalizations as to what it actually does. I for one want students empowered to own their learning, create artifacts, demonstrate conceptual mastery, use their voice, be responsible in online spaces, and connect with the world in authentic ways. From an educator perspective, I also want teachers and administrators to utilize technology and innovative practices to improve teaching, learning, and leadership. However, the principal in me also needs to balance this with clear results. This is a reality for every teacher and administrator that cannot be ignored. It is important to show how students apply what they have learned in relevant ways aligned to the highest levels of knowledge taxonomy. Telling just doesn't cut it anymore.

Think about how you can use data, observation/evaluation, portfolios, and artifacts to showcase success. Not everything has to or can be measured. However, focusing on a return on instruction allows everyone to incorporate multiple measures, both qualitative and quantitative, to determine whether improvement is in fact occurring.

Reflection

Amazing things are happening in education, whether it be through digital learning and leadership or the implementation of innovative ideas. We must always push ourselves to be better and strive for continuous improvement. The more we all push each other on the topic of efficacy, the more our collective goals for education, learning, and leadership can be achieved. The story of Wells Elementary represents a school of dreams and one of the best examples of efficacy in digital leadership. The fact that my daughter loved to learn and was being prepared for her future meant the world to my wife and me. With the compelling learning opportunities she experienced, I hope that she will be further motivated to follow her dreams, no matter what they are.

SUMMARY

Digital leadership is about transforming schools into exciting and stimulating institutions of learning, where students are actively involved in applying and mastering concepts both in traditional ways and through the use of educational technology. It is a call to action for leaders at all levels to become more knowledgeable about society and look for opportunities to connect to the real world that is constantly evolving. The time is now to take a critical lens to our practice in order to provide all learners with the competencies to thrive and succeed in a world that is impossible to predict. We do this by empowering them to think and apply their learning in meaningful ways. Don't prepare learners for something; prepare them for anything!

The Pillars of Digital Leadership provide the framework to initiate meaningful change that can ultimately transform school culture. It is up to the leader, however, to sustain these changes through establishing a clear vision, developing a strategic plan, empowering staff, creating an environment that supports risk taking, giving up a certain amount of control, modeling the effective use of educational technologies, and being the lead learner. With all of the many tools that are constantly evolving, digital leaders need to be on their toes and know where to go for support and training.

Technology has the capacity to allow us to do what we do better while accomplishing the same goals. As important as technology is to digital leadership, human interaction remains the key component of changing education now and in the future. Digital leaders understand this, and when an emphasis is placed on relationship building through these interactions, as well as anticipating needed changes, the Pillars of Digital Leadership will be the guide to move from vision to reality. It all comes down to relationships. Without trust there is no relationship. Without relationships no real learning occurs.

GUIDING QUESTIONS

When it is all said and done, the most important thing we can all do is constantly reflect on our practice. In terms of efficacy in digital learning, consider these questions from your perspective in addition to those under the subheading "Essential Questions" on page 224:

- Did my students learn?

- How do I know whether my students learned?

- How do others know whether my students learned?

- What can be done to improve?

- What point of view have I not considered?

Online Resources

Scan this QR code to access the live links!

Online Resource 3.1 A More Equitable Grading Philosophy (goo.gl/s3jFLK)

Online Resource 4.1 ISTE Standards for Education Leaders (www.iste.org/standards/for-education-leaders)

Online Resource 4.2 ISTE Standards (www.iste.org/standards)

Online Resource 4.3 Future Ready Framework (futureready.org)

Online Resource 4.4 Pillars of Digital Leadership Alignment With the Future Ready Framework (goo.gl/7RN6mS)

Online Resource 5.1 Instagram Project Rubric (goo.gl/mJYEzL)

Online Resource 6.1 Makerspace Resources (tinyurl.com/y6vjtmc4)

Online Resource 6.2 Open CourseWare Sites (goo.gl/oF7EPm)

Online Resource 6.3 Independent Open CourseWare Study (IOCS) at NMHS (sites.google.com/site/opencoursewarestudies/)

Online Resource 6.4 OCW Scholar from MIT (ocw.mit.edu/courses/ocw-scholar/)

Online Resource 8.1 New Milford Athletic Department Twitter Page (twitter.com/NMHS_Athletics)

Online Resource 8.2 New Milford High School Twitter Page (twitter.com/NewMilfordHS)

Online Resource 8.3 Template: Twitter for School Communications and Engagement (tinyurl.com/y8clvas5)

Online Resource 8.4 Sample Principal's Report (tinyurl.com/y7plm9uy)

Online Resource 8.5 Principal's Report Template (tinyurl.com/ycnn8vvj)

Online Resource 8.6 ZippSlip (www.zippslip.com)

Online Resource 9.1 Sample: Student Media Waiver (tinyurl.com/yatt7pdq)

Online Resource 11.1 The Academies @ New Milford High School (goo.gl/8XQ4jv)

Online Resource 12.1 How a New Jersey High School Transformed to Stay Relevant for Students (tinyurl.com/y8g3aaa2)

Online Resource 12.2 Digital Practice Assessment (tinyurl.com/ybyaotlr)

Scan this QR code to access the live links!

References

Anderson, S., & Stiegelbauer, S. (1994). Institutionalization and renewal in a restructured school. *School Organization, 14*(3), 279–293.

Arnold, M., Perry, R., Watson, R., Minatra, K., & Schwartz, R. (2006). *The practitioner: How successful principals lead and influence.* Ypsilanti, MI: National Council of Professors of Educational Administration. Retrieved February 16, 2013, from http://cnx .org/content/m14255/1.1

Barrett, P., & Zhang, Y. (2009). *Optimal learning spaces: Design implications for primary schools.* Salford, UK: Design and Print Group.

Barrett, P., Zhang, Y., Davies, F., & Barrett, L. (2015). *Clever classrooms: Summary findings of the HEAD Project (Holistic Evidence and Design).* Salford, UK: University of Salford, Manchester.

Barrett, P., Zhang, Y., Moffat, J., & Kobbacy, K. (2013). A holistic, multi-level analysis identifying the impact of classroom design on pupils' learning. *Building and Environment, 59*, 678–689.

Barseghian, T. (2011). Straight from the DOE: Dispelling myths about blocked sites. *Mindshift: How we will learn.* Retrieved December 26, 2012, from http://blogs.kqed.org/mind-shift/2011/04/straight-from-the-doe-facts-about-blocking- sites-in-schools/

Boaler, J., & Zoido, P. (2016). Why math education in the US doesn't add up. *Scientific American.* Retrieved November 19, 2018, from https://www.scientificamerican.com/article/why-math-education -in-the-u-s-doesn-t-add-up/

Bouffard, S. (2008). *Tapping into technology: The role of the Internet in family–school communication.* Retrieved September 21, 2013, from http://www .hfrp.org/publications-resources/browse-our-publications/tapping-in to-technology-the-role-of-the-internet-in-family-school-communication

Buchanan, R., & Clark, M. (2017). Understanding parent–school communication for students with emotional and behavioral disorders. *The Open Family Studies Journal, 10*, 122–131.

Carter, D., & White, M. (2017). *Leading schools in disruptive times: How to survive hyper-change.* Thousand Oaks, CA: Corwin.

Casero-Ripollés, A. (2012). Beyond newspapers: News consumption among young people in the digital era. *Comunicar, 20*(39), 151–158.

Cheryan, S., Ziegler, S., Plaut V., & Meltzoff, A. (2014). Designing classrooms to maximize student achievement. *Behavioral and Brain Sciences, 1*(1), 4–12.

Cheu-Jey, L. (2015) Project-based learning and invitations: A comparison. *Journal of Curriculum Theorizing, 1*(3), 63–73.

Churches, A. (2008). *21st century pedagogy*. Retrieved July 1, 2013, from http://edorigami.wikispaces.com/21st+Century+Pedagogy

Couros, A. (2006). *Examining the open movement: Possibilities and implications for education*. Retrieved from http://www.scribd.com/doc/3363/Dissertation-Couros-FINAL-06-WebVersion

Daggett, W. (2016). *Rigor/Relevance Framework®: A guide to focusing resources to increase student performance*. Rexford, NY: International Center for Leadership in Education.

Darling-Hammond, L., Hyler, M., Gardner, M., & Espinoza, D. (2017). *Effective teacher professional development*. Learning Policy Institute. Retrieved August 18, 2018, from https://learningpolicyinstitute.org/sites/default/files/product-files/Effective_Teacher_Professional_Development_BRIEF.pdf

Darling-Hammond, L., Zielezinski, M., & Goldman, S. (2014). *Using technology to support at-risk students' learning*. Stanford, CA: The Alliance for Excellent Education and Stanford Center for Opportunity Policy in Education.

Demski, J. (2012). 7 habits of highly effective tech-leading principals. *THE Journal*. Retrieved December 29, 2012, from http://thejournal.com/articles/2012/06/07/7-habits-of-highly-effective-tech-leading-principals.aspx

Dewey, J. (1910). *How we think*. New York, NY: Prometheus Books.

Dornhecker, M., Blake, J., Benden, M., Zhao, H., & Wendel, M. (2015). The effect of standbiased desks on academic engagement: An exploratory study. *International Journal of Health Promotion and Education, 53*(5), 271–280.

DuFour, R., DuFour, R., & Eaker, R. (2008). *Revisiting professional learning communities at work: New insights for improving schools*. Bloomington, IN: Solution Tree.

Edudemic. (2012). *Pedagogical framework for digital tools*. Retrieved March 23, 2013, from http://edudemic.com/2012/12/a-pedagogical-framework-for-digital-tools/

Edutopia. (2012). *What works in education*. The George Lucas Educational Foundation. Retrieved December 23, 2012, from http://www.edutopia.org

Epstein, J. L. (2011). *School, family, and community partnerships: Preparing educators and improving schools* (2nd ed.). Philadelphia, PA: Westview Press.

Escueta, M., Quan, V., Nickow, A. J., & Oreopoulos, P. (2017). *Education technology: An evidence-based review*. NBER Working Paper No. 23744. Cambridge, MA: National Bureau of Economic Research.

Federal Communications Commission. (2011). *Children's Internet Protection Act (CIPA)*. Washington, DC: Author. Retrieved September 14, 2013, from http://www.fcc.gov/guides/childrens-internet-protection-act

Ferriter, W. M. (2013). Technology is a tool, not a learning outcome [Blog post]. Retrieved July 13, 2013, from http://blog.williamferriter.com/2013/07/11/technology-is-a-tool-not-a-learning-outcome/

Ferriter, W. M., Ramsden, J. T., & Sheninger, E. C. (2011). *Communicating & connecting with social media*. Bloomington, IN: Solution Tree.

Finette, P. (2012, November 1). The participation culture: Pascal Finette at TEDxorangecoast. Retrieved January 5, 2013, from http://www.youtube.com/watch?v=yJMnVieDfD0

Fisher, A., Godwin, K., & Seltman, H. (2014). Visual environment, attention allocation, and learning in young children: When too much of a good thing may be bad. *Psychological Science, 25*(7), 1362–1370.

Fleming, L. (2015). *Worlds of making*. Thousand Oaks, CA: Corwin.

Fleming, L. (2017). *The kickstart guide to guide to making great makerspaces*. Thousand Oaks, CA: Corwin.

Friedman, T. (2005). *The world is flat*. New York, NY: Farrar, Strauss, and Giroux.

Fullan, M. (2001). *Leading in a culture of change*. San Francisco, CA: Jossey-Bass.

Fullan, M. (2011). *The six secrets of change: What the best leaders do to help their organizations survive and thrive*. San Francisco, CA: Jossey- Bass.

Gee, J. P. (2007). *What video games have to teach us about learning and literacy* (2nd ed.). New York, NY: Macmillan.

Gerstein, J. (2013). *Schools are doing Education 1.0; talking about doing Education 2.0; when they should be planning Education 3.0*. User Generated Education. Retrieved March 23, 2013, from http://usergenerated education.wordpress.com/2013/03/22/schools-are-doing-education-1–0-talking-about-doing-education-2–0-when-they-should-be-planning-education-3–0/

Gladwell, M. (2008). *Outliers*. New York, NY: Little, Brown.

Glazer, N. (2009). Outliers, by Malcolm Gladwell [Book review]. *Education Next*. Retrieved December 29, 2012, from http://educationnext.org/nature-or-culture/

Godin, S. (2010). *Linchpin: Are you indispensable?* New York, NY: Penguin Group.

Gordon, D. (2010). Wow! 3D content awakens the classroom. *THE Journal*. Retrieved December 26, 2012, from http://thejournal.com/articles/2010/10/01/wow-3d-content-awakens-the- classroom.aspx

Gronn, P. (2000). Distributed properties: A new architecture for leadership. *Educational Management and Administration, 28*(3), 371.

Harris, A., & Lambert, L. (2003). *Building leadership capacity for school improvement*. Maidenhead, UK: Open University Press.

Hatch, M. (2014). *The maker movement manifesto*. New York, NY: McGraw Hill.

Haystead, M., & Marzano, R. (2009). *Evaluation study of the effects of Promethean ActivClassroom on student achievement.* Retrieved December 26, 2012, from http://www1.promethean-world.com/server.php?show=nav.19203

Henderson, A. T., Mapp, K. L., Johnson, V. & Davies, D. (2007). *Beyond the bake sale: The essential guide to family-school partnerships.* New York, NY: The New Press.

Herold, B. (2016, February 5). Technology in education. *Education Week.* Retrieved January 2, 2019, from http://www.edweek.org/ew/issues/technology-in-education/

Herold, D., & Fedor, D. (2008). *Change the way you lead change.* Stanford, CA: Stanford University Press.

Hopkins, D., & Jackson, D. (2003). Building the capacity for leading and learning. In A. Harris, C. Day, M. Hadfield, D. Hopkins, A. Hargreaves, & C. Chapman (Eds.), *Effective leadership for school improvement* (pp. 84–105). London, UK: Routledge Falmer.

Hoyle, J. R., English, F. W., & Steffy, B. E. (1998). *Skills for successful 21st century school leaders: Standards for peak performers.* Arlington, VA: American Association of School Administrators.

HRTMS. (2016). *Skills or competencies . . . what's the difference?* Retrieved July 7, 2018 from http://www.hrtms.com/blog/skills-or-competencies whats-the-difference

IGI Global & Information Resources Management Association. (2018). *Gamification in education: Breakthroughs in research and practice.* Hershey, PA: IGI Global.

Imordino-Yang, M. H., & Faeth, M. (2010). The role of emotion and skilled intuition in learning. In D. A. Sousa (Ed.), *Mind, brain and education: Neuroscience implications for the classroom* (pp. 69–84). Bloomington, IN: Solution Tree Press.

International Society for Technology in Education (ISTE). (2018). *ISTE standards for education leaders.* Retrieved July 15, 2018, from https://www.iste.org/standards/for-education-leaders

Internet World Stats. (2018). *Internet growth statistics: Today's road to e-commerce and global trade.* Internet Technology Reports. Retrieved May 22, 2018, from https://www.internetworldstats.com/emarketing.htm

Jacob, S. R., & Warschauer, M. (2018). Computational thinking and literacy. *Journal of Computer Science Integration, 1*(1). Retrieved January 1, 2019, from https://inspire.redlands.edu/cgi/viewcontent.cgi?article=1003&context=jcsi

Jacobs, R. (2009). *Leveraging the "networked" teacher: The Professional Networked Learning Collaborative.* Retrieved February 24, 2013, from http://educationinnovation.typepad.com/my_weblog/2009/06/leveraging-the-networked-teacher-the-professional-networked-learning-collaborative.html

Jesdanun, A. (2017, February 10). How Google Chromebooks conquered schools. *AP News.* Retrieved June 9, 2018 from https://www.apnews.com/41817339703440a49d8916c0f67d28a6.

Johnson, S. (2006). *Everything bad is good for you*. New York, NY: Riverhead.

Jones, R. (2008). *Leading change in high schools*. Rexford, NY: International Center for Leadership in Education.

Jukes, I., McCain, T., & Crockett, L. (2010). *Understanding the digital generation: Teaching and learning in the new digital landscape*. Kelowna, BC, Canada: 21st Century Fluency Project [copublished with Corwin].

Junkala, J. (2018). Comfort is the enemy of progress. Medium. Retrieved May 14, 2018 from https://medium.com/@joanijunkala/comfort-is-the-enemy-of-progress-3c861f758a6f

Kelly, F. S., McCain, T., & Jukes, I. (2009). *Teaching the digital generation: No more cookie-cutter high schools*. Thousand Oaks, CA: Corwin.

Kember, D., Ho, A., & Hong, C. (2008). The importance of establishing relevance in motivating student learning. *Active Learning in Higher Education, 9*(3), 249–263.

Kieschnick, W. (2017). *Bold school: Old school wisdom + new school technologies = blended learning that works*. Rexford, NY: International Center for Leadership in Education.

Killion, J. (2013). *Meet the promise of content standards: Tapping technology to enhance professional learning*. Oxford, OH: Learning Forward.

Kouzes, J. M., & Posner, B. Z. (2007). *The leadership challenge* (4th ed.). San Francisco, CA: Jossey-Bass.

Kouzes, J. M., & Posner, B. Z. (2009, January). To lead, create a shared vison. *Harvard Business Review*. Retrieved July 14, 2018 from https://hbr.org/2009/01/to-lead-create-a-shared-vision.

LeLoup, J. W., & Ponterio, R. (2000). *Enhancing authentic language learning experiences through Internet technology*. Report No. EDO-FL-00–02. Washington, DC: Office of Educational Research and Improvement.

Lemke, C. (2008). *Multimodal learning through media: What the research says*. San Jose, CA: Cisco Systems.

Lemke, C., Coughlin, E., & Reifsneider, D. (2009). *Technology in schools: What the research says: An update*. Culver City, CA: Cisco Systems.

Lin, M., Chen, H., & Liu, K. (2017). A study of the effects of digital learning on learning motivation and learning outcome. *Eurasia Journal of Mathematics, Science and Technology Education, 13*(7), 3553–3564.

Maich, K., & Hall, C. (2016) Implementing iPads in the inclusive classroom setting. *Intervention in School and Clinic, 51*(3), 145–150.

Martinez, S. L., & Stager, G. (2013). *Invent to learn: Making, tinkering, and engineering in the classroom*. Torrance, CA: Constructing Modern Knowledge Press.

Merchant, Z., Goetz, E. T., Cifuentes, L., Keeney-Kennicutt, W., & Davis, T. J. (2014). Effectiveness of virtual reality-based instruction on students' learning outcomes in K–12 and higher education: A meta-analysis. *Computers & Education, 70*, 29–40.

Mielke, D. (1999). *Effective teaching in distance education*. Report No. EDO-SP-1999–5. Washington, DC: Office of Educational Research and Improvement.

Murphy Paul, A. (2012). Your brain on fiction. *New York Times*. Retrieved August 3, 2018, from https://www.nytimes.com/2012/03/18/opinion/sunday/the-neuroscience-of-your-brain-on-fiction.html?pagewanted=all

National Association of Secondary School Principals (NASSP). (2011). *Breaking ranks: The comprehensive framework for school improvement.* Reston, VA: Author.

National Research Council. (2012). *Education for life and work: Developing transferable knowledge and skills in the 21st century.* Washington, DC: The National Academies Press.

Niels, J. (2012). *A pedagogical framework for digital tools.* Retrieved from http://www.edudemic.com/a-pedagogical-framework- for-digital-tools/

Olins, W. (2008). *The brand handbook.* London, UK: Thames & Hudson.

Peters, T. (1999). *The brand you 50.* New York, NY: Knopf.

Pink, D. (2011). *Drive: The surprising truth on what motivates us.* New York, NY: Riverhead.

Prensky, M. (2001). Digital natives, digital immigrants. *On the Horizon, 9*(5), 1–6.

Riedel, C. (2012, February 1). Digital learning: What kids really want. *THE Journal.* Retrieved January 5, 2013, from http://thejournal.com/articles/2012/02/01/digital-learning-what-kids-really-want.aspx

Rock, H. (2002). Job-embedded professional development and reflective coaching. *The Instructional Leader.* Retrieved August 18, 2018, from http://www.ascd.org/publications/classroom_leadership/may2002/Job-Embedded_Professional_Development_and_Reflective_Coaching.aspx

Rule, A. (2006). The components of authentic learning. *Journal of Authentic Learning, 3*(1), 1–10.

Saidin, N. F., Abd Halim, N. D., & Yahaya, N. (2015). A review of research on augmented reality in education: Advantages and applications. *International Education Studies, 8*(13), 1–8.

Schrum, L., & Levin, B. (2015). *Leading 21st century schools* (2nd ed.). Thousand Oaks, CA: Corwin.

Scott-Webber, L., Strickland, A., & Kapitula, L. (2014). *How classroom design affects student engagement.* Grand Rapids, MI: Steelcase Education.

Sheninger, E. (2015a). Transforming your school with digital communication. *Education Leadership, 72*(7). Retrieved January 1, 2019, from http://www.ascd.org/publications/educational-leadership/apr15/vol72/num07/Transforming-Your-School-with-Digital-Communication.aspx

Sheninger, E. (2015b). *Uncommon learning: Creating schools that work for kids.* Thousand Oaks, CA: Corwin.

Sheninger, E., & Murray, T. (2017). *Learning transformed: Eight keys for designing tomorrow's schools, today.* Alexandria, VA: ASCD.

Sheninger, E., & Rubin, T. (2017). *BrandED: Tell your story, build relationships, empower learning.* San Francisco, CA: Jossey-Bass.

Skiba, D. J., & Baron, A. J. (2006). Adapting your teaching to accommodate the net generation of learners. *Online Journal of Issues in Nursing, 11*(2). Retrieved January 1, 2019, from http://ojin.nursingworld.org/MainMenuCategories/ANAMarketplace/ANAPeriodicals/OJIN/TableofContents/Volume112006/No2May06/tpc30_416076.aspx.

Spiro, R. J., & Jehng, J. (1990). Cognitive flexibility and hypertext: Theory and technology for the non-linear and multidimensional traversal of complex subject matter. In D. Nix & R. Spiro (Eds.), *Cognition, education, and multimedia* (pp. 163–205). Hillsdale, NJ: Erlbaum.

Stepien, W., & Gallagher, S. (1993). Problem-based learning: As authentic as it gets. *Educational Leadership, 50*(7), 25–28.

Tay, H. Y. (2016). Longitudinal study on impact of iPad use on teaching and learning. *Cogent Education, 3*(1). Retrieved January 1, 2019, from https://www.tandfonline.com/doi/full/10.1080/2331186X.2015.1127308?scroll=top&needAccess=true

Tomlinson, C. (2011). Respecting students. *Educational Leadership, 69*(1), 94–95.

Vest, C. M. (2004, January 30). Why MIT decided to give away all its course materials via the Internet. *The Chronicle of Higher Education*, p. 20.

Wexler, B. E., Iseli, M., Leon, S., Zaggle, W., Rush, C., Goodman, A., . . . & Bo, E. (2016, September 12). Cognitive priming and cognitive training: Immediate and far transfer to academic skills in children. *Scientific Reports, 6*, article 32859.

Whitaker, T. (2003). *What great principals do differently: Fifteen things that matter the most*. Larchmont, NY: Eye on Education.

Whitehurst, G. J. (2009). *Don't forget curriculum*. Washington, DC: Brookings Institution. Retrieved January 1, 2019, from https://www.brookings.edu/research/dont-forget-curriculum/

Willis, J. (2010). The current impact of neuroscience on teaching and learning. In D. A. Sousa (Ed.), *Mind, brain and education: Neuroscience implications for the classroom* (pp. 45–68). Bloomington, IN: Solution Tree Press.

Yildiz, M. N., & Keengwe, J. (Eds.). (2016) *Handbook of research on media literacy in the digital age*. Hershey, PA: IGI Global.

Zhao, Y. (2012). *World class learners*. Thousand Oaks, CA: Corwin.

Zheng, B., Warschauer, M., Lin, C. H., & Chang, C. (2016). Learning in one-to-one laptop environments: A meta-analysis and research synthesis. *Review of Educational Research, 86*(4), 1–33.

Index

Helping educators make the greatest impact

CORWIN HAS ONE MISSION: to enhance education through intentional professional learning.

We build long-term relationships with our authors, educators, clients, and associations who partner with us to develop and continuously improve the best evidence-based practices that establish and support lifelong learning.

A division of
Houghton Mifflin Harcourt

About the International Center for Leadership in Education

The International Center for Leadership in Education (ICLE), a division of Houghton Mifflin Harcourt, challenges, inspires, and equips leaders and teachers to prepare their students for lifelong success. At the heart of all we do is the proven philosophy that the entire system must be aligned around instructional excellence—rooted in rigor, relevance, and relationships—to ensure every student is prepared for a successful future.

Founded in 1991 by Dr. Bill Daggett, ICLE, through its team of thought leaders and consultants, helps schools and districts bring innovative practices to scale through professional learning opportunities and coaching partnerships guided by the cornerstones of our work: the Daggett System for Effective Instruction® and the Rigor/Relevance Framework®. Additionally, ICLE shares successful practices that have a positive impact on student learning through keynote presentations; the Model Schools Conference, Leadership Academy, and other events; and a rich collection of publications. Learn more at LeaderEd.com.

Solutions YOU WANT | Experts YOU TRUST | Results YOU NEED

EVENTS

> > > **INSTITUTES**

Corwin Institutes provide large regional events where educators collaborate with peers and learn from industry experts. Prepare to be recharged and motivated!

corwin.com/institutes

ON-SITE PD

> > > **ON-SITE PROFESSIONAL LEARNING**

Corwin on-site PD is delivered through high-energy keynotes, practical workshops, and custom coaching services designed to support knowledge development and implementation.

corwin.com/pd

> > > **PROFESSIONAL DEVELOPMENT RESOURCE CENTER**

The PD Resource Center provides school and district PD facilitators with the tools and resources needed to deliver effective PD.

corwin.com/pdrc

ONLINE

> > > **ADVANCE**

Designed for K–12 teachers, Advance offers a range of online learning options that can qualify for graduate-level credit and apply toward license renewal.

corwin.com/advance

Contact a PD Advisor at (800) 831-6640 or visit www.corwin.com for more information